Robert Charles.
August 1991
APSA / Washington, D.C.

The Future of Germany and the Atlantic Alliance

The Future of
Germany and
the Atlantic Alliance

Constantine C. Menges

The AEI Press

Publisher for the American Enterprise Institute
WASHINGTON, D.C.

1991

Distributed by arrangement with

National Book Network
4720 Boston Way   3 Henrietta Street
Lanham, MD 20706   London WC2E 8LU England

Library of Congress Cataloging-in-Publication Data

Menges, Constantine Christopher.
  The future of Germany and the Atlantic alliance / Constantine C. Menges.
    p.   cm.
  Includes bibliographical references and index.
  ISBN 0-8447-3731-3
    1. Germany—Foreign relations—1945– 2. Germany—Politics and
government—1945– 3. German reunification question (1945–1990)
4. Europe—Politics and government—1945– 5. North Atlantic Treaty
Organization. I. Title.
DD257.4.M47   1991
327.43—dc20   91-15366
                                                          CIP

AEI Studies 512

The AEI Press
Publisher for the American Enterprise Institute
1150 17th Street, N.W., Washington, D.C. 20036

Printed in the United States of America

In loving memory of three German members of my family who endured, resisted, and transcended the Nazi dictatorship and who were among the millions who participated in the rebuilding of the democratic Germany of today: Johanna Keim Menges, Heinrich Menges, Hedwig Schuman Menges.

Contents

Preface

The historic changes of 1989–1990—transitions to democracy in Eastern Europe and German reunification—offer the hope of a bright future of freedom and peace in the new Europe. At the same time, major historical opportunities, especially those that emerge with drama and suddenness, also entail significant risks.

This book explains why the future foreign policy of the new, reunified Germany may well tilt the balance of the complex forces now reshaping Europe, the Soviet Union, and the U.S.-European relationship—either in the direction of the positive opportunities, or toward the shadows of uncertainty and risk that would accompany a German shift toward de facto neutralism and away from the full security partnership it has had with NATO and the United States. The reunification of Germany in 1990 as a continuing member of the Atlantic Alliance was an enormous accomplishment for the people of Germany, for the Western leaders who steadfastly sought Soviet permission for this result, and for the idea of freedom represented by the West. Now the next challenge is to ensure that the positive international results of German reunification that this book discusses are realized, and to avoid the potential negative effects that might develop despite the current intentions of Germany and all of its Western allies.

My approach to the analysis of the future of Germany and Europe combines both historical optimism and a sense of concern deriving from forces in the present and from the history of this century. It is my view that a reunified Germany continuing as a full political, economic, and security partner of the West can and will make an enormous contribution to increasing the prospects of a successful democratic transition in Eastern Europe, which in turn will be a beacon for the peoples of the Soviet Union.

On the other hand, if as a result of its own internal politics, of changes in the U.S.-European relationship, of the hopes for a new European collective security system replacing NATO, and of the Soviet Union's pursuing its strategic interests the new Germany shifts toward de facto neutralism, this could well undermine the very institutions that have kept peace and promoted freedom in Europe. It is for this reason that both the positive and negative futures need to be conceptualized and their implications assessed, as is done here. The following are among the implications considered: East-West relations, German-Soviet relations, German-U.S. relations, and the future of NATO and of Europe.

In order to better understand the future, this book begins with an overview of divided Germany as a focal point of the cold war, and of the domestic sources of German foreign policy (Part One). Next there is a discussion of the transition to a new Europe, with an analysis of the reasons for the unraveling of communism and of the complex, fast-paced interaction between the internal German and the international aspects of reunification (Part Two). The alternative futures of German foreign policy and their implications are then discussed (Part Three). In conclusion there is a conceptual analysis of what can be learned from the transformations in Eastern Europe and Germany, and drawing upon four decades of evolution in European-Atlantic institutions, a design for a prudent and balanced policy to make the bright future more probable is suggested (Part Four).

Before the dramatic events of 1989, as I was just completing a previous book, it seemed to me that the December 1990 West German elections were going to mark a turning point in that important country's future. For that reason, it seemed a good time to reexamine the relationship between West Germany and its allies. I appreciate the fact that Christopher DeMuth, president of the American Enterprise Institute, and David Gerson, executive vice president, agreed that this work should be done.

I am deeply grateful to the following organizations and individuals who combined to provide the resources that permitted me to write this book: Michael Joyce, president of the Lynde and Harry Bradley Foundation of Milwaukee, Wisconsin; William F. Buckley and Ambassador Evan Galbraith of the Historical Research Foundation of New York; Sir James Goldsmith, financier of wide-ranging interests; James Piereson, executive director of the John M. Olin Foundation of New York; and Daniel McMichael and Richard Larry of the Scaife Foundation of Pittsburgh, Pennsylvania.

I also appreciate the skilled assistance in the final stages of this project by James Sheehan, who is now a research associate in my program on Transitions to Democracy. Robert Egge of Rockford College worked with me as a college intern, compiled much of the statistical data, showed great interest in this project, and has my thanks for his excellent work.

I also wish to thank a number of colleagues and associates for their interest in my work over the past year: at George Washington University, President Stephen Trachtenberg, Dean Maurice East, and Assistant Dean Henry Nau; at the Center for Security Policy, Frank Gaffney, Sven Kraemer, Jennifer White, Roger Robinson, and Rinelda Bliss-Walters. While thanking them and others, I am of course solely responsible for the contents of this book.

My parents opposed the Nazi regime and were fortunate in being able to escape and find refuge in the United States, where I arrived as a four-year-old near the end of World War II. My family—both those who escaped and those who did not—always understood that at times evil regimes may control states, but that no people or group is evil and that individuals are responsible for their actions. I have had the opportunity often to return to Germany and have witnessed the growth of democratic institutions there. I also want to thank my relatives in Germany and the many political leaders and citizens of West Germany whom I have come to know in the course of many visits, starting with my return for a summer as a ten-year-old, and from whom over the years I have learned much about the past, the present, and the future of a Germany that has become an exemplary democracy.

CONSTANTINE C. MENGES
Washington, D.C.

The Future of Germany and the Atlantic Alliance

1
Introduction

Much of this century's most dramatic and tragic history has revolved around the actions and destiny of Germany. The failure of German democracy in the years after World War I—caused by both the rightist and the Communist extremes—opened the way for the Nazi dictatorship and its war on the nations and peoples of Europe.

After World War II the Grand Alliance of the United States, the United Kingdom, and the Soviet Union pledged to permit "free and unfettered elections" to determine the future governments of European countries liberated from fascist control. But the Soviet Union used cunning, deceptively rigged elections, and mostly concealed force to bring pro-Soviet Communist regimes to power in Eastern Europe and in its occupation zone of Germany.

In their three occupation zones, the Western Allies—France, the United Kingdom, and the United States—facilitated and presided over the establishment of a constitutional democracy with a mixed free-market and welfare-state economic system. By 1990 Communist East Germany had a population of about 17 million people and democratic West Germany about 61 million. In the decades after World War II, the different conditions of life in the two parts of Germany and the continuing conflicts over that division exemplified the struggle between democracy and communism, a major focus of international politics.

With Germany poised at the threshold of reunification in 1990, the question arose whether it would occur within the context of continued German participation in the Atlantic Alliance or would require or result in a neutral reunited Germany. In the peaceful protests of 1989 and the free elections of March 18, 1990, the people of East Germany clearly showed their overwhelming rejection of the dictatorship, which as in all Communist countries had combined years of repression, symbolic manipulation, and mass mobilization with a failure to attain its own professed objectives, much less those of the people, in political, cultural, or economic life.

Until the beginning of the end of communism in Eastern Europe

1

in 1989, the historical record showed that Communist regimes could fail in virtually every way that mattered but still could dominate the population and help other pro-Communist or anti-Western groups around the world take and keep power. This record of Communist success in the domain of power provides a sobering context for a review of the opportunities and prospects for Germany and Europe that the events of 1989 have opened.

Two Views about a Reunified Germany and the Atlantic Alliance

In early 1990 the battle lines over Germany were clearly staked out by both sides. After personal consultations with Soviet President Mikhail Gorbachev, on February 1, 1990, the interim East German Communist Prime Minister Hans Modrow, announced that there should be a united, neutral, demilitarized Germany within present borders and that its capital should be Berlin.[1] This position was then explicitly endorsed by Gorbachev and Soviet Foreign Minister Eduard Shevardnadze. The contrary position, stated by West German Chancellor Helmut Kohl in late 1989 and endorsed by the United States and other NATO members, was that if the people in both Germanys voted for reunification in a process of free elections this then should occur, and the reunified Germany should remain in the NATO alliance.[2]

In January 1990 West Germany further proposed that in a reunified Germany there would be no deployment of any NATO troops past the current West German border, that for a time the Soviet Union might continue to maintain some portion of its estimated 380,000 troops in the current East Germany, and that these troops might even have joint exercises with NATO troops, so that Germany might become a place for East-West reconciliation. This West German conception of reunification was endorsed by U.S. Secretary of State James A. Baker III soon after being announced, and again on the eve of Baker's February 1990 negotiations in Moscow.[3] Subsequently, on February 13, 1990, a meeting of NATO and Warsaw Treaty Organization foreign ministers in Canada led to the announcement that the four World War II Allies (the United States, the United Kingdom, France, and the Soviet Union) and the two Germanys would begin formal negotiations for reunification.[4]

Thus, after four decades, the positions of the Soviet Union and the East German Communist leadership on one side and the United States and the West German government on the other had remained virtually the same: in 1952, seeking to block West German rearmament, Soviet Premier Joseph Stalin had proposed reunification and neutrality with "a guarantee of democratic rights to the German people. . . . All democratic parties and associations were to be allowed freedom of activity, including liberty to meet, publish, and decide on their own international relations."[5] In addition, Stalin had proposed that a reunified Germany be free to join the United Nations, and that it "have such armed forces as needed for defense" and be allowed to produce arms, though the types and quantities were to be prescribed by the treaty that established reunification. Further, Germany was to promise not to enter a military coalition directed against any state it had fought between 1939 and 1945, and all Allied forces were to be withdrawn and all foreign bases closed within twelve months.

In the fall of 1954, to block West Germany's movement toward membership in the NATO alliance the post-Stalin Soviet leadership again proposed German reunification, linked to its neutrality.[6] What both the United States and Soviet Union understood then, and even more in 1990, was that the outcome of this longstanding and then renewed political battle for Germany's future would have a major impact in determining the future of Europe; would it be shaped primarily by the values and institutions of freedom, through the free association of sovereign states, or by the Soviet regime's gradual and subtly growing dominance? Rather than seek additional European Communist regimes, in the next few years the Soviet Union wants access on its own terms to a growing share of Western Europe's best technology, its agricultural and industrial products, and its money and directed investments on Soviet territory.

Until July 1990, the Soviet Union held firmly to its demand that German reunification could occur only if Germany left NATO (or became a nominal member of both NATO and the Warsaw Pact). But then, in the context of a summit meeting between Gorbachev and West German Chancellor Helmut Kohl, the Soviets agreed that a reunified Germany could remain in NATO. In return Kohl agreed to provide the Soviets with large sums in financial aid, to accept certain limits on the size and armament of German military forces, and to set the end of 1994 as the date when the 380,000-strong Soviet military forces must withdraw fully from their current bases on the territory of the former East Germany. This study discusses the complex process of international diplomacy and internal evolution within both German states that led to this result—an outcome widely perceived as a significant accomplishment for the Atlantic Alliance and for the governments of Chancellor Kohl and President Bush, both of whom took the lead and worked closely together to attain it.

This study also analyzes the transition to a new Europe and the Soviet decisions made during the 1989–1990 popular protests against Communist rule in Eastern Europe. The results of free elections in

Poland, Hungary, Czechoslovakia, and East Germany in 1990 brought democratic groups to office and showed clearly that only small minorities supported the Communist parties. As these Communist regimes unraveled in the fall and winter of 1989–1990, Gorbachev made the important decision not to use Soviet military force to prop up the national Communist regimes. This decision and the Soviet decision to permit a reunified Germany to remain in NATO were widely perceived as the final evidence of a definitive and irreversible change in Soviet foreign policy, of the end of the cold war, and of the arrival of the day of a new Europe, "whole and free."

But there is another perspective on these historic and positive events. The Soviet leadership initially expected and intended the changes in Eastern Europe to lead to reform Communist regimes, with a change in leadership from the Brezhnev generation to younger, reform-minded "perestroika Communists" like Gorbachev. Such a change was in fact attempted in Romania and Bulgaria, where the Communist leadership changed but there were no genuinely fair and free elections in 1990. As the 1989–1990 events in Eastern Europe moved well beyond reform communism in four of the countries—reflecting the courageously expressed hopes of the overwhelming majorities of the citizens for freedom and independence—the Soviet Union continued to refrain from the use of force. This restraint was practiced in part because of the impact of ten years of warfare and stalemate in Afghanistan on Soviet military institutions, and in part because the Soviet leadership reached two conclusions. First, using force could undo years of effort to establish a new spirit of normal, cooperative relations with the industrial democracies and would jeopardize the large-scale economic and technological assistance they could provide to the Soviets in the post–cold war climate of international relations. Second, should the independent and emerging democratic countries of Eastern Europe be perceived as constituting a threat or obstacle to Soviet purposes, the Soviets could then use political means, coercion, and if necessary force to restore Communist parties to power.

Further, given the long established Soviet goal of neutralizing Germany—meaning its de facto removal from effectively armed membership in a militarily credible Atlantic Alliance—it is quite possible that acquiescence in German reunification within NATO, in combination with the negotiation of a new Soviet-German treaty of friendship and a vastly expanded political and economic relationship, would be seen by the Soviets as providing new opportunities to gradually detach Germany from effective military participation in NATO.

From this perspective, whether or not Germany formally remained in NATO, its neutralization might be accomplished through the cumulative effect of the removal of all or most U.S. and other NATO forces from German territory, through the removal of most nuclear weapons of all types from Germany, though unilateral cuts in Germany's military forces, and through German endorsement of the Soviet view that the countries of the new Europe should rely for defense on a collective security arrangement, to be managed by the thirty-four nations of the Conference on Security and Cooperation in Europe (CSCE), which would include all members of NATO and the Warsaw Pact.

Without question, the beginning of transitions to democracy in Eastern Europe, the reunification of Germany, and Germany's continuing membership in the Atlantic Alliance are immensely important and positive historical developments. Nevertheless, the premise of this study is that while the future of Europe—West and East—is full of hope and promise, now is a time of historical transition, full of risk as well as opportunity. The foreign policy decisions of Germany and the Soviet Union will be among the most important factors shaping events in the coming years.

Therefore, the concluding portion of this study will explore both the future foreign policy of reunified Germany and the transition to a new Europe from two perspectives: first, from one where Germany remains a full member of a functioning NATO and second, from one where the new Soviet-German relationship is part of a complex of causes and trends that bring about the de facto neutralization of Germany. This study will also assess the international political consequences of each alternative future. Of course, determining whether it is necessary to consider carefully the implications of a Soviet strategy to create a neutral Germany depends on judgments about contemporary Soviet foreign policy.

Contemporary Soviet Foreign Policy—Two Views

Many Western observers of the Soviet Union believed by 1990 that it was so weakened by internal economic problems, interethnic clashes, and a spreading, organized opposition to the regime that Gorbachev needed the economic benefits of fully normalized relations with the West, and might even become a convert to genuine democracy. According to this view Moscow no longer had the desire or capability to threaten Western interests.

Yet it is important to recall that the Soviet Union of the late 1940s, which succeeded in helping pro-Soviet Communist movements take power in ten countries,[7] was a country by any objective measure far, far weaker than the Soviet Union of the 1990s. Indeed, it was weaker still in comparison with the United States of 1945, which was victorious in Europe and against Japan. Then the United States produced half the world's economic goods and had 12 million under arms, a nuclear monopoly, and an untouched, prosperous continent, while much of Europe and Asia, especially Germany, Japan, and the Soviet Union, were physically devastated by World War II.

Furthermore, with a government of consent by the governed the United States was the exemplar of the political and military triumph of democratic values over those of fascism and imperial militarism. The war effort had been overwhelmingly endorsed by the people, who showed their support through free and fair elections.

By contrast the Stalin regime conducted a reign of terror during the 1930s that led in its last years to the execution or imprisonment of millions of ordinary citizens as well as a large proportion of the Communist party military and government leadership. After its 1939–1941 alliance with Adolf Hitler failed to prevent a German military attack in June 1941, hundreds of thousands of Soviet troops deserted to fight on the invaders' side. In addition, millions of Soviet citizens, hating the devil they knew (Stalin) far more than the invading forces whom they believed at first to be liberators, had openly repudiated communism and the Soviet regime.

Therefore at the end of World War II the Soviet regime faced a far more powerful United States—not only in economic and military terms (until it reduced its armed forces from 12 million to 1.5 million by 1946) but also in its political support. The massive, internal opposition to Communist rule revealed by wartime events provided a striking contrast to the overwhelming consensus for democracy among the people of the United States. Nevertheless, despite its objectively far weaker situation, the Soviet Union outmaneuvered the United States politically in Eastern Europe and China. This historical context of the immediate postwar era is important to recall as we consider the future of Germany and the Atlantic Alliance in the decade of the 1990s—when the Soviet Union is widely perceived as far weaker than the United States.

The unraveling of the long-entrenched Communist regimes of Eastern Europe in 1989–1990, the far greater openness of discussion (glasnost) about life in the contemporary Soviet Union, the secessionist intentions and actions of the Baltic and other republics, and the new visibility of ethnic minorities, such as the Azerbaijani Moslems, have all encouraged many Western observers to believe that the Soviet regime will also unravel or transform into a social democracy. Gorbachev's welcome decision in 1989 not to use force to preserve the regimes of Eastern Europe is interpreted as indicating a fundamental worldwide change in Soviet foreign policy objectives and methods.

Among the many observers who have reached this conclusion, some argue that the new policy reflects authentically "new thinking" by the Gorbachev regime; others say that international and domestic Soviet failures compel the Soviets to seek economic and technological benefits from the free world; and still others believe in a combination of both factors. An especially widespread opinion holds that the Soviet Union faces such economic catastrophe and severe internal dissent that the regime must pursue a benign foreign policy, lacking the resources to maintain and expand its empire abroad.[8] Those holding this opinion tend to believe that events after German reunification—whatever the political maneuvering—will produce positive results for both a reunified Germany and the free world.

But one can view the actions of the Soviet Union under Gorbachev since 1985 from another perspective: that there is a dual Soviet foreign policy, combining normalization and tactical accommodation with the United States, Europe, China, and Japan with the continued pursuit of key Soviet objectives. These include a neutral Germany, the substantial weakening or dismantling of the NATO alliance, the enhancement of its dominance in strategic nuclear forces, the determination to maintain in power nearly all of the eleven pro-Soviet regimes that Moscow had helped to seize power during the détente of the 1970s, and the continuation of indirect aggression to bring new pro-Soviet regimes to power in key geopolitical and economic areas such as the Persian Gulf oil states (despite cooperation against the aggression of Iraq in 1990) and southern Africa.

Evidence accumulates for the continuing threat from this second dimension of Soviet foreign policy. During the first five Gorbachev years, 1985–1989, the Soviet military budget increased by 15 percent. Soviet strategic offensive forces continued to grow more powerful through modernization, and the Soviet Union seeks to be first with a strategic defense system as well. One million men were added to the military during the first Gorbachev years (the unilateral reduction of 500,000 proposed in 1988 is not yet completed), and Soviet espionage operations have increased.[9] Equally important has been the clear determination of the Gorbachev regime to use diplomacy, propaganda, covert action, and military support to maintain in power virtually all of the eleven pro-Soviet regimes established during the détente of the 1970s. These include the five in countries where armed anti-Communist resistance movements have fought for more than a decade to remove those regimes.[10]

7

The USSR participated in or supported highly visible diplomatic settlements in 1987–1988 for Central America, Afghanistan, and Angola, which were widely perceived as signs of Soviet withdrawal from zones of influence and power. Most of the estimated 350,000 foreign Communist troops were removed from direct combat, and most Soviet forces were removed from Afghanistan by February 1989. At the same time, however, the Gorbachev regime sustained its political and military support for these pro-Soviet regimes, helping them to stay in power. The estimated value of Soviet provided military supplies to those five regimes nearly doubled, from about $6 billion annually in 1985 when Gorbachev came to power to about $10 billion in 1989.[11] The most dramatic example of this continuing Soviet effort to keep and consolidate the victories of the 1970s has been one of the largest military airlifts in history. A reported 4,800 military supply flights were made from February to October 1989 to the pro-Soviet regime in Afghanistan, and these have continued at an estimated 40 flights each day to deliver about $250 million worth of weapons and arms monthly. Further, there has been no indication that relations have ended with longtime Soviet allies such as Cuba, North Korea, Syria, and Libya, the operating bases for much of the violence aimed at free world countries though the indirect aggression and armed subversion.

With the very significant exception of Soviet unwillingness to use military force in Eastern Europe in late 1989 to repress popular demands for political liberalization, contemporary Soviet actions under Gorbachev resemble actions during previous post–World War II efforts at détente. All these efforts point to a duality of method and continuity of purpose in their current foreign policy.

Moreover, the Soviet Politburo and Central Committee have learned the lessons of Russian history. The 1989 events in Eastern Europe have taught them again that dictatorial institutions may remain stable for long periods yet prove brittle under pressure. They understand that while some reforms and limited internal openings may be useful, mistakes can rapidly lead to major threats to the regime. The military intimidation, economic blockade, and other coercive actions to roll back Lithuania's declaration of independence of March 11, 1990, reflect a determination to maintain the authority of Moscow within the entire Soviet Union. Soviet leaders are likely to remember that even during the Great Patriotic War the Stalin regime, although less repressive than during the terror of the 1930s, still maintained control over the government, the military, the secret police, and the people.

Gorbachev and the other key leaders of the Soviet regime want to make communism more open and more economically effective, and they may be willing to introduce some real political competition inside and outside the party. Nevertheless, although they prefer limited and secret coercion, the Soviet leadership will use whatever coercion and violence they think necessary to determine all major Soviet internal and international actions.

Failure by the Gorbachev-led Soviet regime to accomplish its internal and foreign policy objectives in the coming years could well lead to other major shifts, either toward repression or toward far greater liberalization. But during the early 1990s the future of Germany will probably be markedly affected by the actions of a Soviet Union that remains under Communist control, possesses a powerful military apparatus, and pursues its decades-long foreign policy objectives. They include a compliant Germany, one that has become a de facto neutral even if it still officially belongs to NATO. In this way the Soviet regime could gradually dominate Germany and perhaps all of Europe.

Looking to the Future

The current political struggle over Germany's destiny involves not only the Soviet Union, the United States, the NATO countries, and the new leadership in Eastern Europe, but also the nearly 80 million people in the reunited Germany. The last time such a dramatic time of international decisions faced Germany was during the interwar years of the Weimar Republic. At that time a combination of significant political mistakes by well-intentioned German and Western leaders led to the events that permitted Nazi extremists to take power, thereby setting the course toward World War II. Important decisions will again have to be made, not only by well-intentioned Western and German leaders, but by the people of the former West Germany, who have adhered to the ideals and institutions of parliamentary democracy for forty years, and by the East Germans, who have shown by their flight from communism, their peaceful quest for freedom in 1989, and their votes in the 1990 elections that they too want freedom.

German reunification has strengthened the cause of democracy in Eastern Europe and thus in the world. But reunification could also be followed by the de facto neutralization of Germany, whether or not it remains a formal member of the Atlantic Alliance. The final outcome may well have dramatic consequences—for good or for ill. One perceptive American commentator expressed anxiety about the future in these words: "Is there not a terror in millions of human minds and hearts that the nightmare visage of the past may be the

9

face of the future? Did not the two earlier German unifications lead to war?"[12]

Now that German reunification has been achieved, the true nature of the future relationship between Germany and the Atlantic Alliance is an open issue that will be determined by a complex blend of international and German political decisions. This book illuminates the underlying historical and contemporary factors, describes and analyzes the transition to a new Europe and a new Germany, discusses the implications of possible alternative futures, and concludes with suggestions for a Western strategy to ensure that the new, reunited Germany remains a democratic partner of the Atlantic Alliance, in security as well as in economic endeavors.

PART ONE

From Defeat to Division and a Democratic Transition

2
Germany in the Context of International Politics, 1945–1955

On February 12, 1990, the four powers that had defeated Germany in 1945 and the two resulting German states jointly announced that they would begin negotiations on "external aspects of the establishment of German unity, including the issues of the security of the neighboring states."[1] This brief but dramatic announcement brought to a full circle the forty-five years of history that began at Malta in February 1945 with decisions about the occupation zones of soon-to-be defeated Nazi Germany. Later that month at the Yalta summit, Franklin Roosevelt, Winston Churchill, and Joseph Stalin jointly agreed and publicly pledged that the countries liberated from German control would choose their new governments in "free and unfettered elections."

The Western powers expected a cooperative post-war relationship with the Soviet Union, under the rubric of collective security managed by the soon-to-be-established United Nations. Since the Western nations assumed a peace treaty with Germany would be signed soon after the military victory, they had no hesitation in agreeing to four-power joint control of Berlin, the German capital, even though it would be deep within the Soviet zone of occupation.

Germany surrendered unconditionally in May 1945. A month later U.S. and British military commanders learned that they would not be given the expected, normal access needed for the forces moving to Berlin to fulfill their part in the agreed joint occupation of the city. The Soviet military commander, Marshall Georgy Zhukov, "refused to grant his Western colleagues two out of the three railways, one of the two highways and one of the three airfields for which they asked. Moreover, he made clear that what they did receive came as a privilege rather than a right."[2]

This was a disturbing portent, especially since Stalin had sent Walter Ulbricht and a cadre of other German Communists to Berlin in early May 1945 to build a Communist-led political coalition immediately with non-Communist groups. In the words of a former German participant, it had a clear purpose: "The result was to look democratic but the reins must really be in our (Communist) hands."[3] Such Soviet actions in Germany followed a pattern of activities in the rest of liberated Europe that violated in fact though often not in form the Yalta promise of "free and unfettered elections." They indicated that the Soviets had begun to seek dominance in Europe without open warfare and that Germany would be a major focus of this soon to be named cold war.

There have been five major phases in this continuing conflict between the Soviet Union and the West about Germany:

1. occupation and the start of the cold war, 1945–1947

2. the establishment of two competing German states, 1948–1949

3. the integration of both Germanys into the political and military alliance systems of the United States and the Soviet Union, 1950–1955

4. years of often intense confrontation, with the status of Berlin as the symbolic focus, 1958–1969

5. the acceleration of normalization through West Germany's 1970 initiation of *Ostpolitik* (literally, Eastern policy, the attempt to expand West German relations with the East) leading in 1990 back to the Western expectations of 1945 that a peace settlement could bring about a reunified Germany.

Occupation and the Start of Cold War

As a result of the pact the two nations signed in August 1939, the Soviet Union and Nazi Germany both invaded Poland the next month. Secret Nazi-Soviet agreements specified that the Soviet Union could annex about 180,000 square kilometers of Polish territory and the independent Baltic states—Latvia, Lithuania, and Estonia. At the end of the war Stalin was determined to keep these and other annexed territories. Therefore, after the Red Army occupied Poland and eastern Germany in 1945, Stalin detached from pre–World War II Germany a portion of territory nearly equivalent to what the Soviet Union had taken from Poland and decreed it part of the new Poland. The Soviets thereby moved the new eastern border of Germany about 250 miles west, to the Oder and Neisse rivers. These Soviet actions were taken unilaterally, without agreement from the United States and the United Kingdom, and they violated the declaration of the Atlantic Charter promising no territorial aims in the war.

At the Yalta summit, Stalin had proposed that defeated Germany pay $20 billion in reparations (equivalent to about $200 billion in 1990) in money, products, and industrial equipment—half to be given to the Soviet Union. The United States and the United Kingdom would not agree to any specific sum for reparations.

The Potsdam summit in July 1945 was called to prescribe occupation policies. The Soviet Union pressed for Western agreement to the new borders it had established and on the $20 billion in reparations, which would include extractions for itself from the Western zones of Germany, if necessary. From the Western point of view the first priority was to ensure that there was a "sufficient minimum of shelter and food to prevent revolution, starvation, and disease" among millions of displaced persons in Germany and Europe.[4] There were about 10 million German soldiers in detention. In addition, most of the 9 million Germans who had lived in the territory Stalin had placed under Polish control were fleeing or being expelled to make room for the millions of Polish citizens whom Stalin was forcing out of the former Polish territory he had just annexed. And a large proportion of the 3 million Sudeten Germans in Czechoslovakia were also being expelled and were entering Germany.

Despite the war, Germany's industrial capacity was estimated at only about 15–20 percent destroyed, and its 1944 production level had been 20 percent greater than the 1936 level. Its net population had increased between 1939 and 1945, and now the three Western zones faced the need to provide for an influx of about 10 million Germans while resettling about 3 million of the 6 million foreign workers who had been forced by the Nazi regime to maintain and expand wartime production.[5] In addition, millions of Germans who had fled to the countryside to escape the bombing of the cities also sought to return to their homes.

At Potsdam in July 1945, the United States and the United Kingdom threatened to break off negotiations rather than agree to the Soviet demand for $20 billion in German reparations. Instead they proposed that the newly established Control Council which would govern Germany and where each had a veto should work this out. Without Allied consent, the Soviet Union simply began to remove German equipment from its occupation zone, then repeated its demand for $20 billion. The Allies then made two concessions in exchange for Soviet willingness not to specify the $20 billion amount for German reparations.

First, they offered Moscow a portion of the "surplus" economic goods from the Western zones. Moscow took some but soon found it more efficient to leave the factories in East Germany. From 1945 to 1952 the Soviet Union annually extracted an estimated 20 percent of East Germany's production. Second, as described by the British historian Michael Balfour, there was "a virtual Western climb-down over frontiers [the Soviet annexation in Poland and transfer of some German territory to Poland]. . . . Possession proved nine-tenths of the law, but the West's face was saved by a proviso that the final decision on the frontiers should not be taken until the Peace Conference (then expected to occur quite soon)."[6] Soviet-Polish-German borders were thus destined to figure in the negotiations on Germany during 1990. This explained the February 1990 request of the non-Communist prime minister of Poland, Tadeusz Mazowiecki, to participate in the six-party talks on German reunification.[7]

The Protocol of Proceedings drawn up at the Potsdam summit summarized the agreements reached by the Grand Alliance about Germany. It also included a statement of political principles, which can be summarized as denazification, decentralization, and democratization. Political life was to be reconstructed on a democratic basis, with local self-government through elected councils, the encouragement of political parties, and the guarantees of freedom of speech, assembly, and organization.

Although no new central government was established, central administrative departments staffed by Germans were to provide the link between the Control Council and the new local German governments at the state and town levels. But the French opposed the concept of central administration by Germans in any form, as well as nationwide German political parties and trade unions. As a result, the military commanders established German advisory councils in each of the three Western zones, which became more politically significant than originally intended. Balfour notes, however, that "the failure to create a central German administration may have saved the Western powers from having to cope with one which was Communist dominated."[8]

The initial French attitude toward Germany had many points in common with that of the Soviets. Both emphasized the need to punish Germany, both envisioned a politically and economically weak Germany for many years, even decades, and both intended to annex new territory. France sought to obtain the coal-rich Saar region on its western border.

Although President Harry Truman used a nuclear threat to force Stalin to back down from an attempt to annex northern Iran in 1946, much of Eastern Europe was moving into the Soviet sphere through rigged elections. This meant the national Communist parties—with Soviet backing—prevented any genuine freedom during the election campaigns, in voting and in the counting of the ballots. To counter such actions by Stalin and to encourage economic recovery in Europe, the United States shifted its policy on Germany from control and denazification to reconstruction of political and economic institutions. Announcing this policy in Stuttgart on September 6, 1946, Secretary of State James Byrnes declared, "Germany is part of Europe, and recovery in Europe, and particularly in the states adjoining Germany, will be slow indeed if Germany with her great resources of iron and coal is turned into a poorhouse. . . . The American people hope to see a peaceful democratic Germany become and remain free and independent. . . ."[9]

This statement reflected the U.S. view that a democratic, economically viable Germany was essential to prospects for a free and prosperous Europe. Late in 1946 the American and British zones were merged, and in March 1947 Truman proclaimed that the United States would help free people to resist conquest. Greece was then facing a Soviet-aided insurgency, and Turkey faced Soviet threats and demands.

From 1945 to 1947 the United States provided $11.3 billion in economic aid to Europe, including occupied Germany, and another $29 million from private relief agencies.[10] Because of the slow pace of economic improvement, however, Secretary of State George C. Marshall proposed a large-scale U.S. economic aid program in June 1947.[11] France then merged its occupation zone in Germany with the Anglo-American zone; otherwise, it was told, it would receive no Marshall Plan aid.

In February 1948 a quick and deceptive coup led to the establishment of a Communist regime in Czechoslovakia—the last non-Communist state in Eastern Europe. This move cast a more ominous light on Soviet political maneuvering in the Soviet zone of Germany.

The Return of Political Parties

Because of the moral revulsion the Germans felt toward Hitler and his National Socialist German Workers party (Nazi) regime, they looked for ethical standards to guide political life after World War II.

The Three Major Parties. A new centrist party, the Christian Democratic Union (*Christliche demokratische Union* or CDU), was based on Christian and democratic values. From the start it included Catholics, Protestants, non-believers, and members of all economic groups, from both urban and rural areas. A related party, the Christian Social Union (*Christlich sozial Union* or CSU), was established in Bavaria. While maintaining separate structures, the two parties formed a common caucus in the federal Parliament and have functioned at the national level as a coalition, known as the CDU-CSU. Voting center-right on many social issues, this coalition has combined a free-market oriented economic policy with support for the modern welfare state. It calls this policy synthesis the "social market economy."

Dating from the nineteenth century, Germany's Social Democratic party (*Sozial demokratische Partei Deutschlands* or SPD) is one of the oldest political parties in the world. Like the Christian centrist parties of the Weimar Republic, it had been the object of violence by the Communists and of systematic persecution by the Nazis. Although espousing Marxist principles for many decades, the German and other social democratic movements had split in the late nineteenth century from the Communist (Leninist) wing of Marxism. The fundamental difference lay in the Social Democrats' desire for democracy, rather than a "dictatorship of the proletariat" presided over by any "vanguard" party. The social base of the SPD was composed of elements of the working class (especially those in labor unions), elements of the middle-class (especially those in public administration), and elements of opinion-shaping professions such as journalism and teaching. Since the SPD held governmental authority in the Weimar years and its leaders were persecuted by the Nazis, it had members experienced in policy and politics who were known to have been anti-Nazi and who could work in the interim local governments and councils set up during the military occupation. These SPD leaders immediately began to reestablish the party in all parts of Germany.

The Free Democratic party (*Freie demokratische Partei* or FDP) was established by mostly middle- and upper-class Protestants who viewed themselves as liberal in the European tradition: they opposed significant state intervention in economic matters and clerical religious intervention on social and cultural issues. During the Weimar Republic their forerunners were Gustave Stresemann's German People's party and the German Democratic party, both of which were primarily Protestant. The Center party, the forerunner of the CDU-CSU, was mainly Catholic. Despite the concerted effort of the CDU to be nondenominational and despite its interdenominational support in the elections, the FDP became for some "a refuge to those who agree with CDU policies but resent its alleged Catholic domination."[12] Along with the other two parties, it has been a major participant in West German politics—often being the decisive factor in building a parliamentary majority and governing coalition.

An interesting analysis by Gerhard Loewenberg, an American political scientist, compared the vote received by the spectrum of German political groups in the 1928 national parliamentary elections (the last national vote before the world depression) with those in the first national parliamentary elections of the post–World War II era in 1949. In the area of Weimar Germany that became the Federal Republic of Germany, the Christian center and regional parties received 25 percent of the vote in 1928 and 43 percent in 1949; the SPD received 27 percent in 1928 and 29 percent in 1949; the Communist party held 9 percent in 1928 and 6 percent in 1949; and the far right received 13 percent in 1928 and 2 percent in 1949.[13] By the 1960s the three major parties, CDU-CSU, SPD, and FDP, were obtaining more than 90 percent of all the votes cast in the national elections.[14]

The Communist Party. Although small in electoral terms during the Weimar Republic (11 percent in 1928), the Communist party of Germany (*Kommunistiche Partei Deutschlands* or KPD) contributed to the destruction of German democracy. Like the Nazis, the KPD employed political- and paramilitary-extremist methods to polarize German politics and society. Most surviving Communist leaders spent the war years in the Soviet Union. When they were then sent back to occupied Germany to establish Communist power they used Stalin's preferred technique—establishing a "united front" with the Social Democrats. Although this was resisted in the Western occupation zones, some elements of the Social Democrats in the Soviet zone were coerced in June 1946 into joining a Communist-run "united" party, renamed the Socialist Unity party (*Sozialistische Einheitspartei Deutschlands* or SED).

As a result, the 1946 city-wide elections in Berlin were the only place where support for the Communist SED versus the SPD was tested before 1990. The SED had great expectations, not only because of its Soviet support, but also because of the left-wing tradition of Berlin; the Nazis had never obtained a majority of the votes in that city. But in late 1946 the SED received only 20 percent of the city-wide vote, the SPD 49 percent, the CDU 22 percent, and the FDP 9 percent. Following the 1946 city election, the SPD was outlawed in the Soviet zone (not to return until the next free elections, held in March 1990, when the SED received 16 percent of the entire East German vote).[15]

Of the 130 seats in the 1946 Berlin city assembly the Social Democrats won 63, the Christian Democrats 29, the Communists 26, and the Free Democrats 12. When the city assembly then chose Social Democrat Ernest Reuter as mayor the Soviet commandant vetoed the selection, in June 1947. After the election made clear to the Soviet and SED leadership that the electoral process had not yet been manipulated enough to bring East Germany under Communist control, there was a marked increase in repression. In 1990 secret mass graves of thousands of victims were revealed after a democratically elected East German government took office.

In February 1948, the day before the Communist takeover of Czechoslovakia, a Soviet-sponsored People's Congress of Greater Berlin met in the Soviet sector of the city with the apparent intention of supplanting the Berlin city assembly chosen by voters in all four zones and of thereby putting all of Berlin under de facto Soviet governance. Early the next month, March 1948, the Soviet authorities limited travel from their zone to Berlin. This limitation marked the start of Soviet pressure on West Berlin.

Only days later—on March 17, 1948—the first post–World War II defensive alliance among Western states was established when the Brussels Treaty of Western Union was signed by Belgium, the Netherlands, Luxembourg, France, and the United Kingdom. It was intended to protect the participants against the Soviet Union and, potentially, against Germany.

In the spring of 1948 the Organization of European Economic Cooperation (OEEC) was established to administer the Marshall Plan. It became the first institution seeking to foster both economic growth and economic integration in Western Europe. Then the United States, the United Kingdom, and France agreed that their newly merged occupation zones should begin drafting a constitution for a West German federal republic. The Soviet response was to walk out of the Control Council and apply even tighter restrictions on access to Berlin, eventually producing a full Soviet blockade of land access in June 1948. This blockade marked the end of any semblance of four-power governance over Germany, except for Berlin, which would remain under some degree of four-power authority until German reunification.

Two Germanys, Two Coalitions, 1948–1955

The blockade of Berlin was neither accepted nor challenged by Western armed forces. It was leapt over by massive airlift to supply food, shelter, and warmth to the 2.25 million people in the Western zones. The labor government of Britain permitted the United States to station on its territory nuclear-armed B29 bombers capable of reaching the Soviet Union. By November 1948 there were ninety such bombers in Britain.[16]

From the start of the Berlin blockade the Western powers took three mutually reinforcing steps: they established a new German government in the three Western zones; they encouraged economic integration between France and Germany, and then among the Western European democracies; and they established a defensive alliance system. Moscow first tried to impede these actions, then imitated the institutional forms. As a result, from 1948 to 1955 two Germanys and two opposing coalitions evolved.

In the spring of 1948, a British-American-French conference agreed to establish a central German government through the convening of a

> Constituent Assembly [to] draw up a democratic constitution which will establish for the participating states a governmental structure of the federal type which is adapted to the eventual reestablishment of German unity at present disrupted; and which will protect the rights of participating states, provide adequate central authority and contain guarantees of individual rights and freedom.[17]

At the time, among the ministers-president (governors) of the eleven West German states (*Laender*), five were from the SPD, five from the CDU, and one from the FDP. Despite the Berlin blockade, the SPD hoped it might still be possible to cooperate with the Communists in order to obtain German unity. As a result, this Allied proposal for a Constituent Assembly was initially rejected. But ultimately the ministers-president did consent to convene a parliamentary council, elected from among the eleven state legislatures on the basis of population. The parliamentary council was composed of twenty-seven from the SPD, twenty-seven from the CDU, five from the FDP, and two each from three smaller parties, including the Communists. With SPD leader Kurt Schumacher ill, CDU leader Konrad Adenauer became chairman of the council, which began its deliberations on September 1, 1948.

During the next months the German economy began to improve markedly, sparked by the currency reform initiated in June 1948. Under the "social market" policy proposed by the CDU-affiliated economist, Dr. Ludwig Erhard, all German currency was exchanged at a fraction of its nominal value for the new currency, the deutsche mark, and price controls on most items were removed or phased out. By the second half of 1948 there had been a 50 percent increase in industrial production, followed by another 25 percent increase in 1949. By 1953 average living conditions were higher than in 1938, and by 1958 West Germany surpassed Britain and became the world's second ranked exporter.[18] This "economic miracle" derived not only from the new policy but also from the inflow of Marshall Plan aid (about $1.4 billion between 1948 and 1952), from the skilled and

21

plentiful labor force (including millions of German immigrants from the East), and from the replacement by modern facilities of the industrial equipment destroyed by the war or dismantled for reparations.

The sense of crisis created by the Soviet blockade of Berlin produced a political consensus in the United States to build a peacetime alliance building on the 1947 precedent of the Inter-American Treaty of Reciprocal Assistance (Rio Treaty). In April 1949 the North Atlantic Treaty Organization (NATO) was established by expanding the 1948 Treaty of Western Union alliance of Britain, France, and the Benelux nations to include the United States, Canada, and five other European states—Denmark, Ireland, Italy, Norway, and Portugal—making a total of twelve.

At the signing of the North Atlantic Treaty in Washington, D.C., President Truman said, "If it had existed in 1914 and in 1939, supported by the nations who are represented here today, I believe it would have prevented the acts of aggression that led to two World Wars."[19] By making a formal commitment to the defense of Western Europe the United States conveyed a clear signal to the Soviet leadership that Europe was under the protection of American nuclear as well as conventional arms. The overt threat from the Berlin blockade had brought cohesion rather than fear and intimidation to the Western powers. Stalin lifted the blockade on May 6, 1949.

The West German Basic Law. Only days later the new West German constitution, the basic law, was adopted, and on May 23, 1949, the Federal Republic of Germany was formally established. The basic law provided for the full range of civil rights and a bicameral parliamentary form of government, with a president as head of state. The president appoints a chancellor as chief executive, who must be confirmed by a majority of votes in the federal assembly (Bundestag). The Bundestag is chosen through universal suffrage on the basis of population for a four-year term.

The eleven constituent states of the Federal Republic are represented in the federal council (Bundesrat), appointed by the state governments, with the number of representatives from each varying from two to five, depending on the state's population. The Bundesrat must approve all legislation affecting the states, which retain broad responsibilities for such areas as education and law enforcement. And even when its approval is not mandatory, the Bundesrat can veto legislation. To override such a veto the Bundestag must match the vote of the Bundesrat—either a simple majority or a two-thirds vote.

According to the preamble of the basic law, the eleven states were acting for all Germans unable to take part (including those in the Soviet zone and in Berlin) in calling for unification. The basic law also provided a simple means whereby the East German states could join the Federal Republic through a vote of accession. In October 1990 the CDU-CSU–led governments employed this means to bring about full reunification.

The first West German national elections were held on August 14, 1949, and the resulting seats in the Bundestag were: CDU-CSU 139, SPD 131, FDP 52, Bavarian party 17, German party 17, Communists 15, and other parties 31. In a portent of the pattern that would usually prevail for the next forty years, the leading parties, CDU-CSU and SPD, had the choice of a "great coalition" together or of forming a coalition with the FDP. After some weeks of political maneuvering, the Bundestag chose Konrad Adenauer as chancellor by a one-vote margin, and the first CDU-CSU-FDP coalition government took office.

In East Germany, the Soviet authorities set up a People's Congress in March 1948; it established a People's Council, which approved a constitution for the German Democratic Republic in March 1949. In May 1949 another People's Congress was elected on a one-party (SED) list; it then chose another People's Council, which declared itself a provisional government the month after Adenauer became chancellor. As Balfour notes, however, this "did not imply any significant relaxation of the Russian grip."[20]

The Council of Europe. In the Federal Republic, the three Western Allies had agreed that they would give up most but not all of their authority. The Control Council became a High Commission, and after intense negotiations with the German leaders a new Occupation Statute was worked out and formally conveyed to Chancellor Adenauer on September 21, 1949. France insisted upon two features: first, a multinational Ruhr Authority, including the United States, United Kingdom, France, and the Benelux countries to allocate German coal, coke, and steel from the Ruhr among the internal and export markets; and second, recognition for the French "customs union" with the coal-rich Saar region of Germany, which France sought to annex.

From the start, the Federal Republic maintained that the four-power assumption of government authority in 1945 did not affect the continued existence of Germany as a state within its 1937 borders (before it annexed Austria and part of Czechoslovakia). Furthermore, no part of the original German territory could be legally or permanently transferred to another state unless the government of a united

23

Germany gave its consent. This view had the full support of the SPD in 1949.[21]

The Council of Europe was established in July 1949 to encourage unity and political cooperation among ten European democracies. The Federal Republic was invited to join as an associate rather than full member; it became a full member in 1951. The Council was located in Strasbourg, on the French side of the border with Germany, to symbolize hopes for French-German reconciliation. (Strasbourg is also the site of the consultative European Parliament, established as part of the European Coal and Steel Community in 1952 and directly elected since 1979.)

In the spring of 1950 the foreign minister of France, Robert Schuman, took a major step away from his country's initial punitive postwar policy toward Germany and sent Adenauer a letter proposing a French-German Coal and Steel Community as a step toward reconciliation and the economic integration of Europe. Adenauer and his CDU-CSU party were firmly committed to integration with Western Europe, but at that time the Social Democrats were strongly opposed. They believed it would make reunification more difficult and feared it could establish a new form of Allied control.

The 1951 Treaty of Paris, which established the European Coal and Steel Community, brought the end of the Ruhr Authority, the ultimate fading away of the Saar issue, and the establishment of an entirely new level of cooperative relations between Germany and France and among the other four signatories (Belgium, the Netherlands, Luxembourg, Italy). Its success led to other forms of economic integration and to the evolution to the European Community, composed of twelve members committed to creating a single market and closer political cooperation in 1992.

The Challenge to NATO. Only weeks after Schuman made his proposal to Adenauer, in June 1950, Communist North Korea attacked South Korea. The United Nations Security Council (with the Soviet Union absent) authorized military aid to South Korea, and the United States contributed 85 percent of the combat forces. North Korea and Communist China were both backed by the Soviet Union. The war lasted three years and created fears of war in Europe, especially since the American nuclear monopoly had ended in August 1949 with the successful test of a Soviet atomic weapon. At the beginning of the Korean War the military balance in Central Europe had 12 Western divisions facing about 175 (smaller) Soviet divisions in East Germany or nearby. Since the Soviet Union now had an atomic capability and the U.S. nuclear threat had not deterred the North Korean attack, the members of NATO agreed they needed to "greatly improve its strength in 'conventional' (non-nuclear) weapons if its determination to resist aggression was to be made credible to the East."[22]

This meant, first, that NATO needed a functioning military organization. In December 1950 General Dwight Eisenhower was named the first supreme commander of Allied forces in Europe, a multinational combined military staff assembled to command troops from a number of Allied countries that were placed directly under NATO command. It also meant that the NATO conventional forces in the border region between East Germany and West Germany had to be increased—a goal of eighty-five divisions was established (this goal was reduced in 1951 to forty-three divisions with thirty in central Germany). West Germany, then with a population of fifty million, was an obvious source for additional military forces. Moscow had already established a 55,000-strong People's Police, equipped with tanks and artillery in East Germany.

The Question of German Rearmament. In September 1950 U.S. Secretary of State Dean Acheson told a NATO meeting that in order for the United States to remain in Europe, West Germany would have to be rearmed immediately. This rearmament so soon after the war was deeply opposed by many Europeans, as well as by a significant proportion of Germans who favored pacifism or feared that Germany would become the focus of East-West combat and reduce chances for reunification. The Social Democratic party vigorously opposed any form of German rearmament.

While German Chancellor Konrad Adenauer had no wish to see Germany rearmed, he was concerned about the Soviet military threat to Germany. Before the September 1950 NATO meeting, he had agreed to German rearmament if it occurred in the context of a European framework after full sovereignty had been restored to the Federal Republic.

With Churchill in the lead, the Council of Europe called for the establishment of a European army. In October 1950 French Prime Minister René Plevin formally proposed to the Council of Europe the creation of "a European Army attached to the political institutions of a united Europe."[23] This proposal was accepted by the United States, Britain, and France in December 1950. The Occupation Statute was revised in March 1951 to restore German sovereignty in foreign policy. West German officials thereafter took an equal part in the further discussions for a European defense community that would provide for multinational combined staffs and forces.

As these negotiations were moving toward success, in March

1952 Stalin sent his "peace letter." He proposed a four-power peace treaty to permit the reunification of Germany, provided it would be neutral and armed only for self-defense. The Western Allies responded by demanding free elections in all parts of Germany prior to negotiating such a peace treaty—the same position they would take in February 1990. In 1952 the East-West debate about whether free elections or a peace treaty should come first had created an impasse. The continuing Soviet military and economic harassment of the three Allies in West Berlin in 1951 and 1952 reinforced Allied determination to move toward a European defense community.[24]

After officially ending the state of war with Germany in July 1951, the three Western powers in May 1952 replaced the Occupation Statute with a convention on relations with the Federal Republic— the Treaty of Bonn. Besides conferring full sovereignty on West Germany, the treaty committed the United States, Britain, and France to seek the peaceful reunification of Germany while retaining responsibility for maintaining the security of West Berlin. The next day, May 27, 1952, the European Defense Community Treaty was signed in Paris, affirming West Germany's membership and rearmament. This provoked immediate retaliation by Soviet and East German authorities in Berlin as the treaty went before the several European parliaments for ratification.

Adenauer had the votes to secure ratification in the German parliament despite the strong opposition of the Social Democrats. The Soviet Union was determined to block German rearmament. As an example of some of the means used, a forged report allegedly sent from the U.S. chief of naval operations to the National Security Council "revealed" U.S. plans to become dominant in the Mediterranean and to undercut the interests of France and Britain in Europe. This false report was published by the respected French newspaper *Le Monde* and was widely circulated in Europe.[25] William Hyland, a former U.S. government official and observer of the Soviet Union, wrote that the Soviets also sought to block the European Defense Community by promising to help France in its negotiations with the Communist Vietnamese guerrillas (in the first Indochina War, 1946– 1954) if France would refuse to ratify the European Defense Community Treaty.

> Eventually the Soviets struck a bargain with [French Prime Minister] Pierre Mendes-France. In return for Soviet intervention to help settle the remaining issues in Indochina— permitting Mendes-France to make his self-imposed deadline for settlement—the French parliament eventually killed the European Defense Community. Even if no explicit bar-

gain was made (Mendes-France denies it) this was the clear implication and both sides performed according to expectations.[26]

After Stalin died in March 1953, a workers' uprising against Communist rule in East Germany in June 1953 was crushed by Soviet forces when the East German armed units were unable or unwilling to act. The post-Stalin Soviet leadership was pleased when the French parliament rejected the European Defense Community in August 1954. In October 1954, however, Britain proposed a new approach to German rearmament. Instead of the supranational approach of the European Defense Community, the British suggested an organization of sovereign states to be known as the Western European Union. This was in effect an extension of the Brussels Treaty of 1948, but this time both Germany and Italy were invited to join as full members of the Western European Union.

But the October 1954 treaty, which admitted the Federal Republic to NATO, and the Western European Union required Germany to incorporate all its armed forces into NATO; no other member had this requirement. The treaty also required West German renunciation of the right to manufacture nuclear, biological, and chemical weapons on its territory, though not to obtain or control them. Furthermore, West Germany promised never to use force to achieve reunification or the modification of its borders. Germany was to contribute 500,000 men to NATO but would not maintain a separate general staff.

Again seeking to block West German rearmament and its membership in NATO, the post-Stalin leadership of the Soviet Union made a series of proposals promising German reunification in exchange for its neutrality. These were rejected. On May 9, 1955, the occupation of West Germany officially ended with Germany's admission to NATO. Days later, on May 14, 1955, the Warsaw Pact was established by the Soviet Union to include all East European countries except Yugoslavia.

3
From Confrontation to Normalization, 1955–1975

From 1955 to 1975 Germany was at the center of East-West relations. An initial tenuous stability gave way to intense confrontation, with Berlin as the focus. Years of stalemate were followed by a process of gradual normalization. Germany's *Ostpolitik*, a building of ties with East Germany and the USSR, paralleled U.S.-Soviet détente in the 1970s. These events, experienced by the postwar German political leadership, set the context for the international decisions of the 1990s.

Coexistence and Confrontation, 1955–1963

In the era of post-Stalin collective leadership in the Soviet Union and of firmness regarding Germany's rearmament and NATO membership in the West, the initial Soviet policy was to seek normal relations. On May 15, 1955, one day after the Warsaw Pact was signed and only days after Germany joined NATO, the United States, France, Britain, and the Soviet Union concluded the Austrian State Treaty. This provided for the withdrawal of all occupation forces (including all Soviet forces) from Austria and for the restoration of its full sovereignty. It also stipulated an Austrian commitment to permanent neutrality.

The first summit meeting with the Soviet Union held since Potsdam (1945) took place in July 1955 and included Soviet agreement to German reunification by free elections. The West saw this as a major breakthrough, which was followed up in September 1955 when Chancellor Adenauer visited Moscow for consultations. That visit led to the establishment of diplomatic relations between the Soviet Union and the Federal Republic.

Significant events in Moscow contributed to the atmosphere of normalization. At the Twentieth Party Congress in early 1956 Nikita Khrushchev, first secretary of the Soviet Communist party, denounced the crimes of Stalin and called for reforms within the party. This denunciation marked the beginning of the end of mass terror as a threat facing the Soviet people. Khrushchev did succeed in making Soviet communism safe for Communists; thereafter, those purged or demoted were retired rather than killed or imprisoned.

In early 1956 Khrushchev also announced a unilateral reduction of 1,300,000 troops in Soviet military forces; he would call for another 300,000 to be cut in 1958. These reductions would ostensibly be accompanied by cuts in East European military forces. The promised unilateral cuts elicited a positive Western response, but as a high-ranking defector from the Czechoslovak intelligence service would reveal years later, "the satellite nations which were ordered to support the Soviet deception plan received explicit directions from the Soviet Defense Council: announce force reductions but do not actually reduce your forces."[1]

The armed forces of West Germany were established in January 1956. A shortage of manpower due to the enormous German economic expansion caused a sharp reduction in targeted strength; Germany planned to field only 76,000 troops by the end of 1956, about 130,000 by the end of 1957, and 350,000 rather than 500,000 by the end of 1961.[2]

This slowdown in German rearmament occurred while President Dwight Eisenhower and the Atlantic Alliance were reconsidering NATO strategy. Stalin's death, the Korean Armistice (July 1953), and an initially accommodating Soviet foreign policy sharply reduced the perceived Soviet military threat to Germany and Western Europe. Furthermore, none of the major European NATO members could meet their 1952 commitment to the goal of a standing force of ninety-two divisions without substantial U.S. economic assistance.

To deter any Soviet attack on the United States or its Allies, the Eisenhower administration's "New Look" defense doctrine called for the use of nuclear weapons at both the strategic and the tactical level and if necessary massive retaliation. For NATO this doctrine allowed a reduction in the level of planned conventional forces, a smaller Allied presence in Germany, and deployment of tactical nuclear weapons with NATO forces in Europe. This approach was adopted by the NATO members in December 1954 and endorsed by the Adenauer government.[3]

In 1955, however, NATO maneuvers simulating the use of tactical nuclear weapons produced estimates of enormous, "collateral" civilian casualties in Germany. This threat triggered a sustained Social Democratic campaign against any deployment of nuclear weapons on German territory. In one expert's view, "the ensuing debate proved to be the hottest and most divisive one the Federal Republic would experience until the 1980s" (when the SPD vehemently opposed the

29

deployment of intermediate-range nuclear forces in Germany).[4] The SPD argued that nuclear weapons were inconsistent with reunification—yet it "failed to identify persuasive alternatives to Germany's NATO membership or the New Look strategy."[5]

In June 1956 an uprising in Poznan against the Polish Communist regime was crushed, but in October 1956 another uprising took place in Warsaw, and a major anti-Communist revolt was staged against Communist rule in Hungary. On November 1, 1956, a new, independent Hungarian government announced its neutrality and its withdrawal from the Warsaw Pact, and it appealed for Western recognition. But within days Soviet armed forces crushed the uprising in Poland, and after several weeks of combat restored a Communist regime in Hungary.

As in 1953, NATO-member countries took no military action to counter Soviet military repression in Eastern Europe. The SPD continued to oppose nuclear weapons and rearmament, even after the 1956 suppression of the Polish and Hungarian revolts heightened West German fears of Soviet power.

The SPD made German rearmament and nuclear weapons the focus of the 1957 national election campaign. Social Democrats produced vivid posters picturing skulls and carrying the legend "atomic death"; membership in NATO and rearmament, they suggested, sharply increased the risk of an atomic war being fought on German territory. In contrast, the CDU-CSU stood firm on NATO, rearmament, and the need for deployed nuclear weapons.

The CDU-CSU won, receiving 50.2 percent of the vote (up from 45 percent in 1953, and 31 percent in 1949). The SPD received only 32 percent. This third defeat in national elections led the Social Democrats to rethink their policies. In 1959, they adopted the Bad Godesburg program of accepting NATO and rearmament and proposing economic and social policies similar to the mixed-economy perspectives of the CDU. They also abandoned such Socialist economic prescriptions as nationalization of the steel and coal industries.

This SPD step toward foreign policy consensus with the CDU-CSU ensured the 1958 German parliamentary approval of deploying tactical nuclear weapons on German soil. The weapons were authorized by the North Atlantic Council to compensate for its manpower deficiency, but the United States insisted that control of the warheads reside with the president of the United States.

The economic integration of Europe took a major step forward when the members of the European Coal and Steel Community set up the European Economic Community in 1958. The goal of increased economic cooperation had earlier been advanced when France permitted the reincorporation of the Saarland into West Germany in 1956.

In 1954, far earlier than most observers in the West expected, the Soviet Union developed a hydrogen bomb, significantly increasing its military potential. Three years later the Soviet Union became the first country to launch an orbiting satellite, sputnik, and by 1958 Khrushchev boasted that the Soviets were ahead of the West in production of both medium- and intercontinental-range ballistic missiles. Khrushchev had consolidated his control over the Soviet regime in March 1958. After months of a strident propaganda campaign against NATO and German rearmament, Khrushchev issued an ultimatum to the Western powers in November 1958. He spoke of their "unlawful occupation of West Berlin" and the "threat" this occupation posed to the Soviet Union and East Germany. The Soviet government consequently proposed the "demilitarization" of West Berlin—the removal of the 11,000 French, British, and U.S. occupational troops and the subsequent establishment of West Berlin as a "free city." This status could be guaranteed by the four powers alone or together with the United Nations.[6]

Unless these demands were met within six months—by May 27, 1959—Khrushchev threatened to sign a separate peace treaty with East Germany and seal off West Berlin. The military forces of the Soviet Union and the Warsaw Pact countries would support him, Khrushchev said; these countries would view "every violation of the frontiers of the German Democratic Republic" as an attack. He added that "only madmen can go to the length of unleashing another world war over the preservation of privileges for occupationists in West Berlin."[7] Many Western Europeans understood Khrushchev to be threatening World War III unless the Western Allies withdrew from Berlin within six months.

The Western counterproposal was measured and firm, calling for a discussion of Berlin in the context of German reunification. Lengthy conversations ensued in 1959 among the foreign ministers of the four powers—the United States, Great Britain, France, and the Soviet Union. Khrushchev visited the United States and summit talks were held at Camp David in September 1959, followed by a four-power summit in Paris in May 1960. Khrushchev broke off talks in the midst of the Paris summit meeting, "ostensibly because of the shooting down of an American spy plane, but probably because he saw no prospect of emerging from it with any settlement."[8]

Between 1953 and 1961 some 2.5 million of East Germany's 17 million citizens fled from communism to the West, and Khrushchev and East German leader Walter Ulbricht wanted to curtail this loss of skilled manpower. Khrushchev also sought to divide the Western coalition. In 1960 he attacked Chancellor Adenauer and Willy Brandt, the mayor of West Berlin. During a state visit to France in March 1960 he "used all his powers of persuasion to evoke the old French image of a powerful Germany as the hereditary enemy threatening the integrity of France and peace in Europe."[9] In response to Khrushchev's attacks in France, the German government observed that it was "strange that this reproach [was] made by a government that constantly prides itself on its strength and that has no scruples in stating publicly time and again that it is in a position to destroy other countries in a few seconds in the event of war."[10]

In a conciliatory gesture intended to defuse the Berlin crisis, newly elected President John Kennedy held a summit meeting with Soviet Premier Khrushchev in Vienna in June 1961. But this meeting came only weeks after the United States suffered a humiliating defeat at the Bay of Pigs. Cuban President Fidel Castro routed a U.S.-supported armed invasion by anti-Communist Cubans, after Kennedy failed to provide the air cover necessary to ensure their success. Khrushchev took this failure as a sign of Kennedy's indecisiveness, and at the summit meeting repeated Soviet demands concerning Berlin. But he did not specify a deadline.

Kennedy returned from the June 1961 summit meeting quite sobered. He immediately asked Congress for 220,000 more combat forces and an 8 percent increase in the defense budget, adding, "I hear it said that West Berlin is untenable. So was Bastogne. So in fact was Stalingrad. Any dangerous spot is tenable if brave men will make it so. We do not want to fight, but we have fought before."[11] The British and French remained firm, as they had done throughout the crisis.

In addition to overt threats, the Soviets placed intense clandestine pressure on West Germany. A former senior intelligence official of the United States notes that during the two decades following World War II

> the KGB focused its talents on Western Europe, above all on the heart of the capitalist threat, West Germany, and the North Atlantic Treaty Organization. It directed against them the most concentrated, wholesale intelligence barrage in the history of Soviet intelligence.[12]

To give a sense for the scope of the intelligence operations directed against Germany, German court records chronicle more than 2,000 convictions between 1950 and 1953 and more than 8,000 in 1959. This source estimates resident spies for the Soviet Union "operating in West Germany during the mid-1960s . . . at over 5,000."[13]

Instead of forcing the Western powers out of Berlin, on August 13, 1961, the Soviet and East German governments cut off access to West Berlin for the residents of Eastern Germany by employing barriers of troops and barbed wire. Over the next weeks and months those barriers became the Berlin Wall—a visible symbol of the division between the two parts of Europe. President Kennedy responded by increasing the size of the U.S. garrison in Berlin, by sending Vice President Johnson and General Lucius Clay (who had overseen the Berlin airlift) to Berlin, and by continuing diplomatic talks with the Soviet Union.

Although it received 45 percent of the vote in the September 1961 national elections the CDU-CSU lost its absolute majority in Parliament and consequently formed a new government in coalition with the Free Democratic party, which had received 13 percent of the vote (compared with its 8 percent in 1957).

In April 1962 Khrushchev again demanded the withdrawal of Allied troops from Berlin. He followed this in July 1962 with a proposal that the smaller countries of NATO and the Warsaw Pact garrison Berlin, and that the troops from all four powers leave. In October 1962 Kennedy announced the presence of Soviet missiles with nuclear warheads in Cuba and his response to them: the United States would require their removal and would prevent the deployment of any additional missiles or nuclear weapons in Cuba.

After days of tense crisis involving the risk of thermonuclear war, Khrushchev agreed to remove the missiles and nuclear weapons and not to permit the future deployment of any such weapons in Cuba. This episode marked the beginning of the end of the confrontation triggered by Khrushchev's 1958 ultimatum on Berlin. Quite possibly Khrushchev intended the secret deployment of Soviet missiles armed with hydrogen bombs in Cuba—ninety miles from the United States—to change the strategic military balance in the Soviets' favor. Such a shift could have forced the United States first out of Berlin and perhaps out of Germany. In 1964 the Soviet politburo replaced Khrushchev with Leonid Brezhnev as first secretary of the Communist party and Alexei Kosygin as premier.

Continuity and Steps toward Normalization

During the years of the second Berlin crisis, 1958 to 1962, Adenauer consistently advocated a position of strength combined with diplomacy. As an opponent of the Nazis he recalled vividly that the acquiescence of the democracies from 1936 to 1939 had strengthened the Hitler regime and had brought war closer.[14] Another European leader who recalled the tragic consequences of weakness toward an aggressive totalitarian regime was General Charles de Gaulle, who resumed the leadership of France in the spring of 1958. Of approximately the same age, de Gaulle and Adenauer forged an increasingly close relationship, deepened by their shared concerns during the Berlin crisis that the United States and Britain were not always sufficiently firm. In light of the growing Soviet nuclear arsenal capable of reaching the United States, de Gaulle questioned whether the United States actually would honor its commitment to defend Europe if strategic nuclear forces were ever needed.

Both Adenauer and de Gaulle had a strong interest in continuing and deepening the French-German rapprochement. Adenauer wanted to anchor Germany firmly in Western Europe, to avoid lapsing into a foreign policy of swinging between East and West to which Germany's middle European location made it susceptible. De Gaulle wanted a friendly Germany that would support his concept of Europe as a "third force" in world politics, with France at the helm. De Gaulle visited Adenauer in Bonn in 1962 and returned on a state visit in 1963.

In 1963 de Gaulle signed a French-German Treaty of Friendship, announced that France would develop an independent nuclear capability, and called for other members of the European Economic Community to join France in opposing British membership. Although the West German Bundestag overwhelmingly ratified the friendship treaty with France, it also affirmed Germany's commitment to the Atlantic Alliance and called for the inclusion of Britain in the European Economic Community. De Gaulle's decision to leave the NATO military command in 1966 disappointed Germany, but French-German relations continued to improve politically and economically irrespective of some important policy differences.

The 1967 merger of the European Coal and Steel Community (ECSC), the European Economic Community (EEC), and the European Atomic Energy Organization to form the European Community (EC) constituted a major step toward European economic integration. The United Kingdom was admitted in 1973, along with Denmark and Ireland. Greece was admitted in 1981, Portugal and Spain in 1986, bringing the membership of the European Community to twelve. The close French-German relationship has provided an important element of continuity in European integration during the postwar era and was at the core of the continuing process of economic and political integration in Europe through the 1980s. (In late 1989 West German Chancellor Helmut Kohl remarked that visits between the leaders of France and Germany, formerly marked by special fanfare, had as a result of the ever closer levels of cooperation become commonplace. He had participated in seventy-eight during his tenure in office.)[15]

In October 1963 Chancellor Adenauer retired. He was succeeded by Dr. Ludwig Erhardt, the economist who devised the social market policy credited with spurring Germany's economic revitalization. The CDU-CSU government under Erhardt undertook a "policy of movement" toward the East. Adenauer had insisted on the doctrine of one Germany represented only by the Federal Republic, although he had been willing to negotiate East-West German trade agreements and to take a number of steps in relations with the Soviet Union to open the way for normalization with East Germany. In the 1960s West Germany established trade relations and opened trade missions in five East European Communist countries. This new policy represented a marked departure from the earlier West German practice of terminating diplomatic relations with countries that recognized the East German government.

In addition, agreements were negotiated with East Germany between 1963 and 1966 that permitted more than a million West Germans to visit relatives in East Germany over the Christmas holidays.

The 1965 national elections ushered in a three-year-long coalition government between the CDU-CSU and the SPD. This coalition marked the first time the SPD participated in a national government since the Federal Republic was established in 1949. Former CDU member of parliament and state governor Dr. Kurt Georg Kiesinger became chancellor, and former SPD mayor of Berlin Willy Brandt became foreign minister.[16]

Since 1959 the SPD had continued to move away from Marxist views on economic and social policies, toward the centrist position of the CDU-CSU. Now in the Great Coalition of 1966 to 1969 the CDU-CSU approached the SPD position concerning normalization with the East. The SPD perspective had been summarized in 1963 by Egon Bahr, an SPD member of the Parliament and a key advisor to Willy Brandt, as: "nearness will bring change."[17] After much internal debate the CDU issued a new party program in 1968 calling for liberalization of its social, economic, and foreign policy—the Berlin program.

The Federal Republic then made overtures to East Germany for "regulated coexistence." As Karl Kaiser observed, "By establishing communication with the GDR [East Germany], by proposing its inclusion in a European system of mutual renunciation of the use of force, and by accepting it as the *effective* though not *legitimate* ruler over the East Germans," the CDU-CSU-SPD coalition government took the first steps toward a two-state view of Germany.[18]

Ostpolitik and the Eastern Treaties

In the September 1969 national elections the SPD received 43 percent of the vote, the FDP 6 percent, and the CDU-CSU 46 percent. But the governing coalition the FDP chose to join was led by the SPD rather than the CDU-CSU. Thus for the first time in the twenty years since the founding of the Federal Republic the SPD headed the government. Its leader Willy Brandt now became chancellor, and the chairman of the FDP, Walter Sheel, became foreign minister.

Brandt was determined to normalize relations with the Eastern bloc countries, including East Germany, but he emphasized that reconciliation with Eastern Europe and the Soviet Union was prudent only for a West Germany securely integrated with the West. In the United States the administration of the newly inaugurated Richard Nixon (1969–1974) was also interested in improving its relations with the Soviet Union. Nixon viewed the 1968 Soviet invasion of Czechoslovakia as a regrettable but clear sign that the Soviets would continue to control Eastern Europe.

Brandt initiated long and complicated negotiations with the Soviet Union and Poland, and in August 1970 the Federal Republic and the Soviet Union signed the Treaty of Nonaggression. This treaty explicitly recognized the "present borders" in Europe and the "territorial integrity of all states in Europe."[19] These were key Soviet demands, since Moscow did not want West Germany or any coalition of states ever to challenge its 1940 annexation of the Baltic states, its 1945 annexation of Polish and other territories, or its compensating grant to Poland of pre-1937 German territory.

In exchange for this concession from West Germany, the Soviet Union accepted an important stipulation—that West Germany recognized no conflict between this treaty and the political goal of a German people reunified in free self-determination. Furthermore, the Soviet Union authorized West Germany to inform the United States, Britain, and France that it was the view of both signatories that the treaty would not affect the rights and responsibilities of the four occupying powers in Germany, especially in Berlin. Last, West Germany stipulated that its ratification of the treaty would depend on the successful conclusion of a four-power agreement about Berlin. That four-power agreement, signed in 1971, removed Berlin as a focus of Soviet and East German pressure and threats.

Brandt signed the Polish-German Treaty in Warsaw in December 1970. In this treaty again, the Federal Republic declared that it accepted as "inviolable" the current border between Poland and East Germany along the Oder-Neisse line. For its part, Poland agreed that "people of indisputably German nationality" living in Poland who wished to emigrate to either East or West Germany could do so, provided they respected Polish rules and regulations. Along with West Germany's subsequent monetary compensation to Poland, the Polish-German Treaty opened the way for thousands of ethnic Germans to leave Poland and resettle in the Federal Republic.[20]

As these Eastern treaties went before the West German parliament for ratification in May 1972, President Nixon prepared to meet General Secretary Brezhnev for the first formal U.S.-Soviet summit meeting since 1960. After Soviet relations with the People's Republic of China had approached military confrontation in 1969, Nixon began secret talks with China that culminated in his visit there in early 1972. The U.S. efforts at détente with both China and the Soviet Union paralleled the West German efforts at détente with the East. At the May 1972 Moscow summit the United States and Soviet Union signed accords limiting strategic weapons and anti-ballistic missile systems.[21] And in Bonn the West German parliament overwhelmingly approved the treaties with the Soviet Union and Poland.

In 1973 Brezhnev made a state visit to Bonn—the first visit by a Soviet head of state to a non-Communist German state in more than sixty years. In his round of meetings with German industrial leaders Brezhnev projected the prospects of long-term Soviet-German economic cooperation and pictured "the two countries as advancing from coexistence to interdependence, a process which would necessarily bring with it both external and internal relaxation."[22] At the time, this visit was perceived as marking the end of the cold war.

Also in 1973 the United States, the Federal Republic, and the other NATO countries accepted the Soviet proposal first made in 1954 and now modified to include the United States and Canada—that a Conference on Security and Cooperation in Europe (CSCE) should be convened. Beginning its work in Helsinki in July 1973, this conference sought to establish goals and standards in four fields: security, disarmament, economic cooperation, and human rights.

In 1974 the revelation that one of Chancellor Brandt's closest SPD aides was an East German spy and had been one for years forced Brandt's resignation. In his place the SPD-FDP coalition named Helmut Schmidt, an SPD leader who had served both as minister for economic affairs and minister of defense. Schmidt continued the *Ostpolitik* of his predecessor, just as President Gerald Ford, who took office in August 1974, continued the détente policies of Nixon. United States-Soviet summit meetings were held in 1972, 1973, and twice in 1974, the first three involving Brezhnev and Nixon, the last Brezhnev and Ford.

Détente and normalization with the Soviet Union were further promoted by the Helsinki Final Act of 1975. The members of NATO and the Warsaw Pact, along with nearly all other European states, agreed upon broad goals and standards of conduct in the four CSCE fields and planned periodic follow-up conferences to assess the results and decide on future activities. The Soviet Union and the European Communist regimes made those commitments with no provision for independent verification, enforcement, or sanctions for noncompliance. In exchange the Western countries recognized the existing European borders—implicitly including all Soviet annexations—as the permanent borders of Europe. This recognition had long been a Soviet goal. From the German perspective it was merely an affirmation of a de facto arrangement it had already acknowledged in the Eastern treaties. It was the price of normalization.

4
Domestic Politics and Foreign Policy, 1975–1989

With détente and *Ostpolitik* both in place in 1975, Germany's two major political parties began to make the foreign policy decisions that would affect their responses to the 1989–1990 opportunities for reunification. The CDU-CSU had opposed aspects of *Ostpolitik*; a majority of its members abstained in the 1972 votes on the Eastern treaties. But in 1975, with both center-right and center-left factions powerful within the party coalition, the CDU-CSU had to decide whether to accept the need and value of *Ostpolitik* as a continuing aspect of German foreign policy.

The SPD, whose participation in the governing coalition of 1966 to 1969 and whose subsequent leadership of the government had raised its political stature, faced a different decision. The SPD would have to decide whether to remain committed to the Atlantic Alliance and a Western-oriented security policy even as it pursued further détente with the East.

Three Political Stages

The political history of the Federal Republic has evolved in three political stages.[1] In the first, from 1949 to 1966, the CDU-CSU governed primarily in concert with the Free Democratic party (FDP). This period was followed by a brief transition, lasting from 1966 until 1969, when the large coalition between the Christian Democrats and Social Democrats held office. This coalition had the important effect of making the SPD appear capable of governing.

In the second stage, from 1969 to 1982, Germany was governed by an SPD-FDP coalition. The FDP broke away in 1982 and reestablished a coalition with the CDU-CSU because of differences with the SPD on economic and social policy issues.

The third stage began with the CDU electoral victory of 1983 and the formation of a CDU-CSU-FDP coalition. This was renewed in the

TABLE 4–1

WEST GERMANY—THREE POLITICAL STAGES, 1949–1990

National Election	Percent of the Vote Received				Government Formed by
	CDU-CSU	SPD	FDP	Others	
1949	31	29	12	28	CDU-CSU-FDP
1953	45	29	10	16	CDU-CSU-FDP
1957	50	32	8	10	CDU-CSU
1961	45	36	13	6	CDU-CSU-FDP
1965	48	40	10	2	CDU-CSU-FDP
1969	46	43	6	5	SPD-FDP
1972	45	46	8	1	SPD-FDP
1976	49	43	8	–	SPD-FDP
1980[a]	45	43	11	–	SPD-FDP
1983	49	38	7	6 (Greens)[b]	CDU-CSU-FDP
1987	44	37	9	8 (Greens)	CDU-CSU-FDP
1990[c]	44	33	11	12	CDU-CSU-FDP

a. In 1982 the governing coalition changed without a national election as the FDP left the SPD and the coalition became the CDU-CSU-FDP.

b. In 1983 and 1987, the Green party accounted for almost the entire vote in this category, but in 1990 it received only 4% of the national vote.

c. First national elections in a reunified Germany. Data for this December 2, 1990, election are taken from Marc Fisher, "Grateful Germans Vote to Keep Kohl," *Washington Post*, December 3, 1990.

SOURCES: Data for 1949–1976 are taken from Gerhard Loewenberg, "The Development of the German Party System," in Karl H. Cerny, ed., *Germany at the Polls* (Washington, D.C.: AEI Press, 1978), pp. 18–19. Data for 1983 and 1987 are taken from Stephen F. Szabo, "Political Shifts in West Germany," *Current History* (November 1988), p. 361. Data for the CDU in 1980 are taken from Michael Balfour, *West Germany—A Contemporary History* (New York: St. Martins Press, 1982), p. 258. Data for the SPD and the FDP in 1980 are taken from Helmut M. Müller, Karl Friedrich Krieger, and Hanna Vollrath, *Schlaglichter der Deutschen Geschichte* (Mannheim, Germany: Bibliographisches Institut, 1986).

1987 election, and again after the December 1990 vote, the first national election of the reunified Germany. (See table 4–1.)

Along with economic, social, and environmental issues, foreign policy was of signal importance in the elections of the 1970s and 1980s. As table 4–1 shows, the vote for the CDU-CSU increased to nearly its highest level by 1983, while the vote for the SPD decreased continually from its highest level of 46 percent in 1972. Considered in the light of the rise of the Green party and its left-wing views on foreign policy issues, the vote for the left on foreign policy matters could be viewed as a combination of the SPD and the Green votes; it was about 45 percent in 1987 and 37 percent in 1990.

When Helmut Schmidt replaced Willy Brandt as chancellor in 1974 he chose as his foreign minister Hans-Dietrich Genscher of the FDP. In the coalition with the SPD and later with the CDU-CSU, Genscher served as a symbol of continuity in German foreign policy. The CDU-CSU recognized that just as their success in the 1953 and 1957 elections had ratified Adenauer's *Westpolitik*, so too the SPD success in the 1972 and 1976 elections endorsed the SPD's *Ostpolitik*. After another extended internal debate, the CDU-CSU accepted détente and *Ostpolitik* in conjunction with a NATO-centered defense strategy and political and economic integration with Western Europe. Three American presidents representing both political parties pursued détente with the Soviet Union in the 1970s while maintaining deterrent military forces and a commitment to the Atlantic Alliance. The CDU-CSU similarly determined in the late 1970s that Germany could and should pursue a foreign policy anchored in the West but reaching toward normalization with the East.

Soviet Actions

Soviet leader Brezhnev proclaimed the end of the cold war when he visited Bonn in 1973, after the 1972 U.S.-Soviet summit agreement had spoken of a new framework of peace. Yet a second, hostile dimension to Soviet foreign policy continued during the détente years of the 1970s. The Soviets continued their strategic military buildup; the Warsaw Pact conventional forces on Europe's central front continued their modernization and expansion; and most ominously, the Soviet Union began deploying nuclear warheads on new intermediate-range missile launchers. These missiles were clearly targeted at Western Europe, including Germany. By the early 1980s the Soviet Union had deployed nearly 1,500 such nuclear warheads— on missiles having a range of 600 to 3,400 miles, known as intermediate-range nuclear forces (INFs).

The Soviets engaged in many covert aggressive actions. They supported Egypt's attack on Israel in the 1973 Yom Kippur War. They participated in an intense covert effort to bring the Communist party of Portugal to power between 1974 and 1976, after the demise of that country's authoritarian regime. They backed the Communist government of Hanoi in its violation of the 1973 Indochina peace accords, and when it mounted a massive invasion to bring Communist regimes to power in South Vietnam, Cambodia, and Laos in 1975. By 1979 eight more third world countries were ruled by newly established pro-Soviet dictatorships, empowered after many years of Soviet support. And the Soviet Union was engaged in a large-scale military supply of foreign Communist troops to help the pro-Soviet regimes of Angola, Mozambique, Ethiopia, and Cambodia to consolidate and keep power. In Afghanistan, the Soviet Union sent in 120,000 of its own forces in 1979 to prop up the Communist regime that had seized power in 1978, and Moscow supplied more than $3 billion in arms during the decade after the Sandinistas took power in Nicaragua, also in 1979.

At the same time, in the mid-1970s, West Germany, Turkey, Italy, and other NATO nations became the targets of systematic terrorism by small, radical-left groups. The Soviet Union provided important assistance to these groups, and so did its allies, including several East European countries (East Germany, Czechoslovakia, Bulgaria), Syria, Libya, Cuba, and North Korea. The wave of terrorist attacks in Germany was particularly intense in 1977 when a federal prosecutor, a prominent banker, and the leader of the National Employer Federation were kidnapped and killed. The terrorists even hijacked an aircraft. The Schmidt government enacted strong antiterrorism legislation in 1978, but the attacks continued. An estimated 41 persons were killed (21 of whom were terrorists), and 400 were sentenced for terrorism from 1977 to 1980.[2]

These events and especially the deployment of INFs aimed directly at Germany and Western Europe were certainly not the responses to détente and *Ostpolitik* expected by the SPD (or the U.S.) leadership. After debate within the party Chancellor Schmidt requested that the NATO alliance deploy its own intermediate-range nuclear armed missiles and agreed that some portion of these could be stationed on German territory. At the same time, the Schmidt government fully supported the 1979 NATO decision both to move forward on missile deployment and to engage the Soviet Union in negotiations for the removal of intermediate-range missiles on both sides. This double track NATO decision, widely supported in Germany, became part of the SPD's platform as it moved toward success in the 1980 elections.

The SPD Moves Away from the Atlantic Alliance

The mood of détente was broken in December 1979 for most Westerners when Soviet military forces invaded Afghanistan to prop up the Communist government the USSR had helped establish in a military coup the year before. The United States imposed economic sanctions against the Soviet Union, curtailing the sale of wheat and other commodities and urging its allies to do likewise.

But Germany resisted. Factions of both the SPD and the FDP favored as much trade as possible with the East. The Schmidt government continued Germany's growing commercial relationship with the Soviet Union and the Eastern Europe countries. As one German political analyst put it, "This cooperative behavior paid handsomely as both the Soviet Union and its East European allies profited economically."[3] In 1980 Chancellor Schmidt visited Moscow to urge a resumption of U.S.-Soviet negotiations; he wanted to pursue both *Westpolitik* and *Ostpolitik*.

The Soviet Union did not reciprocate. Instead it mounted a massive political action campaign "to mobilize the West Germans against Schmidt's government and to create public pressure against honoring the missile deployment pledge to NATO."[4] The Soviet leadership evidently believed that if it kept its nuclear armed intermediate-range missiles pointed at Western Europe and prevented NATO countries from deploying equivalent deterrent weapons, it could prevent the United States from defending Western Europe, in appearance if not in fact. According to this reasoning, without a European-based nuclear deterrent the United States would be forced into the first use of intercontinental ballistic missiles in the defense of Europe. As such an occurrence would not be credible to the Western Europeans, theoretically U.S. nuclear deterrence and the defense of Europe would be "decoupled."

Former Secretary of State Henry Kissinger offers a telling example of Soviet persistence in attempting to remove the protection of U.S. strategic forces from Western Europe. He writes that the Soviets proposed to the United States in 1972 that both countries secretly agree that any conventional or tactical nuclear East-West European war would not affect the territory of either superpower.[5]

Apparently the Soviet Union wished to create a sense of its overwhelming military preponderance in Western Europe, thus increasing its ability to obtain the political and economic concessions it wanted. To this end it built up its own and its allies' conventional, chemical, and nuclear forces steadily through the 1970s and it unilaterally deployed its nuclear-armed intermediate-range missiles. The leaders of the NATO countries, including Germany, believed that the counterdeployment of their own INF forces could thwart this plan.

In the early 1980s the Soviet Union used propaganda, political action, and threats to discourage the SPD-led German government and other West European governments from deploying these NATO INF missiles. For many observers these actions amounted to a second cold war.

As a result of economic and social policy differences, the Free

Democratic party in 1982 left its coalition with the SPD and instead formed one with the CDU-CSU. This brought Helmut Kohl to office as interim chancellor, until the elections of 1983 confirmed the new coalition and began the third stage of the political cycle—a return to CDU-CSU-FDP government. The left wing of the SPD, led by former chancellor Willy Brandt, now became dominant on foreign policy issues.

In 1983 the SPD formally renounced its request to NATO for deployment of the INF missile forces on German territory.[6] Since deployment was the critical issue facing the Atlantic Alliance, this SPD action at its annual congress represented a sharp turn away from the alliance and from the SPD's earlier endorsement of a close security relationship with the United States. As one American observer put it, Chancellor Schmidt's policy had been defeated "by the left wing of his own Social Democratic party, led by former Chancellor Willy Brandt. The radicals scuttled Schmidt and his chances for victory for a decade rather than support Schmidt's commitment to NATO and a new generation of U.S. missiles on German soil."[7]

Two factors account for this profound change in the SPD foreign policy of the 1980s. First, the generation of leaders surrounding Willy Brandt seemed in effect to rescind their approval of *Westpolitik* and returned to some assumptions the SPD held in the early 1950s. Second, the social demography of the SPD had changed as a result of Germany's economic success and the radicalization of the universities in the late 1960s and the 1970s.

In the 1950s about 45 percent of SPD members were blue-collar workers; by the late 1970s only about one quarter came from this traditional base, and about 40 percent of the enlarged membership of the party came from " 'the new technical intelligentsia' consisting of white-collar employees of large organizations, civil servants, teachers, and journalists."[8] Many of these new SPD members were younger, were educated in the highly radicalized universities, and belonged to the New Left or Young Socialist movements. They began to exert an important leftward influence on the party during the 1970s.

By the early 1980s the political agenda of the German New Left—including environmentalism, pacifism, feminism, and anti-authoritarianism—had led to the formation of the Green party. The Greens began to obtain parliamentary representation in 1983, garnering a share of the national vote approaching that of the FDP. The Greens explicitly opposed continued German membership in NATO.

The SPD leadership interpreted votes for the Green party as a loss of the leftist constituency of their own party. To reclaim these

44

voters, some SPD leaders felt that their foreign policy positions should move further to the left during the 1980s, and hence further away from the Atlantic Alliance and the United States.

The ideas behind this new SPD foreign policy, however, had preceded these social and political changes. Having been accused in the Weimar Republic days of not being nationalistic enough, the SPD leadership had expressed its nationalism in the early 1950s through its strong objections to economic integration with the West, to German rearmament, and to the NATO alliance. They argued that German reunification could be achieved only through accommodation with the Soviet Union, which called for a foreign policy of neutrality rather than commitment to the West.

By the late 1950s the SPD had devised a plan for Germany that "called for a phased withdrawal of all [foreign] military forces from both parts of Germany, coupled with the gradual political and economic integration of the two Germanys within a confederated entity."[9] Walter Hahn called this SPD plan "a reflection of a proposal for a German 'confederation' contrived by Soviet leader Nikita Khrushchev and East German chieftain Walter Ulbricht three years earlier as a last ditch effort to reverse the FRG's entry into NATO."[10]

More than a decade later, when Willy Brandt became the SPD chancellor of Germany in 1969, his intellectual strategist Egon Bahr officially revived elements of this approach. During the 1960s Bahr "not only had worked out a comprehensive strategy and a game plan for *Ostpolitik* but had already shaped some of its essentials in secret meetings with the East Germans and leaders of the Italian Communist party, the latter acting as a go-between for the Soviet bloc. Bahr's strategy became the hidden agenda for Brandt's *Ostpolitik*. . . ." The four steps of the Brandt-Bahr plan conceptualized in the late 1960s were described by Hahn as follows:

1. the establishment of direct relations and a modus vivendi between the Federal Republic of Germany and the German Democratic Republic
2. the conclusion of a renunciation of force pact with the Soviet Union, which would open the way for West German diplomatic ties with all the East European satellites
3. U.S.-Soviet negotiations leading to a substantial thinning out of NATO and Soviet conventional forces in both parts of Germany
4. the ultimate dissolution of NATO and the Warsaw Pact and their replacement by a "European collective security system" embracing the continental nations.[11]

Concerning German reunification, Bahr projected that in the changed European environment the two German states would grow together in fact if not formally.

The first two steps were taken with the Eastern treaties of 1970 to 1972. The third became the focus of the negotiations on conventional force reduction in Europe, resulting in the Treaty on Conventional Forces in Europe signed on November 19, 1990, among thirty-four states including all members of NATO and the Warsaw Pact (see chapter 9). The Soviet Union repeatedly proposed the fourth step—dissolution of both alliances—as its preferred approach to peace in Europe. In late 1989 the Soviets stated that this dissolution would be the price for German reunification.[12]

During the 1983 election campaign the SPD claimed to be best able to bring peace to Germany and Europe. It implied that a CDU government would bring a new "Ice Age" to East-West relations, and that the CDU-CSU was "incapable of fostering peace." After the CDU-CSU won the elections and Kohl was confirmed as chancellor, East German Communist leader Erich Honecker indeed threatened a new Ice Age if Kohl should meet the German commitment to NATO and permit deployment of INF missiles in the Federal Republic.

Despite Soviet threats and massive opposition demonstrations by the SPD, the Greens, and others, the Kohl government did permit INF deployment as scheduled in November 1983. The Soviet Union responded initially by suspending arms control talks, but it returned to the negotiating table in 1985. Nevertheless, the 1986 SPD party congress again voted to urge the CDU-CSU-FDP government unilaterally to dismantle the INF missiles and to remove them from German territory.

Another facet of the SPD's turning away from the values and commitments of the Atlantic Alliance was its blurring of the moral and political distinctions between prodemocratic and antidemocratic groups and regimes abroad. The split between Social Democrats and Communists in the late nineteenth and early twentieth centuries concerned the issue of political democracy: the democratic socialists, including the SPD, were committed to democracy as a fundamental principle and purpose of political action. In contrast, the Marxist faction, which later became known as Leninists or Communists, favored the "dictatorship of the proletariat"—meaning absolutist control during the years or decades of transition to a truly "classless society."

After World War II, when the democratic socialist parties of Europe met in 1950 to establish the Socialist International to coordinate their political activities and to formulate their basic political principles, they reaffirmed the distinction between genuinely demo-cratic political movements and nondemocratic ones. The democratic socialists called for opposition to dictatorships of the left, even if Marxist, as well as dictatorships of the right. They defined one-party Communist regimes as dictatorships.

But in 1978 a new policy arose. The left wing of the SPD had become increasingly powerful under the chairmanship of Willy Brandt, and it exercised a strong influence on foreign policy toward the third world. At the meeting of the Socialist International, nonde-mocratic political parties such as the Sandinistas of Nicaragua and the New Jewel movement of Grenada were for the first time voted support and the right to participate in its meetings. As a result, factions of the SPD began to provide important political and material support to groups such as the new Sandinista regime of Nicaragua and the PLO. These factions of the SPD included those working in the Socialist International and in the SPD political foundation, which had an annual budget of about $50 million allocated to political action around the world. In June 1989 the SPD officially recognized the PLO as the representative of the Palestinian people, and SPD chairman Hans-Jochen Vogel invited a delegation for an official visit to Bonn.[13]

Having become aware of the extent and negative impact of these activities in Central America, the Reagan administration attempted to persuade the German Social Democrats not to help antidemocratic forces. It was especially disturbing to the United States that the German SPD and the Socialist International endorsed the Commu-nist-led guerrilla coalitions in Central America. During the 1980s the Soviet Union and Cuba provided these guerrillas with military and covert support to wage illegal war in countries south of the United States.[14]

During the 1980s the left wing of the SPD seemed to carry this failure to distinguish between the genuinely democratic and the nondemocratic regimes even into its approach to East Germany and Eastern Europe. As part of his "change through rapprochement" strategy, Chancellor Brandt had in the early 1970s stopped espousing the hope and cause of German reunification. But Chancellor Schmidt had remained hopeful, saying in 1979, "I do not foresee under what auspices and conditions the Germans will get together again, but they will. . . . One Germany is not something which anyone thinks of as being around the next corner, or even the corner after next. It is a real desire in the soul of the German nation, whether in the West or the East."[15]

By 1984 Brandt contended that the "meaningless debate" over German reunification should be ended by ignoring this issue. Even as the East German regime was unraveling and thousands were fleeing to the West in October 1989, the SPD mayor of West Berlin, Walter Momper, illustrated how his party had turned away from reunification when he announced that progress toward peace in Europe must not be "delayed by a superfluous discussion about reunification, a discussion which leads to a dead end."[16] He also said, "Anticommunism must disappear from our minds. This is what prevents the development of a European way of thinking"[17]—voicing a sentiment widespread in the SPD.

Brandt and his faction within the SPD had given up on reunification, opting instead to enter into direct conversations and even negotiations with the Communist party of East Germany. Meanwhile they ignored the small and courageous prodemocratic opposition groups inside East Germany. The SPD called these years of conversations and joint party-to-party agreements reached with the Communist party of East Germany its "second phase of *Ostpolitik*." This policy produced party-to-party agreements between the SPD and the East German Communist party on steps to limit nuclear and chemical weapons in the two Germanys, and in Kohl's view it amounted to a "parallel foreign policy."[18] By 1987 the SPD and the East German Communist party established a commission to explore "common values." Egon Bahr reportedly declared that any discussion of German unity is "political environmental pollution." Meanwhile, the deputy chairman of the SPD's group in parliament, Horst Ehmke, said that the West German government should acknowledge "its own responsibility for the division of Germany."[19]

Equally remarkable, especially in the light of the Helsinki Final Act (1975) requirements for a single standard of behavior on human rights in both East and West, was the SPD recommendation to dismantle (as "unnecessary") the West German organization responsible for monitoring human rights abuses by the East German regime. The SPD also recommended that the hallowed right of East Germans to automatic West German citizenship and social and pension benefits be rescinded.

The SPD was engaged in a step-by-step legitimation of communism in East Germany and Eastern Europe, with no apparent, tangible concern for the struggle of genuinely democratic opposition groups there. Perhaps the best single example of this process was Willy Brandt's refusal to meet with Lech Walesa, the founder and chairman of the Polish Solidarity movement, during Brandt's 1985 visit to Poland.

In 1987 three events had serious implications for the SPD's foreign policy. The first was the state visit of East German Communist leader Erich Honecker to West Germany. Honecker had responded to the SPD's *Ostpolitik* and the Eastern treaties in the 1970s with a policy of *Abgrenzung*—in English, "distancing." Instead of growing more accommodating, the East German regime stressed the political, historical, and cultural differences between the two Germanys. It even wrote a new constitution, in which "all references to unification were deleted, and [which] explicitly declared that the GDR [German Democratic Republic] was no longer a 'socialist state of the German nation' but rather a 'socialist state of workers and farmers.' "[20]

But in the 1980s Kohl's firmness on INF deployment, combined with East Germany's economic problems and the Kohl administration's pursuit of normalization and willingness to provide generous loans and credits, far from leading to the "new Ice Age" resulted in major steps toward normal relations between the two governments. Honecker's 1987 state visit to the Federal Republic symbolized this.

The second event occurred in December 1987, when the United States and the Soviet Union signed a treaty on intermediate nuclear forces. This treaty provided for the total elimination of two categories of nuclear-armed missiles. On the Soviet side they included those armed with about 1,500 nuclear warheads, and on the NATO side those with about 400.[21] This agreement demonstrated the wisdom of Schmidt, Kohl, and Reagan: the way to elicit the removal of the Soviets' nuclear-armed missiles was both to deploy an equivalent counter against their forces and to continue negotiating their reduction or removal.

The third event was the decline of the SPD in the 1987 national election—it received only 37 percent of the vote. These election results did not lead the SPD back towards the center, however. Apparently the increase of the more leftist Green party vote from 6 percent to 8 percent and the strength of the 1960s-generation "young Socialist" faction of the SPD stirred a move to return to a Marxist orientation on domestic issues. That move failed, but in foreign policy the SPD continued on its eastward course.

At the SPD Party Congress in the summer of 1988 the party's future foreign and defense policy brought on a major debate. Among the major decisions taken by the 1988 SPD Party Congress regarding European security and disarmament were the following (emphasis added):

• "The social democratic concept of common security aiming at a European order and *the overcoming of the system of mutual deterrence* is gaining ever more support in East and West. . . . It is especially important that the disarmament process now receives additional impetus, and that it is made irreversible. . . .

49

- "On the basis of the eastern treaties which we concluded, the European post-war order must now be transformed into a European peace order. In the long term the CSCE [Conference on Security and Cooperation in Europe] process is to lead to a contractually secured European peace order which *will replace the military alliances.*

- "In contrast to the global strategic questions, for which the two world powers bear special responsibility, . . . in Europe this responsibility calls for European initiatives.

- "The SPD supports the idea of a 'European pillar' within the Atlantic Alliance, through which the European Alliance members would be able to do justice to their responsibility for the structuring of peace in an organized form. We, however, do not aim at the creation of a new military superpower. We strive for a European peace order which overcomes the military alliances so far dividing Europe."[22]

The 1988 SPD Congress further listed a number of dangers facing Germany, including "the erroneous belief that more security is achieved with more weapons," "delaying negotiations," and "striving to offset the military options which have been lost to the INF Treaty . . . through the development of new weapons."[23] Not a word was said about dangers posed by the military forces of the Soviet Union or its Warsaw Pact allies. In fact, the SPD catalog of dangers might be labeled as an example of "blaming the Atlantic Alliance first."

The resulting agreements, entitled *European Security 2000*, offered detailed suggestions for a 50 percent reduction in NATO and Warsaw Pact forces and for "peace and disarmament in Europe."[24] In this detailed plan for the reduction of military forces in Europe, the SPD made a number of proposals that would shift key security responsibilities from NATO to the Conference on Security and Cooperation in Europe (CSCE). Recognizing the importance of verification in the SPD plan to cut forces by 50 percent, for example, the report proposed entrusting this issue to the CSCE rather than the Atlantic Alliance.

Many of the SPD's 1988–1989 proposals reflected arms-control and reduction-negotiating objectives that might have been supported by bipartisan consensus in most NATO countries. But the main objective of the SPD was a "contractually secured European peace order which will replace the military alliances."[25] Explicitly, this meant the effective elimination of the Atlantic Alliance. Implicitly, it meant the withdrawal of the United States as a military presence in Europe and specifically in Germany. Implicit also was the assumption that no political movement toward genuine democracy was needed in Eastern Europe or the Soviet Union as a prerequisite for establishing this "European peace order." Despite decades of historical evidence to the contrary, the SPD believed that a collective security agreement among European states could replace what it called the "post-war order." Even the SPD's expectation of perpetual Communist power in the Warsaw Pact countries did not undermine this belief.

As discussed, in the 1950s the SPD opposed West German participation in NATO and in West European economic integration, contending that this reduced the chances for reunification. Three decades later, in 1988, the SPD declared reunification impossible for the foreseeable future and proposed that a European collective security system replace the Atlantic Alliance. The consistent element in these apparently contradictory positions was the SPD confidence that a demonstrated Western readiness for peace would be sufficient means of achieving it; collective security agreements written on paper would be adequate guarantee of the Soviet Union's good faith. With the 1990 reunification of Germany and the transition toward political democracy so dramatically under way in a number of East European countries, the SPD may well urge the replacement of NATO by a CSCE collective security system.

CDU-CSU Perspectives

In the early 1950s Chancellor Adenauer spelled out the CDU-CSU's basic view of Germany's future in international politics as follows:

> There are three courses that Germany (theoretically) can take. . . . One is that we join Soviet Russia. The second is that we join the West. And the third is that we join neither, but stand on our pride and depend upon our own resources. Soviet Russia would like to see us take the last stand. I deliberately refrain from using the word neutralization for that is no neutralization. A neutral country is one which has the power, if the need arises, of defending its neutrality against all comers. A country that survives only by the tolerance of others is not a neutral. . . . We want the integration of Europe, and we want to be allied with the West.[26]

Underlying Adenauer's concept was the premise that without an alliance with the West—including the United States—to counterbalance the Soviet Union's overwhelming military power, neither Germany nor Western Europe could truly defend itself.

The continuity of this CDU-CSU foreign policy appeared in its

51

1988 party program, entitled "Our Responsibility in the World Today." It pressed the following conclusions:

- "Improved superpower relations have given greater operating freedom to both East and West Europe—and thus to Germany. The CDU's German policy is aimed at . . . the unity and freedom of Germany in a free and united Europe. . . .
- "The Federal Republic of Germany is especially vulnerable to political and military threats and therefore particularly dependent on the protection of the United States and its partners in the western alliance.
- "As a member of the European Community and of the Atlantic Alliance, the Federal Republic of Germany . . . [rejects] any neutralism in the East-West conflict.
- "NATO is irreplaceable because it protects Europe against war and political blackmail. . . . Europe needs America. America needs Europe.
- "Christian Democrats consider that peace is more than mere absence of war. Stable peace can exist only in a social order founded on the principles of justice and liberty where human rights are fully recognized. Therefore arms control and disarmament alone cannot ensure peace. . . . As long as the conflict between freedom and oppression persists, the free nations must be capable and ready to defend themselves. Security by military means and a policy of active dialogue, defense readiness, and readiness for rapprochement are not contradictions, they presuppose and complement each other. They are the foundation of our Christian Democratic policy of détente."[27]

The contrasts between this program and the 1988 SPD program were significant. The CDU affirmed the Atlantic Alliance; the SPD favored a "European peace order." The CDU said genuine peace required internal political changes in the Warsaw Pact countries, leading to full recognition of human rights and liberty; the SPD was silent on this issue. The CDU said arms control and disarmament must be complemented by military deterrence; the SPD was ambiguous on this issue. These differences grew even more important after the dramatic events of 1989.

The CDU foreign policy of solidarity with the Atlantic Alliance combined with rapprochement toward the East worked well during the 1980s. The 1983 decision to deploy nuclear-armed missiles maintained Atlantic Alliance cohesion and strengthened the U.S. negotiating position for seeking the phased elimination of all INFs.[28] The Atlantic Alliance's growing strength in conventional arms, in which

Germany played the largest part, also contributed to an increased Soviet interest in reducing forces in Europe. And the Kohl administration negotiated a series of agreements with East Germany under the rubric of its "policy of small steps" from 1987 to 1989, permitting more than 10 million East Germans to visit West Germany[29]—a success that confirmed the merit of Kohl's 1983 rejection of Honecker's threatening demands.

The Alliance Paradox—Public Support and a Gathering Anti-NATO Coalition

Support for the Atlantic Alliance was always strong among the citizens of West Germany. In fact, among the major European NATO countries, the citizens of West Germany have consistently given the highest level of support to the Atlantic Alliance (see table 4–1). From 1969 until the end of 1988 public support for the statement, "NATO is still essential to my country's security," was higher than 80 percent. The October 1988 figure showed 76 percent of Germans considering NATO essential and only 13 percent considering it "no longer essential."[30]

Soviet President Gorbachev's policies of normalization toward Western Europe certainly contributed to his personal popularity in virtually all the NATO countries. But even in 1984, before the Gorbachev era, about 47 percent of West Germans did not feel threatened by the Soviet Union—a proportion about equal to the combined 1983 vote for the SPD and the Greens. By late 1988, 75 percent of West Germans felt no threat from the East, yet nearly the same large majority of Germans continued to support a public consensus that the alliance remained necessary.[31]

Much attention was paid to the 1987 opinion polls showing a plurality (not a majority) of West Germans and Britons trusting Gorbachev more than Reagan to reduce international tensions.[32] The response was surprising, but it probably reflected a broad hopefulness in the West and a particularly positive Western media image of Gorbachev. By contrast, Reagan's media image suffered because many citizens had disagreements with his domestic and foreign policies.

Only a tiny minority of Germans suggested the Federal Republic should withdraw from NATO (an average of 3 percent in the 1970s and 9 percent in the 1980s).[33] But in 1987 more than 70 percent were in favor of "withdrawing all nuclear weapons from Europe."[34] And although 51 percent in 1988 still said military deterrence was necessary to their security, 32 percent said it was not necessary. On the

FIGURE 4–1
EUROPEAN VIEWS ON THE NEED FOR NATO, 1969–1988

Question: Do you believe NATO is still essential to your country's security?

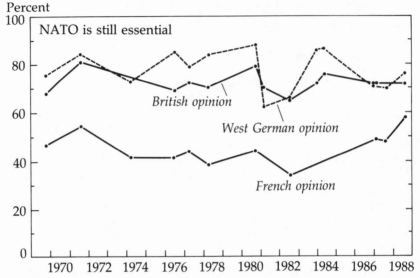

NOTE: In the October 1980 and prior surveys, this question was asked only of those who had heard or read about NATO. To standardize data, percentages have been recalculated on the base of those asked the question.

SOURCE: Surveys conducted under the auspices of the U.S. Information Agency, using local firms in each country. Published in *Public Opinion*, May/June 1989 (Washington, D.C.: American Enterprise Institute), p. 21.

issue of a continued U.S. military presence in Europe, 32 percent in 1988 said they would welcome the withdrawal of American troops, 30 percent were undecided, and 38 percent were opposed to this action.[35] These data suggest that even before the hopeful developments of 1989 and 1990 in Eastern Europe and despite overwhelming public support for NATO membership, a strong sector of public opinion in West Germany favored an effective reduction of NATO's ability to provide credible military defense for Germany. Such a reduction would eliminate all nuclear weapons and, potentially, remove all U.S. and other allied troops.

By 1988, among politically relevant leadership groups there were two broad coalitions on NATO. One favored continuing full German participation in NATO; the other rhetorically endorsed the Atlantic

Alliance, but it proposed unilateral actions that could effectively end any functioning military alliance.

The NATO-supporting coalition was rooted primarily in the CDU-CSU and a group within the FDP, its coalition partner. It probably included some elements of the business sector, a small minority of religious leaders, and a very small element of the national media.

The coalition for de facto neutrality through a "restructing" of Germany's relationships with the United States and with NATO included the SPD and the Greens (together accounting for 46 percent of the electorate), a significant proportion of organized labor, and a range of business firms seeking expanded opportunities for trade with Eastern Europe and the Soviet Union. This view was also shared by many politically active religious leaders, a group that had been moving to the left since the 1970s, and by the majority of the media, which had also become largely self-identified with the views of the left in German politics. To this cluster of left-neutralism could be added small groups of the far right, which also rejected the existing relationships with the United States and with NATO.

Before the events of 1989 in Eastern Europe, it seemed that in the 1990 elections the SPD would avoid directly challenging Germany's membership in NATO, instead proposing arms control and reduction initiatives and a reformed relationship with U.S. forces. Such moves could have led in time to a de facto neutrality for Germany. For example, the SPD submitted an eighteen-page "major parliamentary question" to the Kohl government in March 1989, and stated that "the equal rights which the Federal Republic enjoys in the alliance can no longer be reconciled with the fact that the [foreign] forces stationed in the Federal Republic of Germany have retained the privileges which the sending states were granted at the end of World War II in their function as occupying powers."[36] The U.S. ambassador to Germany, Vernon Walters, stated that the new limitations and restrictions proposed by the SPD on the United States and other Allied forces stationed in Germany would render Germany incapable of defending itself.[37] Before the events of 1989, it seemed that the SPD's intended approach to the 1990 elections was to focus public attention on the already objectionable activities of NATO and especially American armed forces in Germany. It could then demand a major renegotiation of the rights of such Allied military forces.

If Kohl's CDU government had refused to support these SPD objectives, the SPD could depict the CDU-CSU as being subservient to U.S. and NATO interests at the expense of the West German people. Together with a package of proposals for disarmament and

55

for restructuring NATO forces to make them capable only of defensive operation (to be done in conjunction with a similar restructuring by Warsaw Pact forces), this refusal might have permitted the SPD to court the political left and appeal to German nationalism. Such SPD "neutralist nationalism" (the phrase is Walter Hahn's) could have turned the 1990 elections into a referendum on reducing the role of U.S. and NATO forces in Germany, thereby moving Germany away from the Atlantic Alliance.

Thus by the summer of 1989, on the eve of the dramatic transformation of Eastern Europe, both West German coalitions had established their positions regarding the major issue facing a reunified Germany in the 1990s: whether it should and would remain a full member in the Atlantic Alliance. The CDU-CSU, in coalition with the FDP, had demonstrated its belief that the best foundation for an effective *Ostpolitik* was a secure and reliable *Westpolitik*—it could pursue both with vigor. The SPD, while continuing a rhetorical commitment for the immediate future to the Atlantic Alliance, in fact rejected many of its key security concerns, ignored the democratic opposition in East Germany and Eastern Europe, abandoned prospects for German reunification, and legitimized the East German Communist regime. It furthermore undercut the interests of Germany's key ally, the United States, in Nicaragua and other third world conflicts. In effect, while the CDU-CSU held firmly to its commitment to the West and simultaneous pursuit of détente with the East during the 1980s, the SPD tilted strongly toward the primacy of *Ostpolitik* and the abandonment of any Western-oriented security policy. The events of late 1989 in Eastern Europe would render a judgment on these two different political perspectives.

PART TWO
The Transition to a New Europe

5

The Democratic Opening of Eastern Europe, 1989–1990

Poland ten years, Hungary ten months, East Germany ten weeks, Czechoslovakia ten days. . . .

> Slogan written during the protests
> against communism in Czechoslovakia,
> November 1989

The year 1989 marked the transition to a new Europe. Acting with enormous courage and determination, the people of Eastern Europe brought a new momentum to their decades-old quest to end Communist rule and establish political democracy. The surprising and dramatic events of 1989 began with a process of coalition between democratic and Communist groups in Poland. Soon a number of Communist regimes were unraveling, and a liberalization process in East Germany opened the door for German reunification.

Certain East European countries fulfilled the promise of free and fair elections in 1990, inaugurating new democratic governments. Others held partially rigged elections and maintained Communist regimes in power. Even in the countries where democratic movements succeeded a dark shadow remained: the hard-line elements of the Communist party, the secret police, the pro-Soviet military personnel, and unknown proportions of the national bureaucracies. These elements all portended the possibility of communism's restoration at some time in the future.

The continuing struggle between prodemocratic and hard-line Communist Eastern Europeans may in the future significantly depend on the international actions of a reunified Germany. A Germany firmly aligned with the West would help strengthen the prodemocratic elements in East European governments and communities, while an effectively neutral Germany would not. De facto neutrality would mean accommodating the wishes of the Soviet Union; Germany in this case would be less likely to use its resources and political experience to assist other nations' efforts to establish democratic institutions.

The 1989 turning away from communism can be better understood by recalling the late 1940s turn toward communism and the subsequent efforts of the East European people to steer away from that unwanted course. The establishment of Communist regimes between 1944 and 1948 was done through a process combining subtlety, deception, and hidden Soviet force. Virtually all the Communist parties of Eastern Europe changed their names—as they did again in 1989. They dropped the word "Communist" and called themselves the "Polish Workers party" in Poland, the "Socialist Unity party" in East Germany, and the "Hungarian Socialist Workers party" in Hungary. They used coercion and deception to create coalitions with non-Communist parties and then forced these parties to remain in the sham coalitions for decades, most of them until 1989. As in the Soviet Union, the national Communist parties also exploited the electoral process to establish a specious legitimacy through the ballot. They became expert at manipulating both the initial election campaigns and the final counting of the votes. The national Communist parties established all-pervasive secret police forces, with networks encompassing hundreds of thousands of informers among the population and with detailed dossiers on suspected political opponents and significant nonconformists. Non-Communist institutions such as civic, religious, professional, and ethnic associations were thoroughly infiltrated, suppressed, or supplanted by paralleled Communist organizations.[1]

During the decades of Communist rule the people in a number of countries made it clear that they wanted independence and political liberalization. In 1953, when a workers' uprising in East Germany could not be contained by the East German army and police, Soviet troops intervened to crush it. In 1956 Nikita Khrushchev denounced Stalin's purges and executions of Communist party officials and officially launched a Communist reform in the Soviet Union, promising some political liberalization, greater freedom of expression, and economic reform through decentralization. Khrushchev's reformist pronouncements inspired a number of Communist leaderships to loosen their repressive reins. In China, for example, Mao Zedong launched the period of letting "one hundred flowers bloom" to encourage more free expression (when these flowers bloomed into a bouquet of opposition to his rule, Mao cut them down). In Poland the words of Khrushchev led to demands for greater freedom, to a change in Communist leadership, and to a growing momentum of strikes and demonstrations. In Hungary the party also replaced leaders of the Stalin generation, and the new Communists rode the wave of national opposition to continued Soviet occupation. In late October 1956 Hungary announced its intention to become neutral and to withdraw from the Warsaw Pact. But a large-scale invasion by Soviet armed forces crushed the Hungarian revolution and its aspirations for independence.

Other Stalin-generation leaders were removed in the early 1960s. In Bulgaria Todor Zhivkov took power, pledging some degree of liberalization and an end to the "excesses" of the Stalin era; in Romania Nicolae Ceausescu similarly ascended to power, professing to be a Communist reformer of the Khrushchev era.

Interestingly, the last site of this generational change in Eastern Europe was Czechoslovakia. Not until 1968 was the Stalin-imposed leader Antonin Novotny replaced by a member of the post-Stalin generation, Alexander Dubcek. Representing a faction within Czechoslovakia's Communist party that sought a great deal of reform, Dubcek pledged adherence to the Warsaw Pact and loyalty to the Soviets in international affairs—but he launched a series of internal liberalizing changes that came to be known as the "Prague Spring." In late July 1968 the Soviets met with Dubcek and the entire Czechoslovakian Communist leadership amid disarming smiles and toasts of mutual appreciation, reassuring the Czechoslovakians that all was well in their relationship with Moscow. Their guard was lowered and they were encouraged to permit key party and armed forces officials to take their planned vacations in August 1968. On August 20 the Soviet Union, employing troops from East Germany, Hungary, and Poland, invaded Czechoslovakia, crushed the reform effort, brought Dubcek and his colleagues to Moscow in chains, and installed Gustav Husak as the new, reliably pro-Soviet ruler.

As if by some law of dictatorship, each of the Khrushchev generation of Communist reform leaders of the 1960s ruled with increasing repression and rigidity, abandoning their initial steps toward liberalization.

The Helsinki Final Act of 1975, signed by thirty-three European states, the United States, and Canada, stipulated that all countries live up to international standards of human rights. The Soviet purpose in seeking and signing the Helsinki accords was to ratify the post–World War II borders it had set with Poland and between Poland and Germany. Having previously committed themselves to the same principles of human rights, as members of the United Nations and as signatories to the International Convention on Human Rights, the Soviet and East European regimes had no reason to refrain from yet another unenforceable set of broad promises. Within some East

European countries, however, the Helsinki promises catalyzed the political efforts of small, courageous, prodemocratic groups, in many cases affiliated with and encouraged by religious institutions. From the mid 1970s to the late 1980s these small citizens groups monitored their governments' compliance with the Helsinki accords and became the nucleus of the growing political democracy movements.

The Unraveling

Across Eastern Europe, the tightly spun fabric of communism began to unravel.

Poland. After the attempted "bread and freedom" rebellion of 1956 the Communist regime reestablished control, but it permitted certain liberal concessions. The Catholic church was allowed to function autonomously, and most of the country's agriculture was permitted to remain in private hands. As Poland's economic problems mounted in the 1970s, the regime welcomed billions of dollars in credit and financial aid from the West—mainly Germany. This was an aspect of normalization associated with détente and the Eastern treaties. In 1980 the independent Polish labor movement, Solidarity, was established and quickly began to grow into a national movement of protest against the Communist regime. Its success derived in part from the government's reluctance to avoid cuts in the flow of Western economic credit and trade opportunities. Underestimating the movements' speed of growth, the Communist regime faltered in suppressing it.

Initially organized at the Gdansk shipyard, the Solidarity movement's genesis came in the attempt to secure better working conditions and wages for its members. It was closely affiliated with the Catholic church and with a broad current of intellectual opposition to the Communist regime—opposition that was to be nonviolent at all times. The appointment of a Polish cardinal as the Roman Catholic pope in 1978 provided an added inspiration for opposition to the Polish Communist regime. This was intensified by the triumphal visit of the first Polish pope, John Paul II, to Poland in 1979.

By late 1981 the membership of Solidarity approached 10 million, formidable in a country whose estimated adult working population was 25 million. In late 1980 the Soviet Union had massed a large formation of troops near the Polish borders and there were signs of preparation to occupy Poland and dismantle Solidarity. On December 13, 1981, the Polish regime, led by General Wojciech Jaruzelski, used the secret police and paramilitary police to arrest nearly the entire leadership of the movement and to repress it in one night.[2]

Solidarity was officially abolished in 1982, and years of persecution and labor unrest ensued during the 1980s. But by the end of the decade Solidarity gradually became a visible participant in the Polish political economy. In early 1989 the Jaruzelski regime decided to invite the Solidarity movement to join in a Communist-led coalition government seeking the labor peace the Communists believed necessary both to improve the country's deteriorating economic situation and to obtain increased Western financial aid and credit. This invitation included an opportunity for Solidarity to run its candidates in new elections for a national parliament.

Solidarity had boycotted previous elections because it considered them rigged by the Communists. The Communist strategy in 1989 was "to persuade Solidarity . . . to participate in a restructured political system in which a powerful president—presumably Jaruzelski—would preside over a Parliament divided by fiat into blocks of 65 percent for the Communist-led alliance and 35 percent for the opposition."[3] When Solidarity rejected this proposal of a token coalition government, the Communist minister of interior proposed that a second house of Parliament, a Senate, be added to the existing Parliament, called the Sejm. But membership in this second house would be predominantly Communist. One of the Solidarity leaders is reported to have responded, "You can violate democracy once but not three times"—referring to the presidency, the existing house of Parliament, and the new house of Parliament that the regime sought to control while giving Solidarity token representation.[4]

Intending the new Senate to have very limited powers, the Communists then proposed that elections for that 100-member body be free and open to Solidarity. The Communists expected Solidarity to obtain little support in the countryside; with only two months remaining before the elections, the urban, labor-based movement would presumably be unable to augment this support. Communist polls showed relatively few people supporting Solidarity, most respondents declaring themselves to be "independents."

After much internal debate, Solidarity accepted the Communist proposal. Open elections for Parliament and the Senate—with two senators to be selected from each province—were to be held on June 4, 1989.

Using a countrywide network of activists, the Catholic church, and a variety of civic organizations opposed to the Communist regime, Solidarity campaigned nationally. It was permitted to contest 161 seats in the Sjem—35 percent of the total, 65 percent being reserved for the Communist-led alliance—and all 100 seats in the Senate. On June 4 the people of Poland decisively repudiated the

Communist party. Solidarity won 260 of 261 open seats, including 99 in the Senate.

The assumption that the Parliament would choose General Jaruzelski once again to be president underlay the negotiations leading to the April 7, 1989, agreement between the Communist regime and Solidarity. Continued Communist control of the secret police and the military was also accepted. Thus on July 19 the Parliament chose Jaruzelski as president with the minimum number of required votes. But instead of then forming a parliamentary coalition with the Communist party to establish a new government, Solidarity leader Lech Walesa persuaded his party to ally with two small, non-Communist parties that had been coerced into alliances with the Communists for years. The Peasant party and the Democratic party were still represented in the Parliament, and they agreed to give their votes to Solidarity so it could form a new government. On August 24, 1989, longtime Solidarity activist Tadeusz Mazowiecki was confirmed as the new prime minister of Poland, the first non-Communist government in Eastern Europe since 1948. He headed a twenty-three-member coalition cabinet in which only four members were Communists.

Confronted by this unexpected Solidarity-led coalition intending to form a new government, the Polish Communists reportedly consulted Moscow. Press reports said that Gorbachev held a telephone conversation with the Polish Communist leadership on August 22 urging that it permit a Solidarity-led government.[5] Jaruzelski told a Western journalist in September 1989, "There is a Government and parliamentary majority going one way [Solidarity]. . . . [But] the civil service, the army, the security apparatus are guided by the ideology of the minority [Communists]."[6] This statement suggests Jaruzelski felt confident that as long as the Communist party remained intact and controlled the secret police, the military, and the bureaucracy, it could also control the Solidarity-led government.

June 4, 1989, the day of the limited free elections that inaugurated Poland's transition from Communist rule, was also the day the Chinese Communist regime bloodily suppressed the thousands of young people who had called for liberalization and democracy in the People's Republic of China. The people of Eastern Europe had before them on June 4 two alternative visions of the future—brutal repression in Beijing and free elections in Poland.

Hungary. In May 1988 the reformist wing of the Hungarian Communist party forced out János Kadar, the party boss installed in 1956 by the Soviet Union's armed forces. The Hungarian Communist leadership had established its control after a thorough purge of all institutions—and an estimated 40,000 people were executed or imprisoned after the Soviet army crushed the Hungarian revolution in 1956.[7] From that time, the Soviets maintained a large diplomatic and secret police presence as well as some 70,000 troops in Hungary.

In the 1960s the Hungarian Communist leadership decided to adopt economic and political liberalization themes from the Soviet Union in what came to be called "goulash communism." This meant some decentralization of the state's role in the economy and a marked reduction in visible repression. By the 1970s Hungarian Communist rule seemed less harsh than that of East Germany, Bulgaria, or Romania. The Soviet invasion of Czechoslovakia in 1968 contributed to the public perception that reform in Hungary could happen only with the party, not against it.

Drawing on Gorbachev's proposals for openness and reform in the Soviet Union, on January 11, 1989, the Hungarian Communist leadership permitted the Parliament to legalize freedom of assembly and freedom of association for non-Communist groups. One month later, on February 11, the Communist central committee moved to permit the creation of independent political parties. In May 1989 Hungary began dismantling the barbed wire fence and lethal barriers lining its border with neutral Austria, thus becoming the first Soviet bloc country to open its border with Western Europe. This action was intended to symbolize the political rebirth inside Hungary and to attract more Western financial support for the country. In the next months it produced an entirely unanticipated result.

Although the Helsinki agreements of 1975 had committed the Communist signatories to permit their citizens freedom of travel, none of them actually honored this commitment. The citizens of Eastern Europe did, however, enjoy freedom of travel within and among the Communist countries. Thus when Hungary removed its border fences with Austria first hundreds, then thousands of East Germans came to Hungary in the hope of crossing over into Austria and then onward to West Germany and freedom. As word spread that it was possible to slip over the border, more and more East Germans flocked to Hungary in the summer of 1989. Complete families—men, women, and children—camped out in places where the Western media was permitted to interview and film them.

These East Germans demonstrated a dramatic rejection of communism, repeatedly declaring as their reason for wanting to leave East Germany a desire for freedom, not simply for better living conditions. This event happened to coincide with the fiftieth anniversary of the August 1939 Hitler-Stalin pact, an occasion widely observed in Europe. On August 22, 1989, the day before the fiftieth anniversary, Hungarian foreign minister Gyula Horn decided to permit East Germans peaceful passage through Hungary to Austria and West Germany, despite the East German regime's protests.

This decision violated a 1968 Hungarian–East German treaty, but it was in keeping with the Helsinki Final Act and with a 1989 CSCE agreement signed by Hungary in Vienna, and with a United Nations protocol on refugees, also signed by Hungary. The 1989 UN protocol prohibited Hungary from forcing refugees to go back to their country. Horn said, "The agreement that we signed in 1968 was an anti-human agreement. We have to look for the humanist solution no matter what sort of conflict might arise. It was quite obvious to me that this would be the first step in a landslide-like series of events."[8]

The "landslide" was to have an important effect in East Germany, Czechoslovakia, and Hungary. In September 1989 the Hungarian Communist regime agreed with the newly established opposition parties that a multiparty political system with free and fair elections should be created in 1990. Then in October 1989 the Hungarian Communist party renounced Marxism and renamed itself the Hungarian Socialist party. This was the first explicit rejection of Marxism-Leninism as an ideological system by a ruling Communist party. Later that month Hungary was proclaimed a free republic, and the "People's Republic" phrase was dropped from its official name.

In April 1990 as promised, free and fair elections were held. The renamed Communist party received 9 percent of the vote and democratic opposition parties won, establishing a new non-Communist government.[9]

East Germany. From 1945 the East German Communist party maintained tight control over the 17 million people of East Germany. No major challenges to the regime arose after Soviet troops crushed the 1953 rebellion. More than 2 million East Germans fled during the 1950s for West Germany, where they had the right to immediate West German citizenship—including passports and access to all social and health insurance benefits, equivalent to their employment situations in East Germany. But this emigration ended in 1961 with the building of the Berlin Wall.

The East German regime was among the most active in collaborating with the Soviets in hostile international activities, and among the most confident of the East European Communist regimes concerning its capacity to keep power. East Germany worked diligently with the Soviet Union to prevent the deployment of the intermediate-range nuclear forces in West Germany in 1983. Part of the Communist propaganda campaign was aimed at promoting peace movements, especially among religious organizations in West Germany.[10] A group of Protestant and Catholic clergymen in East Germany also established peace organizations and sought positive initiatives from the East German government toward the relaxation of tensions with the West. They also sought the reduction of the 180,000-strong East German army and the 380,000-strong Soviet military presence within their country.

Despite constant harassment by the Communists these church-affiliated peace organizations spread throughout East Germany. Poland's 1989 installation of a non-Communist government and the Hungarian Communist party's reforms and permission for East Germans to transit Hungary to West Germany gave these dissident movements a sense of momentum and hope.

From the Hungarian regime's fateful decision in late August 1989 to the middle of September 1989, more than 13,000 East Germans fled to West Germany through Austria. The eyes of all of Europe—West and East—were focused on these families as they made their journey to freedom. Many of the refugees had their own automobiles and enjoyed a comfortable living standard. They told the Western media again and again that they were not going to West Germany primarily to seek material prosperity; rather, they were going to seek freedom. Seizing the opportunity for escape, thousands of additional East Germans went to Hungary and then to Czechoslovakia, where they established vast temporary tent settlements near the East German diplomatic missions in an effort to obtain permission to leave for West Germany. In late September 1989 the hard-line regime in Czechoslovakia reached an agreement with the East German regime that permitted more than 17,000 East German refugees to leave for West Germany, often on special trains that went through East German territory. Western television—visible in East Germany—nightly portrayed the hopes of the East Germans as they obtained permission to leave, their symbolic acts repudiating the regime, such as throwing their East German money and passports out of their trains to West Germany, and the joy of their arrival in West Germany. A mood of expectation grew inside East Germany, as the actions of these thousands of families revealed the extent and depth of discontent with the East German regime.

Throughout these weeks Erich Honecker, the East German ruler installed during the Khrushchev era, was absent because of a serious illness, operation, and postoperative recovery. Honecker returned in time to greet visiting Soviet leader Gorbachev on October 7, 1989, for the celebration of the fortieth anniversary of the establishment of the East German Communist state. Gorbachev was cheered by the East

German people much as he had been during his May 1989 visit to the People's Republic of China, as a Communist representing change and reform. In his speeches and reportedly in his meeting with the East German politburo Gorbachev made two key points to the East German Communist leadership: first, that it should not isolate itself from the people or it would lose its right to exist; and second, that "it was up to each Communist party to find a way to renew itself."[11]

Two days later the center of Leipzig, East Germany's second largest city, was described as follows:

> It resembled an armed camp. Riot police backed by water cannon stood watch over intersections around the broad Karl Marx Platz. . . . Lines of armored cars were placed up on nearby side streets, packed with thousands of police "battle groups" of the Communist party's militia and special fighting teams of the feared State Security organ, the "Stasi." Nearby at St. Nicholas Church, a huge crowd of people filled the pews, aisles, and entryway and were spilling out the door. They were praying and waiting for a mass demonstration scheduled to begin at 6:00 P.M., a protest against the hard-line regime of Erich Honecker.[12]

Hard-line East German Communists had publicly spoken about the need for a Tiananmen Square–type repression in East Germany to crush the growing spirit of democratic protest. And the preparations made by the police and other Communist groups to attack the demonstrators on that October 9 clearly suggested that Honecker's intended crackdown would have resulted in enormous human casualties that evening.

That afternoon, however, Kurt Masur, conductor of Leipzig's symphony orchestra, had called three Communist party leaders and three opposition activists to meet at his home. After discussion they agreed on a joint statement, which was broadcast only minutes before the 6:00 P.M. demonstration was to begin. In this joint statement the Leipzig Communist leaders made this commitment: "We all need a free exchange of opinions about the continuation of socialism in our country. Therefore we promise all citizens that we will use our full power and authority to insure that this dialogue will occur not only in the Leipzig area but with our national government."[13] The acting Communist party chief of Leipzig then delivered this statement personally to the local police commanders and thereupon reportedly "the police snapped off their lights, cut the engines of their trucks and water cannons, and withdrew from the line of march."[14]

When asked later the reason for this unprecedented concession of granting legitimacy to the protesters, local Communist leader Karl Mayer, a member of the party for thirty-one years, responded, "We kept waiting and waiting for change to come from Berlin but nothing came. But the straw that broke the camel's back was the massive departure of our young people who were going to the West. Honecker said there were no problems to solve. That's the point where I said to myself 'this can't go on any more, we will have to do something.' "[15]

On the night of October 9, 1989, 70,000 people demonstrated in Leipzig against the regime, peacefully chanting "We are the people" and "No violence." A week later the regular Monday night vigil in Leipzig grew to 100,000 people, the largest unauthorized demonstration in East Germany since 1953. Two days later a meeting of the East German politburo removed Honecker and replaced him with Egon Krenz, Honecker's much younger protégé and longtime party secretary for internal security issues. Krenz moved immediately to bring colleagues of his generation into party leadership positions. In a ploy to gain favor with reformist elements of the Communist party and the growing democratic opposition groups Krenz publicly exposed and criticized the luxurious lifestyle and failings of the Honecker group.

But revelations of posh villas and gourmet food, rumors of foreign bank accounts in gold and in dollars, and televised exposure of the East German Communist elite's self-indulgent lifestyle only further angered the population. Krenz promised that the party would reform, but the number of East Germans trying to flee increased—more than 2,000 a day sought to escape through Czechoslovakia or Hungary. On November 1 the Krenz regime attempted to end the flight of East Germans by promising there would be freedom of travel for all East Germans, and he duly lifted restrictions. The result was the flight of more than 50,000 East Germans to West Germany through Czechoslovakia in the week of November 1–8, 1989.

On November 7, 1989, Krenz removed his prime minister and the entire cabinet, promising to establish a more moderate government, but the exodus continued. On November 9 the East German regime declared the Berlin Wall would be open and would no longer be a barrier between the two Germanys. Krenz intended this dramatic act as a visible guarantee to East Germans—who clearly did not trust the regime—that there would be permanent freedom of travel in the future. But immediately after the wall was opened, hundreds of thousands of East Germans poured into the long-forbidden West Berlin, where they were joyfully welcomed, and another 500,000 East Germans demonstrated in East Berlin for freedom and against the regime. This largest demonstration in East Germany's history reflected the people's enormous yearning for freedom and their growing expectation of having an impact. As the exiled poet and protest singer Walt Biermann said, "I must weep for joy that it happened so quickly and simply. And I must weep for wrath that it took so abysmally long."[16]

On December 1, 1989, the Communists permitted the Parliament to change the constitution, eliminating the party's guaranteed monopoly on power. Two days later the party's entire ruling politburo and central committee resigned, along with Egon Krenz. Krenz was succeeded on December 9 by Gregor Gysi, a lifelong Communist known as a reformer and an attorney who had defended dissidents in East Germany. The party also changed its name from the Socialist Unity party to the party of Democratic Socialism. The new party leadership in turn selected a well-known Communist reformer, Hans Modrow, as premier of a new government. Clearly the Communist party hoped that by bringing its best reform leaders forward it would be able to maintain authority. Modrow promised free and fair elections in early 1990.

The election date was set for March 18, 1990, and an extraordinary election campaign ensued. The Communists' former captive coalition partners, the Christian Democrats and the Social Democrats, declared themselves independent of their former Communist affiliations, changed their leadership, and forged new alliances with their West German counterparts. As a result the election campaign in February and March 1990 was conducted by both East and West German political leaders, who toured East Germany and spoke for their respective democratic parties. The East German Communists promised reform and moderation—but they received only 16 percent of the vote. The election was won by a CDU-led coalition, the Alliance for Germany, which had favored rapid reunification. The Alliance won 48 percent of the vote, the Social Democrats 24 percent, and the Free Democrats (linked to the West German FDP) 5 percent. In April 1990 East Germany's first non-Communist government was formed by a coalition between the CDU-led Alliance and the Social Democrats. The new prime minister, Lothar de Mazière, favored rapid reunification and negotiated an agreement with West Germany's Chancellor Kohl for the economic merging of the two Germanys to occur on July 2, 1990.

Czechoslovakia. After the 1968 invasion the Soviets installed a new hard-line Communist party leadership in Czechoslovakia. A large Soviet diplomatic, KGB, and military presence (about 73,000 troops) further ensured that there would be no need for another overt invasion.

By 1989 some members of the Czechoslovakian Communist party were beginning to catch the new spirit of perestroika and glasnost and they argued for political and economic reforms in Czechoslovakia similar to those in the Soviet Union. Prime Minister Ladislav Adamec took this position, but he was opposed by the Soviet-installed Communist party general secretary Milos Jakes. Reportedly, Gorbachev summoned the two to meet with him at his vacation villa in the summer of 1989. The purpose was to encourage some degree of liberalization in Czechoslovakia, but as the senior party official in charge of state security later commented, the two Czechoslovakian leaders "knew there was no way they could survive perestroika."[17] By November 1989, the events in Poland and East Germany as well as the successful flight of tens of thousands of East Germans through Czechoslovakia had emboldened the small democratic opposition groups there. On November 17 some thousands of young people congregated in the main square of Prague, the Czech capital, to demand human rights. At about 10:00 P.M. they were attacked by police, who had surrounded the entire square. Hundreds of demonstrators were seriously injured. This event occurred one day after Jan Fojtik, the Communist party's ideology chief, was summoned to Moscow and informed that the Soviet Union would join the new governments in Poland and Hungary in publicly repudiating the 1968 invasion. As one observer said, "coming from Moscow, that would deprive Jakes of the last shred of legitimacy."[18]

On November 19 more than 10,000 prodemocracy demonstrators rallied in Prague. On the same day the Civic Forum was founded as a prodemocratic reform movement. Never in the twenty-one years since the crushing of the Prague Spring had the secret police permitted more than a handful of people to gather for unauthorized demonstrations. As the Communists debated the use of violence against the demonstrators, more than 200,000 rallied in Prague on November 20, demanding free elections and the resignation of the hard-line Communist leaders. Similar demonstrations occurred in other cities.

The Communist party politburo was reported to have decided by a margin of two votes not to use violence against the protesters.[19] On November 24 Milos Jakes and other hard-line leaders resigned. The man whom they had removed in 1968 with the help of Soviet bayonets—Alexander Dubcek, whom they had forced to live in obscurity and work as a menial laborer—then addressed 250,000 prodemocracy demonstrators in Prague. On November 27, 1989, millions of

Czech workers staged a general strike in support of the prodemocracy movement.

Czechoslovakia's dramatic "ten days in November" unfolded rapidly. On November 28 the Communist party's leading role in Czechoslovakia was repudiated. On November 30 the government announced plans to remove the fortifications along the border with neutral Austria and to lift virtually all travel restrictions to the West by early December. On December 7 Premier Ladislav Adamec resigned and was replaced by Marion Calfa. On December 10 a new government was sworn in with non-Communist ministers in the majority, for the first time since 1948. The hard-line president, Gustav Husak, thereupon resigned. He was replaced by the poet, author, and former political dissident Vaclav Havel, who became interim president on December 29, 1989.

These changes brought a second Prague Spring to Czechoslovakia. The new interim government permitted democratic political parties to organize, to receive legal recognition, and to prepare a campaign for elections to be held in June 1990. In the new atmosphere of openness newspapers and periodicals reflecting a variety of political viewpoints were established. The new government removed the fortifications on the Austrian border and opened opportunities for travel for its citizens and for visitors from the West.

Internationally, the new Havel government announced an end to all intelligence cooperation with the Soviets against other countries, and to trafficking in lethal devices, such as the Semtex plastic explosives the Czechoslovakians had sold to Libya. Furthermore, Havel promised that all Soviet troops would be withdrawn by the end of June 1991.

After a vigorous and unrestricted campaign, national elections were held on June 8 and 9, 1990. The Communists received 14 percent of the vote. The Civic Forum and its affiliated party in Slovakia, the Public Against Violence, won 47 percent of the vote for Parliament. These two prodemocratic parties then united and together with a new Christian Democratic party, which received 12 percent of the vote, formed a democratic coalition government with no Communist component.[20]

Bulgaria. Having been under the domination of the Ottoman (Turkish) Empire for 500 years, Bulgaria looked to Russia for protection from Turkey after it achieved independence in 1908. Furthermore, a small Communist party had operated in Bulgaria even before Communist rule came to Russia in 1917. These two factors distinguish Bulgaria from the other East European countries, which had long histories of opposition to the power of Russia and later the Soviet Union.

In 1944 a new Bulgarian government rejected an alliance with Hitler's Germany and sought peace terms with the Allies, but it was overthrown by the Soviet-supported Fatherland Front and the nation was invaded by Soviet troops. As the Communists did throughout Eastern Europe, the party in Bulgaria used deception and pseudo-coalitions to ensure its full power. In 1947 the Bulgarian Communist party adopted a constitution patterned after the Soviet Union's, and it renamed the country the People's Republic of Bulgaria. By 1949 Vulko Chervenkov, known as the Stalin of Bulgaria, had completed a bloody purge of the party and emerged as ruler.

Chervenkov was replaced in 1961 by Todor Zhivkov, who denounced his predecessor for "Stalinist excesses" and "violations of socialist legality," much as Khrushchev was denouncing his predecessor. Initially Zhivkov embarked on a limited program of economic decentralization and liberalization, but the Soviet invasion of Czechoslovakia in 1968 ended this initiative.[21] From 1961 to 1989 the Zhivkov regime remained closely allied with the Soviets. Bulgaria was useful: it bordered two key NATO countries, Greece and Turkey, and it had in 1989 a Turkish minority of nearly 1 million among its 9 million people. The Soviet Union made extensive use of Bulgaria for a variety of hostile and sensitive international actions against the West, such as the attempt to violently destabilize Turkey between 1978 and 1980 and the attempt to assassinate Pope John Paul II in 1981. The Bulgarian regime of Zhivkov, enjoying control for decades, was one of the most subservient to the Soviet Union of all those in the post–World War II Eastern Europe.

Like the other long-established East European regimes, Zhivkov's rule was marked by repression, economic decline, overinvestment in heavy industry, massive pollution, cronyism, and corruption; the country also accumulated a $10 billion foreign debt to the West. Zhivkov's "Brezhnev style" of rule clearly was not compatible with Gorbachev's approach, and reportedly Gorbachev had refused to meet with Zhivkov.

Unlike the other East European countries we have discussed, Bulgaria maintained an exceptionally pervasive repression that permitted few if any prodemocratic groups to emerge. The unraveling of the Zhivkov regime occurred entirely within the Communist party.

For nineteen years Petar Mladenov, a loyal party member, was the regime's foreign minister. In early 1989, in an effort to improve Bulgaria's international image, Mladenov signed an international accord on human rights in Vienna. Only months later Zhivkov launched another wave of vicious persecution of the nation's nearly 1 million Turks—forbidding the Turkish language from being spoken in public and, by autumn, forcing about 310,000 men, women, and children to flee to Turkey.

By late October 1989, Mladenov had decided to remove Zhivkov. Undoubtedly the events in Poland and Hungary and the October 18 ouster of Honecker in East Germany made this seem more feasible. Mladenov persuaded the Bulgarian minister of defense, Dobri Dzhuro, to join his plot. Reportedly Zhivkov was preparing for "ruthless repression of all deviants," including not only dissidents but also younger, change-oriented Communists such as Mladenov.[22] On November 9, 1989, the day the Berlin Wall was opened, Bulgaria's nine-member politburo met. Zhivkov's earlier attempts to deploy ministry of interior and state security troops in his own support had been countered by Dzhuro's movement of his military forces. Now the politburo by a reported five-to-four vote removed Zhivkov, and Mladenov took over.[23]

On November 18, 1989, more than 50,000 Bulgarians demonstrated for democratic reforms—the first such gathering in decades. On January 15, 1990, the post-Zhivkov regime permitted the National Assembly to formally end Communist dominance and to give independent parties the right to compete in future elections. An Extraordinary Congress of the Bulgarian Communist party convened from January 30 to February 2, 1990. Afterward the party declared its commitment to reform by issuing a new manifesto and party statutes, and by changing its name to the Bulgarian Socialist party. Mladenov continued as head of state until July 1990, but the Party Congress named Aleksandur Lilov as the new head of the party and another reputed reform Communist, Andrei Lukanov, as prime minister. All these self-identified reform Communist leaders had histories of close association with the Soviets—associations that continued.

During the six months leading up to the June 1990 elections, the democratic parties were allowed to establish themselves, organize, and recruit members. Independent labor unions were also organized, and the formerly Communist-controlled labor unions declared themselves members of an Independent Labor Federation no longer operating under Communist control. Changes in the secret police leadership were also announced, and during the 1990 election campaign the opposition political groups had some access to the state-controlled electronic media and opportunity to circulate their own newspapers.

This political opening was only partial, however. The post-Zhivkov Communist regime used the full resources of the state to help the Bulgarian Socialist (Communist) party in the election campaign. The secret police continued to exist; their move to new buildings in Bulgaria's capital "may be interpreted as a sign of expansion rather than reduction of the organization," in the view of the main democratic opposition party.[24] The new head of the secret police, General Atanas Semerdzhiev, was a lifelong Communist and a graduate of two Soviet military academies. He was a reportedly close associate of the minister of defense, himself a staunch ally of Moscow, and during the entire election campaign Semerdzhiev refused to disclose publicly past strengths and budgets or present operations of the secret police.

In February 1990 a Bulgarian observer noted that "the model for [the new regime of] Bulgaria remains Gorbachev's perestroika. It does not lie in Warsaw, Prague, or Budapest."[25] This statement proved to be accurate. The Bulgarian self-styled reform Communist party could permit some preliminary steps but not a full opening to free elections or political competition. Not surprisingly, in the June 1990 elections for a new national Parliament, the Bulgarian Socialist party obtained a majority of the seats in Parliament (211 of 400), and claimed to have received 47 percent of the vote.

Sixteen democratic opposition groups had joined together to form the United Democratic Front (UDF), and the organization's leaders complained during the campaign that they were not able to compete fairly. A few days before the election the UDF had charged that "analyses have pointed to locales, mainly in Sofia [the capital], where up to 30 percent of the citizens eligible to vote have been excluded from the electoral lists."[26] Western election-observers reported that they did not believe there was an atmosphere of free competition in the Bulgarian countryside, where the majority of voters lived. Genaro Arriagada, a Chilean who had directed the election campaign against Pinochet in his own country, observed, "You have the security forces and a Communist army and a mayor that is not a mayor but a projection of the informers and the state police. It is always the same under dictators, under the Sandinistas, here [in Bulgaria]. . . . The real element is fear."[27]

An indication of the extent of the people's fear is apparent in the words of one voter on the eve of the June 17 election: "I don't believe the Socialist [Communist] party and will never believe it. People are frightened. They have been telling my parents that they will lose pensions and medical benefits. I am ashamed at Bulgarians who voted for the Communists because there have been no changes."[28] Another person said, "The people are afraid. I was also afraid and if you had had a camera I would not have dared to speak with you."[29]

After the second round of the Bulgarian elections on June 17, 1990, Western international observer teams reported "incidents that indicated a pattern of intimidation in several areas of the country."[30] This pattern included the presence of uniformed military and local militia outside polling stations and "the failure to observe voting secrecy in some polling booths."[31] Soldiers who had voted for the UDF in the first round of the elections were reportedly "being sent on training sessions for the weekend to stop them from voting in the second round."[32]

A preponderance of evidence suggests that the Bulgarian elections were neither fair nor free. The dominance of the regime party during the electoral campaign, the problems with assuring fair voting lists, the inability of the democratic opposition to campaign effectively in the countryside, the observed irregularities during the election, the assumed, unobserved irregularities, and the unknown factor of how fairly the ballots were counted all point to tainted elections. The Communist party's victory should thus be seen as a continuation of its traditionally rigged successes.

Romania. In March 1945 Soviet troops entered Romania as the Nazi armies retreated, and King Michael was forced to appoint a Communist-led "coalition government." In keeping with standard Stalinist practice this "coalition" became a Communist-dominated regime, formally declared as a People's Republic in December 1947. The king was then obliged to abdicate and go into exile.

In 1965 Nicolae Ceausescu became the new Communist ruler in Romania. To symbolize his repudiation of Stalinism he changed Romania's name from People's Republic to the Socialist Republic of Romania. Ceausescu adopted a new constitution and indicated an intention to be more independent of the Soviet Union in international matters. Yet despite Romania's refusal to participate in the invasion of Czechoslovakia in 1968, both Ion Pacepa, a senior defector from the Romanian Intelligence Service, and former U.S. Ambassador to Romania David Funderburk have provided evidence suggesting that, although independent in some areas, the Ceausescu regime provided a great many useful services to the Soviets.[33]

Nevertheless, by 1989 the Ceausescu era came to resemble the later Brezhnev era in Moscow—stagnant and heavily involved in corruption and cronyism. In addition, Ceausescu conceived an irrational plan to destroy 8,000 peasant villages and forcibly move their residents into high-rise apartment complexes in the countryside. He also stepped up the persecution and forced relocation of thousands among the 1.8 million ethnic Hungarians living in Romania.

By December 1989, when the feared Securitate (secret police) began persecuting an ethnic Hungarian Protestant pastor who had protested the forced relocation of Hungarians, thousands demonstrated to support him. On the orders of Ceausescu, hundreds and perhaps thousands of these protesters were killed on December 19, 1989. On December 20, in the small town of Timisoara where the killings occurred, 10,000 anti-Ceausescu demonstrators marched. Having just returned from a state visit to Iran, Ceausescu put Romanian troops on a nationwide alert.

On the following day security forces and the military attacked anti-Ceausescu demonstrators in Bucharest, reportedly killing dozens of people. This provoked larger mass protests, and on December 22 the military joined the demonstrators against Ceausescu, who fled. Elements of the Ceausescu secret police battled the army for some days while hundreds of thousands of Romanians demonstrated for democracy and showed their rejection of communism by removing the hammer and sickle emblem from thousands of Romanian flags.

On December 25 Romanian state television, which had taken the side of the anti-Ceausescu demonstrators, reported that Ceausescu had been captured, tried, and executed; it later showed a videotape of the execution. Only after the bodies of Ceausescu and his wife were shown on Romanian television did the 30,000-strong secret police force curtail its sniping and attacks against the Romanian military.[34] Reportedly, the army turned on Ceausescu in part because he had ordered the execution of General Vasile Milea, the defense minister who had refused to order the army to fire on civilian demonstrators. Also, it was reported that at Timisoara forty-two Romanian soldiers were "executed on the spot during the operation for refusing to fire on the crowd."[35] Yet there are also reports suggesting that the Soviet KGB was in collusion with elements of the Romanian military to prepare a pro-Soviet coup against Ceausescu, and that an already existing plan was simply accelerated when the events of December 1989 provided an unexpected catalyst.[36]

Out of the battle came a group of Romanian Communists calling itself the National Salvation Front, establishing an interim regime led by Ion Iliescu. Iliescu is said to have studied agricultural techniques in the Soviet Union and to have been a former classmate and personal associate of Gorbachev. All the key figures in the new Front regime were longtime members of the Romanian Communist party; none of the prodemocratic leaders was given any significant role in the interim government that prepared the way for elections in May 1990.[37]

Iliescu described the purpose of the interim Front regime as follows: "We have fought to put an end to dictatorship, to bring about a democratic system, to make free elections the basis for this democracy."[38] And the Front did permit democratic opposition parties to form and to begin competing for votes in the May 1990 elections. On April 30, 1990, however, the five leading democratic opposition parties announced they would boycott the elections unless they were postponed some weeks to provide the opposition with a better chance to organize and compete. These democratic political parties were deeply concerned that the Front regime was continuing the Communist pattern of a rigged election process. They believed that although it was providing a little more room for them, it still did not really intend to permit a fair campaign or vote.

A number of circumstances raised serious concerns during the election campaign. First, the Front used all the regime's resources and unlimited public funds in its campaign. This included a nearly total domination of the "free Romanian television," which had played an important anti-Ceausescu role during the events of December 1989. Subsequently, however, it gave democratic opposition parties little opportunity to convey their point of view to the Romanian people.[39] Second, the dreaded Ceausescu secret police, though transferred to the ministry of defense, were in fact continuing their work as before the fall of Ceausescu.[40] Third, a campaign of systematic harassment waged against democratic opposition figures reminded one analyst of the Communists' intimidation tactics using controlled mobs during "the terror of 1945–1947."[41] The U.S. Department of State on May 7, 1990, publicly criticized the Front regime's intimidation tactics and use of violence against the democratic parties; on May 10 it withdrew the U.S. ambassador in protest. Nevertheless, the regime refused to give the democratic opposition a fair chance by postponing the election.

Ion Iliescu, the Front presidential candidate, did not obtain Ceausescu's customary 98 percent of the vote, but he did claim to receive 83 percent. And in the vote for the parliament the Front obtained a 66 percent majority. A member of the U.S. delegation observing the Romanian elections said "this was the most unfair campaign" he had ever witnessed.[42] But the U.S. Department of State, while criticizing "irregularities and instances of violence and intimidation," nevertheless decided to recognize the election as having been proper. The Romanian democratic leadership felt this was a mistake and protested that a significant proportion of votes had been lost through fraud perpetrated by the Front regime.[43]

In June 1990 the Front regime revealed its hand. Responding to continuing democratic party protests that the election had not been fair, President-elect Iliescu called on miners from a distant part of the country to come to the city to "protect" the government. In tactics exactly reminiscent of those used by the Communists in taking power in the mid-1940s, the miners were brought to Bucharest, where they beat anyone they decided looked like a member of the democratic opposition. They also destroyed totally the headquarters of the democratic opposition parties and the homes of the democratic leaders. The prime minister of the Front government referred to these events as "unpleasant moments."[44] The United States reacted to the brutal events of June 14 and 15 by declaring it would "withhold all nonhumanitarian aid from Romania until the democratic process has been restored."[45] The Iliescu regime had demonstrated that it intended to continue ruling as a Communist dictatorship.

A Perspective on the Events of 1989–1990

Understandably the dramatic and hopeful unraveling of six Communist regimes in Eastern Europe in 1989 led to a conventional view that "the Cold War is over, communism has been defeated."[46] After the elections of 1990 many commentators observed that the Eastern European countries were now free to decide their futures based upon the decisions of elected governments.

Yet in looking at the future of a reunited Germany in a Europe in transition, two questions need closer examination: (1) What is the extent of the positive changes in Eastern Europe, and are they irreversible? and (2) What was the Soviet role, and what does this portend for future Soviet actions?

For decades every close observer of Communist-dominated societies has understood that the overwhelming majority of the people and even many in the party elite reject Communist ideology. That discovery is not new. But the ability of Communist regimes to remain in control decade after decade has depended not on the adherence of broad masses to their professed belief system, but rather on their operational capabilities in the domain of power. A closer look at the six transitions in Eastern Europe shows that questions about the future must remain.

In Romania and Bulgaria the new Communist regimes have given themselves the trappings of reform and democratic elections; but they are continuing as pro-Soviet dictatorships, permitting some liberalization in the hope this will improve matters and also bring in more Western economic aid. In Poland the non-Communist government is responsible for the economy, it seeks to open the economic system and obtain increased Western aid, and a free vote led to the election of Solidarity-founder Lech Walesa as president in December

1990. But, as General Jaruzelski candidly observed, the Communist minority continues to retain influence in the secret police, the military, and a large segment of the bureaucracy. Even in Hungary and Czechoslovakia, where the spirit of democracy and open competition was manifest in free elections, the democratic leadership's efforts to dismantle the secret police have proven more difficult than anticipated. Although the people of East Germany, Hungary, and Czechoslovakia have overwhelmingly repudiated the national Communist parties, they will need more time to fully remove the coercive apparatus of the hard-line Communists. The secret police, Communists in the national military establishments, and a significant Soviet presence continue to some unknown extent.

While professing reform and the wish to "rectify the mistakes of the past," the Communist parties in these six East European countries have all shown that they still consider themselves best qualified to rule. Despite large-scale defections from the Communist parties in all of them except Romania and Bulgaria, the hard-core elements seem to have remained intact—surprisingly so, given the liberalizing changes in East Germany, Poland, Hungary, and Czechoslovakia. Most disturbing and most indicative of the continuing existence of the hard-core Communist nexus are the reports of continuing secret police operations in these four countries, despite their moving in the direction of democracy. One month after the March 1990 East German elections, Ottfried Hennig, the West German Parliament member responsible for Inter-German Relations, reported that the East German secret police continued to remain active. "The Stasi people continue to be there, although under different authorities. . . . Listening operations continue, mail is censored, and there are still attempts to keep the whole machinery working, even after the SED's loss of direct power."[47] And press reports in 1990 indicated that the Soviet Union had taken the most sensitive files and records as well as personnel of the East German secret police for safekeeping either to Soviet military bases in East Germany or to Soviet territory.

In Hungary, despite the months of pledges for democracy from the reformed Communist party, a defector from the secret police revealed in early 1990 with videotapes and other documentary evidence that the secret police were continuing large-scale spying operations and penetrating democratic opposition groups.[48] In Czechoslovakia, whose interim president Havel was a democratic dissident and a former political prisoner, listening devices were still being discovered in the president's office five months after he assumed power. After one non-Communist minister of internal security had been unsuccessful in dismantling the Czechoslovakian secret police, Havel replaced him with a member of the Civic Forum. A senior Czechoslovakian official, admitting that progress was slow, guardedly observed, "Resolving this is much more tricky than we can reveal. . . . There is an obvious situation, and then there are the wheels within wheels."[49] Another senior official of the new government noted early in 1990 that "the KGB has special sources" for financing the operations of the Czech secret police, and "by utilizing these resources the foreign branch could continue to function for five to ten more years."[50]

Obviously, if the Soviet Union decided at some future time to sweep away the new governments of Eastern Europe through military invasion, it could do so. The national armies of the East European countries singly or in combination would be no match for concerted Soviet military assault, and the armed forces of NATO would not protect the post-Communist East European governments—history has demonstrated this fact many times since the 1953 rebellion in East Germany. A question to consider for the future is, Could the combination of Soviet operatives and remaining national indigenous Communist groups restore Communist rule in some of these countries without open Soviet military action?

The following conceptualization suggests that there are ten stages in the transition from dictatorship to democracy. Each one needs to be traversed before a post-dictatorial political situation is substantially irreversible. Table 5–1 provides an overview of these ten stages and shows how they fit the contemporary transitional situations in the six Eastern European countries.

Based upon this conceptualization, Eastern Europe is at the beginning of the final transitional process rather than at the end. In fact, fully free and fair elections to determine the national government have been held in only three of the six countries—Hungary, East Germany, and Czechoslovakia. Although those governments have been duly chosen, they still must succeed in stages 8, 9, and 10. At the same time they must meet the continuing challenge posed by the remaining indigenous and Soviet-supported Communist apparatus, and they must make complex economic changes. In Poland the elections of June 1989 were only partially free, in that competitive elections accounted for only 35 percent of the more important chamber of the national parliament. Free and fair local elections were held in June 1990, and for the presidency in December 1990 but elections have not yet been held for the full national Parliament. In Bulgaria and Romania, neither the election process nor the elections them-

TABLE 5–1: STAGES OF THE TRANSITION TO DEMOCRACY IN EASTERN EUROPE, 1977–1990

Stages	Poland	Hungary	E. Germany	Czechoslovakia	Bulgaria	Romania
1. Rise of visible prodemocratic groups	1979–81 1986–	1987	1982	1977	—	—
2. Regime repression begins to fail	1988	1988	Aug. 1989	Nov. 1989	—	Dec. 1989
3. Communist party leadership shifts to reformist faction	1989	May 1988	Oct. 1989	Nov. 1989	Nov. 1989	Jan. 1990
4. Communist regime legitimatizes prodemocratic groups (by legalizing or negotiating with)	Apr. 1989	Feb. 1989	Dec. 1989	Nov. 1989	Jan. 1990	Feb. 1990
5. Communist regime promises free and fair elections	Apr. 1989	Sept. 1989	Jan. 1990	Dec. 1989	Feb. 1990	Feb. 1990
6. National elections held	June 1989 (free but limited)	Mar. 1990 and Apr. 1990	Mar. 1990	June 1990	June 1990 (not fully free and fair)	May 1990 (not fully free and fair)
7. New, elected government takes office	Aug. 1989	Apr. 1990	Apr. 1990	July 1990	July 1990 (Communist regime)	May 1990 (Communist regime)
8. Continuing tension and competition between prodemocratic and antidemocratic groups including the remaining hard-line Communists and far right or ultranationalist elements	Since Aug. 1989	Since Apr. 1990	Since Apr. 1990	Since June 1990	Since June 1990	—
9. Second round of national elections	—	—	—	—	—	—
10. If elections are free and fair, beginning of the consolidation of democratic institutions	—	—	—	—	—	—

SOURCE: Author.

selves were fully fair or free. In both countries pro-Soviet Communist regimes—proclaiming reformist intentions—remain in power.

These facts tell much about Soviet purposes. Many in the West give Gorbachev credit for the dramatic transitions, and even ascribe to him the intention of unraveling communism in Eastern Europe. This view assumes that he secretly wants to bring genuine democracy to the Soviet Union also. If this were correct, it would have enormous implications for the future of Europe and a reunified Germany. The military capability of the Atlantic Alliance would be far less crucial if the Soviet Union were committed to the success of genuine democracy in Eastern Europe and, ultimately, in the Soviet Union.

An alternative view interprets Romania and Bulgaria as more closely reflecting what Gorbachev had in mind for Eastern Europe— replacing an older generation of Communist leaders with his contemporaries, who would put a more modern, reformist face on Communist rule. The process of unraveling began in Poland, and it was in Poland that the Soviets consented to an arrangement with a clearly limited purpose: to bring the Solidarity movement into government, where it would assume responsibility for the economy. The Jaruzelski regime could then presumably have obtained labor peace within Poland and new large-scale infusions of Western economic help for Poland.

The unexpected and poignant defection of thousands, then tens of thousands of East Germans provided the impetus to speed up Honecker's removal. The next step would be to help the next generation of Communist leaders take power in Hungary and in Czechoslovakia. Quite possibly these processes began with some Soviet encouragement and in cooperation with the successor Communists, who were oriented toward perestroika and limited, Gorbachev-style reforms. But the hopes of the general populations in these countries simply went far beyond the original intentions and purposes of the Soviets and national Communists. As popular demonstrations for freedom swelled, Gorbachev faced a decision: Should he use the nearly 600,000 Soviet military forces available in Eastern Europe to back national Communist hard-liners who sought to limit the extent of the political changes? This step had been taken in 1953, 1956, and 1968, and Gorbachev did not repeat it. But that does not mean that he welcomed or even expected the extent of the Communist disintegration in East Germany, Hungary, and Czechoslovakia.

We must remember that Gorbachev had spent more than three years establishing a new, benign image for the Soviet Union in all the industrial democracies, and he had requested and expected billions of dollars in economic aid. This would be cut off if Gorbachev used force. An additional inhibition might have been the "lessons of Afghanistan," which affected both the Soviet political and military leadership. Some 300,000 Soviet, Vietnamese, and Cuban troops had been in combat for more than a decade with armed anti-Communist resistance movements in Afghanistan, Cambodia, Angola, Mozambique, and Nicaragua. Only months earlier (in February 1989) Soviet troops had withdrawn from Afghanistan after ten bloody years and failure to crush the armed anti-Communist resistance movements.

Thus, Gorbachev's reasons for not using Soviet military forces in Eastern Europe might include a combination of possible factors. Initially, he may have been politically overconfident about communism's ability to hold power. He may have been concerned with maintaining détente and access to Western resources. He may have felt unwilling to risk prolonged combat against East European resistance movements emboldened by the military stalemate forced upon Soviet and other foreign Communist military forces in the developing regions.

Furthermore, the economic needs of the Soviet Union would argue strongly against using troops in Eastern Europe—the Western capital, trade, and technology that Gorbachev seeks from détente with the United States, Europe, and Japan would be jeopardized. The Soviets recalled the consequences of their invasion of Afghanistan in 1979: a suspension of détente with the United States and a significant reduction in financial opportunities for the Soviet Union.

Finally, we can consider the hypothesis of a former Soviet citizen and current analyst of Soviet issues, Lev Navrozov. He suggests that in the face of unraveling Communist rule, Gorbachev and the Soviet politburo decided to cut their losses and settle for a "Finlandized" Eastern Europe. Like Finland, these countries would be non-Communist but militarily nonthreatening, allied with no powerful countries. By tolerating this "concession" they could hope to achieve the benefit of the de facto neutralization of Germany, and thus the likely expulsion of the United States from Europe. The Soviets sought to maintain the institutions of the Warsaw Pact military alliance until early 1991, when they announced it would be dissolved in April 1991. In doing so, Gorbachev's spokesman repeated that the Soviet Union hoped that in exchange NATO would be dismantled.[51]

These perspectives suggest that a transition to a new Europe is indeed under way, thanks to the events of 1989 and 1990 in Eastern Europe. But whether democracy will become more secure in the new Eastern Europe or the receding presence of the United States will open new ambiguities may well depend on where the road after German reunification ultimately leads that important nation.

6

The Road to German Reunification

A European Germany, rather than a German Europe.

THOMAS MANN

For decades the reunification of Germany was perceived as a distant possibility. It seemed in fact so distant that the German Social Democratic party ceased even to speak of it as a rhetorical goal of German foreign policy during the 1980s. Yet in a matter of only months the distant possibility was transformed to a reality. Thousands of East German men, women, and children fled to West Germany in the last months of 1989, a formal agreement was reached between NATO and the Warsaw Pact foreign ministers in February 1990 to begin talks on German reunification, the four occupying powers gave up all their rights in a treaty they signed in September 1990, and full reunification took place on October 3, 1990.

The process by which German reunification occurred in 1989–1990 combined internal political decisions and events in both Germanys with progressively intensifying U.S., Soviet, and West German diplomatic engagement. Examining this process is not only an interesting endeavor but also an important guide to the future. The largest undecided issue looming over the emerging order of Europe is, Will a reunified Germany remain in the Atlantic Alliance, or will it evolve into a neutral state?

Four phases characterized the road to German reunification:

1. From August to October 1989, the people of East Germany demonstrated their rejection of the regime.

2. From October 1989 to January 1990, the East German Communist party sought to maintain its control through an increasing tempo of political accommodations.

3. From February to March 1990, the East German election campaign marked the beginning of de facto unification.

4. From April to October 1990, the election of a democratic East German government opened the way to the beginning of serious negotiations between the two Germanys. Negotiations intensified

among the Soviet Union, the United States, and the German states in a political context where each passing month increased the prospects for reunification with Germany remaining in NATO.

Phase One—The East German People Reject the Regime

In the spring of 1989, U.S.–West German security relations were focused on the usual issues of alliance policy. The West Germans felt reluctant to modernize short-range nuclear weapons stationed on German territory, and the Bush administration and Prime Minister Thatcher were trying to persuade them to maintain the credibility of the nuclear deterrent based in Europe. In May 1989 President Bush proposed that the United States and the Soviet Union reduce their European-based forces to roughly equal levels of 290,000 each. This proposal would entail the withdrawal of about 30,000 U.S. forces and 300,000 Soviet forces. It was endorsed by the May 1989 NATO meeting.

In June 1989 Soviet leader Gorbachev paid a state visit to Bonn, where he received an enthusiastic welcome from both the Kohl government and the West German people. Gorbachev endorsed Bush's plan for cuts in conventional forces in Europe, but at the same time he called for negotiations to eliminate all short-range nuclear weapon—a position contrary to that of the United States and to the agreement just reached at the NATO summit. The joint Soviet-German declaration of June 13, 1989, agreed on the need to prevent war and guarantee the right of self-determination; but it said nothing about German reunification. Only Chancellor Kohl spoke of reunification, calling the continued division of Germany an "open sore." Gorbachev spoke of "a common European house," as he had for a number of years. And a Soviet official traveling with Gorbachev privately deplored the East German shootings of would-be escapees crossing the barbed wire at the internal border. He added that Moscow hoped one day there would be two "comfortable German apartments with lots of doors between them" in the common European house.[1]

When the reformist faction of the Hungarian Communist party dismantled its border fences with Austria in May 1989, it little expected the major impact this move would have on East Germany. During the summer of 1989 thousands of East Germans decided to use a vacation in Hungary as a stepping-off point to flee through Austria and then settle in West Germany. By the end of September 1989 some 30,000 East Germans had already fled to West Germany through Hungary and Czechoslovakia.

Gorbachev's decision to participate in the fortieth anniversary celebration of the East German Communist regime on October 7, 1989, was reported as perceived by "Western diplomats . . . as an indication that Moscow wants to ease pressure on East Germany's troubled leadership. . . ."[2] According to this view, Gorbachev regarded "Honecker as the archetypical aging leader whose rigidity is the chief obstacle to making communism work effectively"; but his interest in a stable and friendly East Germany argued for supporting him.[3] The East German Communist leadership was facing the crisis of tens of thousands of people continuing their efforts to flee the country.

By the time Gorbachev arrived in East Berlin on October 7, 1989, an estimated 45,000 East Germans had fled, and tens of thousands were demonstrating for greater freedom. Perceiving Gorbachev as a reformer, they shouted, "We are the people," "No violence," "Freedom," and "Gorby! Gorby!"[4] On October 9, 1989, Honecker met with visiting Chinese Deputy Prime Minister Yao Yi Lin. Thereafter the regime threatened that continuing demonstrations would be met with a Tiananmen Square-style crackdown. The official East German press agency reinforced this threat by reporting that "the two [East German–Chinese leaders] agreed there was evidence of a particularly aggressive antisocialist action by imperialist class opponents with the aim of reversing socialist development. In this respect there is a fundamental lesson to be learned from the counterrevolutionary unrest in Beijing and the present campaign against [East Germany] and other socialist states."[5]

The Kohl government had immediately welcomed the East German immigrants and declared that the exodus signified the desire of the East German people for freedom. The Social Democratic party reacted much more tentatively during this first phase. In September 1989 it intended to continue its party-to-party dialogue with the East German Communist party. Since the SPD leadership had publicly affirmed the right of East Germans to emigrate freely, however, the East German government canceled meetings planned with the SPD for mid-September 1989.[6]

One important international reaction to the East German exodus was President Bush's August 1989 statement that the United States continued to support German reunification, as it had always done in the past. U.S. Ambassador to West Germany Vernon A. Walters also took a strong affirmative stand on reunification and on freedom, as fundamental U.S. interests. This early and positive support for reunification from the U.S. president and his able ambassador in Bonn would continue and prove of great importance.

Phase Two—The East German Communist Party
Seeks Control through Reforms

Honecker's removal by younger leaders of the Communist party on October 18, 1989, marked a major turning point in German and European politics. The change in the top leadership was accompanied by the dissolution of the twenty-one member East German politburo, its replacement with a ten-member group, and the resignation of the entire forty-four member East German cabinet. The new East German leader, Egon Krenz, had long been in charge of the internal security organizations in East Germany and had been Honecker's close associate. Krenz said East Germany would now move toward reform as the Soviet Union was doing, stating, "We want a socialism that is economically effective . . . and most of all, has its face turned to the people."[7]

Soviet policy at this stage was visible in the results of a Warsaw Pact members meeting. This October 1989 meeting was the first to include representation of a government without a Communist majority—Poland's. The new Polish prime minister urged that the Warsaw Pact be transformed into more of a political than a military alliance and called for a "radical reconstruction of Comecon," the Communist trading bloc.[8] Speaking candidly, Soviet Foreign Minister Eduard Shevardnadze said, "We might not fully like the fact that it is non-Communists who are in the leadership of Poland, but we respect the will of the Polish nation."[9] At the same time all seven Warsaw Pact nations issued a joint communiqué opposing German reunification, criticizing West Germany's provision of automatic citizenship to East German refugees, and warning in classic Communist propaganda terms of the "danger of stepped up neo-Nazism" as a result of the demands for changes in East Germany.[10]

Peaceful demonstrations by hundreds of thousands of East Germans continued, as Krenz sought to demonstrate the reformist intentions of East Germany's new Communist leadership and to stop the continuing exodus. He pardoned all those guilty of fleeing from East Germany, a crime punishable by prison. Krenz promised in late October 1989 that travel restrictions would be relaxed, allowing East Germans to visit the West at least once a year.[11] From November 1 to 8, more than 50,000 East Germans showed their distrust of how long the regime's sudden openness might last by using the new travel opportunity to escape to West Germany; as a result about 2,000 persons each day continued to leave.

Expressing a view typical of those leaving, Ulrich Freiteger, a twenty-seven-year-old construction foreman, said, "We never became part of the system. You can say we are anti-Communists. We are not going to West Germany to have the luxuries, to eat bananas, or to drive a better car. We didn't want to live in a jail."[12]

On November 4, 1989, more than 500,000 East Germans marched peacefully for democratic reforms in Berlin. On November 9 the Berlin Wall was opened, and de facto unification began. West Germans welcomed the tens of thousands of East German visitors who came to see the West.

Despite the conciliatory efforts of the Krenz regime, once the borders were open the exodus of East Germans to West Germany increased. As one East German explained, "They said we could go and I don't believe the changes are here to stay. The government didn't do this. It was the pressure from the people. So the government will try to stop it as soon they can quiet the people."[13]

To counter the continuing mistrust of the people reflected by the accelerating exodus, the East German Communist party convened an Extraordinary Congress in early December. Krenz was replaced as party leader by Gregor Gysi, a Communist lawyer who had frequently defended dissidents. The party promised to undertake major reforms and said it would consider permitting independent political groups to organize and have legal status. The Krenz politburo and central committee resigned and were partially replaced by Communists perceived as more committed to reform. These events followed the East German Parliament's December 1 alteration of the constitution, eliminating the Communist party's guaranteed monopoly on power.

Kohl's Ten-Point Plan. At the end of October 1989 Chancellor Kohl offered his first thoughts on how the reunification of Germany could be achieved. In an address to German and American leaders and scholars, he said that when East Germany attains genuine democracy, "then the people of both German states can decide by free secret ballot whether they want to reunify, and this could happen only if the citizens of both Germanys agree."[14] Kohl, like Adenauer, emphasized that reunification must occur under "a European roof" and that membership in the Atlantic Alliance and the European Community (EC) must continue. Further, Chancellor Kohl reaffirmed his commitment to the original goals of European political unification as defined by the 1958 Treaty of Rome, which established the European Economic Community. Kohl contended that the West German government should help facilitate reforms in East Germany; it should neither be too passive nor push too hard. There was no point in the West German government's telling the East German regime what to do, he said, because the people of East Germany were already doing that in a very clear voice.

On November 28, 1989, Kohl presented a ten-point plan for German reunification. He pointed out that a new relationship had developed between the people of East and West Germany in the past several years because of the 10 million visits by East Germans to West Germany. These years had coincided with his administration, and Kohl believed the new level of normalized relations with East Germany he had fostered had helped the East German people under-ˈ stand life in West Germany. His plan proposed that East Germany first become genuinely democratic; then the peoples in both German states could decide whether to implement reunification.[15]

The SPD Response. During the dramatic weeks from the summer of 1989 to the removal of Honecker and the opening of the Berlin Wall, the response of the Social Democratic party of Germany provided a sharp contrast to that of the CDU.

Weeks after Honecker's removal and days after the Berlin Wall was opened, Walter Momper, a leading Social Democrat and the mayor of West Berlin, accused Chancellor Kohl of "spectacular failure during this decisive situation in German history."[16] The failure that Momper had in mind was Kohl's "deep dislike of the GDR's democratic development and its right to self-determination. He has not understood that the people in the GDR are not interested in reunification."[17] A leading SPD member of the Parliament (Bundestag) and its speaker for foreign policy, Karsten Voight, declared later in November 1989 that reunification would have to mean the end of German participation in the Atlantic Alliance.[18]

On December 18, 1989, the SPD held an Extraordinary Party Congress to debate the dramatic developments in East Germany. In the face of the overwhelming evidence, this congress reversed years of SPD policy and concluded that reunification was only a matter of time, as Willy Brandt put it, and the people of East Germany should have the right to determine the future of their state. The SPD consequently ended its longstanding close relations with the East German Communist party and instead took up the cause of the East German people directly.[19]

This decision came as the result of the events in East Germany, Czechoslovakia, and Bulgaria, which together shook the SPD's belief that Communist domination of Eastern Europe would continue in the foreseeable future. In Bulgaria the long-ruling Communist leader Zhivkov had been unseated by a younger Communist faction on November 10; in Czechoslovakia the process of unraveling began with

mass demonstrations on November 17 and ended with the installation of a non-Communist government on December 10. At the December 1989 U.S.-Soviet summit meeting in Malta, Gorbachev expressed a Soviet commitment to national self-determination. And the
December 4, 1989, meeting in Moscow of the leaders of five Warsaw
Pact countries—Bulgaria, East Germany, Hungary, Poland, and the
Soviet Union—had pronounced the 1968 invasion of Czechoslovakia
"illegal" and an "interference in [Czechoslovakia's] internal affairs."
The Soviet Union further issued a separate statement expressing
regret for its role in the 1968 invasion and calling its rationale
"unfounded."[20]

The Soviet Response. Those actions certainly created the impression
that Gorbachev meant what he said in July 1989: "The social and
political orders in particular countries have changed in the past and
may change in the future. This change is the exclusive affair of the
people of that country."[21] At the same time, Soviet spokesmen made
it clear after the opening of the Berlin Wall that the "common
European home" the Soviet Union was seeking would have no
Atlantic Alliance. An adviser to Gorbachev was quoted on November
10, 1989, as saying, "We have said many times that we are ready to
disband the Warsaw Pact tomorrow if NATO were also disbanded. We
think that these questions must be solved in the context of an all-
European political process."[22]

In retrospect it seems that the Soviets expected for a reformist
Communist regime such as Gorbachev's, committed to glasnost and
perestroika, to succeed the Honecker regime in East Germany. They
suggested this was an opportunity to end both alliances and thereby
bring about the de facto neutralization of Western Germany and,
perhaps, much of Western Europe.

The official Soviet spokesman made it clear immediately after the
Wall was opened that reunification was not on the Soviet agenda:
"Bonn should take into account that any policies considering changes
in borders would not be suitable to any government in Europe and
would cause deep distrust. A new regime has started on the East
German side of the border, *but the border does remain* [emphasis
added]."[23] One of Gorbachev's closest advisers, Alexander Yakovlev,
said he believed the United States, Britain, and France did not really
want the reunification of Germany and secretly hoped the Soviet
Union would prevent it.[24] In November 1989 Gorbachev's official
spokesman, Gennadi Gerasimov, pointed to Poland as an example of
what the Soviets had in mind for changes in Eastern Europe: "Poland
is a good member of the Warsaw Pact, and in Poland you have a

91

coalition. You don't have a Communist government there; governments may change, international obligations remain."[25]

Following the November 28 Kohl proposal for German reunification and the December U.S.-Soviet summit, Gorbachev criticized Kohl's plan as an attempt to "extract selfish benefits" from the process of change in Europe. Gorbachev said those changes could "open the way to cooperation" between two German states on a number of issues, but warned, "Let us not push or force the issue [of reunification]. History itself will decide this question."[26]

The U.S. Response. The United States responded to the unraveling of the Honecker regime and the opening of the Berlin Wall in several ways. There was praise for the Eastern Europeans, East Germans, and Gorbachev. President Bush said on November 10, 1989, "The process of reform initiated by the East Europeans . . . is real, offers us much hope, and deserves our continuing encouragement."[27] At the same time, according to Secretary of State James Baker, the Soviet Union was warned by the United States that any attempt to use repressive force in Eastern Europe would create serious problems in the U.S.-Soviet relationship. Baker pointed out further that while the end of the Berlin Wall "could well be the start of a new world, nobody really knows what the next step will be. It is a very long step from free travel to free, fair, and democratic elections[;] when you talk about the distance from . . . free travel [to] such questions as German reunification, there is an even bigger jump there."[28]

While describing "NATO as an alliance destined to last" and promising a U.S. determination to "continue to be a very involved partner in NATO and to act in a manner that makes this clear to everyone," Bush also offered another message on the eve of the U.S.-Soviet summit in December 1989. He said there could be significant reductions in U.S. troops in Europe and that NATO could extend its role beyond defense to a number of cooperative issues.[29] The United States also consistently stated that after reunification the German people should decide as a sovereign state whether they wished to continue as members of the Atlantic Alliance and should be able to do so if that were the decision.

A potentially serious split in the Western position occurred in early December, following a summit meeting between French President François Mitterrand and Soviet President Mikhail Gorbachev. Even though Chancellor Kohl had issued his ten-point plan for German reunification only days before, speaking in the Soviet Union Mitterrand said France must be prepared to "speak the truth" to Bonn on the issue of German reunification:

None of our countries—and especially one whose weight is so great and whose geographical position is such—can act without taking into account the balance of Europe. We should not begin by talking about changing borders. Seen from the West it is more urgent to reinforce the structure of the European Community.[30]

This agreement between France and the Soviet Union to oppose German reunification, along with the coolness of the United Kingdom, might have caused some in the West German government to reflect on an earlier era of European international politics—when France, Britain, and Russia established an entente to "contain" Germany.

Phase Three—East Germany Promises Democratic Elections, the Soviets Accept German Reunification

The clear intention of the East German Communist party and the Soviet leadership to have a reformed Communist East Germany but not German reunification was undermined by a series of internal pressures. The reformist Communist faction that took over in early December included Gregor Gysi, the new Communist party chief, and Hans Modrow, the new prime minister. They established a weekly dialogue with the already visibly organizing prodemocratic groups, thus providing a means for consultation until free elections could determine a new government in the spring of 1990.

The most hated symbol of the Communist dictatorship was the *Staatssicherheitsdeinst*, or State Security Service, commonly known as the Stasi. With an estimated strength of 85,000 personnel, it had about 130,000 regular informers and kept computerized files on some 5 million East Germans.[31] Gysi and Modrow promised that the secret police were being disbanded, but at the end of December both said the regime would establish a new internal security and intelligence service—as Gysi put it, in order "to protect us from nasty surprises, be they military, political, or economic."[32] Modrow's professed justification was the reported increase in neo-Nazi activities in East Germany. But a leader of the opposition Social Democrats in East Germany accused the regime of attempting to introduce "hysteria" with warnings of neo-Nazism simply as a pretext for keeping the secret police.[33] The democratic opposition groups told the regime they would cancel their weekly dialogues unless they were shown proof that the secret police were being disbanded and that no security service would be reconstituted, except by an elected government.

In mid-January 1990 the West German minister of the interior

93

said there was "no sign that agents have been withdrawn. The division of the Stasi responsible for espionage, the *Hauptvervaltung fur Aufklarung* [HVA, or Main Administration for Reconnaissance], is functioning as it was in Honecker's time."[34] Along with these revelations a number of incidents occurred that broke the little confidence the new East German Communist leadership had been able to gather. A spray-paint desecration of the Soviet war memorial in East Berlin, for example, had the earmarks of a Stasi operation. As Kohl put it, the attempt to establish a secret police "was the symbol of what they had just overthrown in their peaceful revolution, the symbol of communism that had a catastrophic effect on the people."[35]

By the end of 1989, 350,000 East Germans had left through the newly opened borders. By the third week of January 1990, another 50,000 had joined them. The exodus increased as confidence in the reform Communists dwindled. The East German Communist party saw its membership decline from 2.4 million in 1989 to about 1.2 million at the beginning of 1990. On January 20, 1990, in an attempt to counter a loss of support within the party as well as the disaffection of the East German people, the party leadership expelled fourteen former leaders, including Egon Krenz.[36] The deputy chairman of the East German Communist party and mayor of Dresden, Wolfgang Berghofer, led forty key officials out of the Communist party, after failing to obtain its dissolution at an emergency meeting of the party leadership. Berghofer lamented that "the old SED [Communist party], and its leadership have ruined East Germany politically, economically, and morally in a shameful and irresponsible way."[37]

By the end of January 1990, the democratic opposition groups in East Germany had moved a long distance on the issue of reunification. Initially, most members of the New Forum and some other opposition organizations expected a "third way" of East German social democracy to be established. Increasingly numerous revelations about the hidden control exerted by the East German Communists, however, changed this position; even the reformist Communist leaders were intending to establish a new secret police. Furthermore, the pro-unification views of nearly all West German political leaders persuaded many democratic opposition groups to endorse reunification as the best guarantee of freedom and democracy in East Germany. By the end of January 1990, the New Forum, the CDU-CSU–affiliated Democratic Awakening movement, and the East German Social Democratic party had all voted to endorse reunification.[38]

On January 30, 1990, the East German Communist party reluctantly dropped its opposition and endorsed step-by-step, gradual unification; Prime Minister Hans Modrow cautioned that it must be achieved within the context of a new European security structure. Modrow and Gysi went to Moscow to persuade Gorbachev there could be a form of German reunification acceptable to the Communist parties of both East Germany and the Soviet Union. Gysi later reported that Gorbachev supported his view that "the end of the unification process will be a demilitarized Germany without foreign troops."[39] Gysi went on to say that for Germany "neutrality is not enough. We want demilitarization."[40]

Gorbachev Accepts Reunification. Following this meeting in Moscow with Gysi and Modrow, Gorbachev dropped his objection to reunification, but said "it is essential to act responsibly and not seek the solution to this important issue on the streets."[41] Perhaps he was referring to the hundreds of thousands of East Germans demonstrating each week for reunification, or the 400,000 who had already left the country since August 1989.

To encourage Communist acceptance of reunification, Germany and the United States acted promptly. West German Foreign Minister Hans-Dietrich Genscher announced that a reunified Germany would remain in NATO, but NATO troops would not be moved into the formerly East German territory.[42] President Bush proposed at the end of January 1990 that the United States and the Soviet Union both cut back their forces to 195,000 troops in Central and Eastern Europe; the Soviet Union currently had 565,000 and the United States 255,000.

As part of a regular process of U.S.-Soviet consultations, Secretary of State Baker visited Moscow from February 8 to 9, 1990. The meeting prompted Gorbachev to announce that "the USSR accepts [President Bush's] proposal to reduce the Soviet and American troops in foreign territories in Europe down to 195,000. If this proposal does not suit you we suggest the figure of 225,000 for the entire European region."[43] In recounting the discussion of Germany, Baker said, "I pointed out that unification has been a policy goal of the United States for over forty years. . . . I indicated that the United States does not favor neutrality for a unified Germany, that we favor a continued membership in or association with NATO."[44]

Immediately after Baker's visit, Chancellor Kohl arrived in Moscow for three hours of negotiations with Gorbachev and Shevardnadze. At the end of the talks on February 10, 1990, Kohl said, "General Secretary Gorbachev assured me unmistakably that the Soviet Union would respect the right of the German people to decide to live in one state and that it is a matter for the Germans to determine the time and the method."[45] Shevardnadze confirmed this, but at the same time he repeated the Soviet position and agreement with the

95

view of the East German leadership: both German states should leave their respective military alliances and form a neutral Germany, in a gradual unification process. Shevardnadze described a neutral demilitarized Germany as "a good old idea," reminding his audience that it had first been proposed by the Soviet Union in the early 1950s.[46] His pronouncements marked a turning point: from this time the issue at the focus of international and German politics was not whether Germany would be reunified, but whether it would be neutral or part of the Atlantic Alliance.

The twenty-three foreign ministers of the NATO and Warsaw Pact countries met for the first time on February 12–13, 1990, in Ottawa, Canada. The original reason for the meeting had been to consider "open skies" types of verification measures for the reduction of conventional forces in Europe. But the focus turned out to be Germany and the U.S.-Soviet proposals for the reduction of foreign troops in Europe.

The United States would reduce it forces to 195,000 in Central Europe and keep an additional 30,000 troops in Europe but the Soviets should be limited to 195,000. Secretary of State Baker pointed out the U.S. need for these extra forces to compensate for being "an ocean away, whereas large numbers of Soviet troops would remain in the European part of the USSR."[47] The United States, West Germany, Britain, and France also agreed that two-plus-four talks should be held as a means of resolving the international issues of German reunification. The "two" referred to the two German states, the "four" to the four Allies responsible for Germany after its defeat in World War II. The Soviet Union accepted both proposals: the United States could maintain 225,000 troops in Europe, and the two-plus-four process of negotiation could be used to decide the international issues of German unification.[48]

These Soviet concessions were viewed as an important breakthrough, but only days later Soviet leaders repeated their concerns about Germany's future international role. Shevardnadze said in late February that reunification would not occur "as quickly as they imagine in Bonn. It requires several years."[49] Both Gorbachev and Shevardnadze then repeated their opposition to a reunified Germany's membership in NATO. Taking up a theme he was often to voice, Gorbachev said a united Germany should not "spell a threat or harm the national interests of neighbors or anybody else for that matter," and that only a peace agreement "can finally determine Germany's status in the European structure in terms of international law."[50]

While these events were occurring, East Germans were moving

to West Germany—85,000 of them in the first six weeks of 1990. In mid-February Prime Minister Modrow and Chancellor Kohl met in Bonn to discuss Modrow's request for a $6–9 billion infusion of West German resources to help East Germany's crisis-ridden economy. In contrast with their first meeting in Dresden, East Germany, the previous December, it was now clear to both leaders that reunification was only a matter of time. Kohl offered to provide $300 million in medical aid and credits for East Germany. Instead of the large-scale infusion of aid requested, however, he suggested the two countries begin planning for East Germany's adoption of the West German deutsche mark as its own currency. Modrow agreed, saying "a new chapter in German history has begun. The unity of Germany is closer."[51]

Free Elections. Just how close unity had come became apparent in the weeks before the March 18, 1990, national elections—the first free elections for East Germany since 1933. As the campaign began in late January, leaders from the major West German parties visited East Germany frequently to campaign for their affiliates. Undoubtedly the East German Communist leaders who opened the borders never imagined that only months later the banners, symbols, and leaders of West German parties—well known to East Germans from television—would be visible in campaign rallies throughout East Germany. On February 20, for example, more than 100,000 East Germans greeted Chancellor Kohl with chants of "Helmut! Helmut!" as he spoke in Erfurt, East Germany. Kohl said, "We are one Germany. We are one people."[52] And Willy Brandt made frequent appearances for the East German Social Democrats, quoting his formula for reunification: "What belongs together will grow together." By February 1990 opinion polls showed 75 percent of East Germans in favor of reunification, and except for the SPD, the major parties of West Germany and their East German correlates wanted it to be effected rapidly.[53]

At the start of the election campaign there were sixty political groups, but by March 1990 consolidation had reduced that number to twenty-three listed on the ballot. The fair and open campaign process, the close involvement of West German political parties, and the political history of East Germany all contributed to a result in which 70 percent of the votes were cast for parties affiliated with either the CDU-CSU or the SPD. As table 6–1 shows, the CDU-CSU–backed Alliance for Germany obtained 48 percent of the votes, the Social Democratic party of East Germany 22 percent.

With 94 percent of those East Germans eligible to vote participating, the election was judged by Western observers to be free and fair.

TABLE 6–1

Results of the March 18, 1990, Election in East Germany

Party	Percentage of the Vote	Seats
Alliance for Germany (Christian Democratic-led coalition)	48	193
Social Democratic Party	22	87
Party of Democratic Socialism (renamed Communists)	16	65
Free Democratic Party	5	21
Others	9	34
	100	400

Source: *The Economist* (London), June 23, 1990.

It provided a ringing endorsement for rapid German reunification. The major difference between the CDU-led Alliance for Germany and the SPD was that the center-right parties urged a rapid process of reunification while both the West German and East German SPD proposed a much slower process. Since the SPD was the leading party during the Weimar Republic era in the region that became East Germany, it had expected to win the election. Receiving only 22 percent of the vote thus disappointed the party. According to polls conducted at the time of the election, 91 percent of the voters in East Germany favored reunification. One German analysis concluded that this sentiment, along with a general disenchantment with socialism, explained the positive vote for the CDU-led coalition.[54]

The Communist party received 16 percent of the vote—and within East Berlin almost 30 percent. Although this share of the vote was larger than many expected, the election was nonetheless a massive repudiation of communism, reform communism included. A similar repudiation occurred in the subsequent free elections in Hungary (April 1990) and Czechoslovakia (June 1990). The dramatic fact and results of a reasonably free election in East Germany ushered in the post-Communist era and facilitated reunification.

Phase Four—The Accelerating Momentum of de Facto Unification

For forty years the Christian Democratic party of East Germany was a captive member of the Communist-led pseudo-coalition regime. Once Honecker was removed and political liberalization became possible, however, the Christian Democrats replaced their collaborationist leaders. With extensive political and material help from the West German Christian Democrats, they forged a new party in the months leading to the March 18, 1990, elections. Chancellor Kohl himself visited East Germany six times and addressed hundreds of thousands of people at mass rallies.

The new chairman of the Christian Democrats was Lothar de Maizière, a former musician who, as an attorney, had defended political dissidents against the Honecker regime. After the election victory, de Maizière and the Alliance for Germany could have constructed a majority government by entering into coalition with the Free Democrats—a replication of the coalition in West Germany. But the Christian Democratic chairman hoped for a broader coalition of all the major democratic parties, including the SPD. He issued an invitation to them, saying, "From a sense of national responsibility and to make possible a broad base for decisive and effective actions by the government to be formed, we want to create a coalition as broad as possible."[55] De Maizière also outlined the issues requiring priority attention by the new government:

• to reach quick agreement with West Germany on a common currency and to establish economic and social union
• to replace East Germany's fifteen administrative regions with its original five largely autonomous states, similar to those in West Germany. This change would eventually permit direct accession of those states into West Germany, under Article 23 of the West German constitution. De Maizière believed such direct accession would hasten integration and facilitate automatic membership in the European Community
• to move quickly toward reunification within the broader context of European unity
• to ensure that East Germany fulfill existing treaties and obligations, including those to the Soviet Union.

Initially the East German Social Democratic party chairman, Ibrahim Boehme, rejected this invitation to join in forming a government. He contended that the East German Social Democrats would not enter into any coalition with either the Communist party or the German Social Union party—a sister party to West Germany's Christian Social Union (CSU). In West Germany, some Social Democratic leaders urged post-election unity with the CDU in East Germany—but not Oskar Lafontaine, the designated SPD opponent of Chancellor Kohl in the scheduled December 1990 West German elections. Lafontaine criticized Kohl (and indirectly the East German voters) for his promises of quick economic unification, saying, "The people put trust in the man who promised a lot of money. That's Kohl. We'll be reminding him daily of his promises."[56]

In the course of several weeks of negotiations the East German Christian Democrats attempted to persuade the Social Democrats to join them in a grand coalition government. These negotiations were possibly facilitated by the March resignation of Boehme, who was accused of having been an informer for the East German secret police for many years.[57] On April 9 a grand coalition was agreed upon; it would encompass the CDU-Alliance for Germany, the Free Democrats, and the SPD. Among the twenty-four members of the new cabinet, the Christian Democrats would have fourteen ministries, the Social Democrats seven, and the Liberal Democrats three. De Maizière would be the prime minister. Markus Meckel, a Lutheran pastor and the acting chairman of the East German Social Democrats, would be the foreign minister. Another Lutheran clergyman, Rainer Eppelmann, leader of the small Democratic Awakening party, was appointed defense minister.[58]

In the negotiations for the grand coalition these East German democratic parties all agreed on a program to do the following:

- move rapidly toward reunification
- participate in the two-plus-four international negotiations on reunification
- exclude Communists from government
- keep a reunited Germany in NATO.

This last important commitment—undoubtedly a shock to the Soviets—was qualified by the stipulation that NATO renounce the first use of nuclear weapons and partially reorient its military strategy.

The elected East German democratic government also took a number of immediate, symbolic steps. In contrast to the Communist governments, which had always denied East German responsibility for Nazi crimes or reparations, the new East German government formally recognized "the responsibility of the entire German people for the past" and promised to "provide material support" to those who had been persecuted.[59] Concerning the Holocaust, the new East German government admitted "joint responsibility on behalf of the German people for the humiliation, expulsion, and murder of Jewish women, men, and children. . . . We feel sad and ashamed and acknowledge this burden of German history."[60] The new democratic government also formally apologized for having participated in the invasion of Czechoslovakia in 1968. To Poland, anxious about the integrity of its borders after the reunification of Germany, the new government said the Polish people "should know that their right to live within safe borders will not be questioned by territorial claims from us Germans, either now or in the future."[61]

Economic Unification. By early March 1990, 465,000 East Germans had crossed into West Germany, seeking asylum and resettlement. The exodus was continuing at a rate of more than 2,000 per day. As soon as the new East German government was formed, Chancellor Kohl moved to begin negotiations for economic and social union by the target date of July 1990. On April 23 Kohl agreed to exchange East German marks for West German deutsche marks at a one-to-one rate, for up to 4,000 deutsche marks per individual. The official exchange rate had been three East German marks for one West German deutsche mark, and the black market rate was five to one. With Kohl's offer an East German family of four could obtain 16,000 West German deutsche marks (about $9,400) for 16,000 East German marks. In addition, all social insurance and pension payments from East Germany would be converted into West German currency and ultimately moved to a comparable level as economic unification occurred. For an estimated 2.7 million retirees in East Germany, for example, the April 1990 pension of about 420 East German marks would be converted first into West German deutsche marks and over time would likely rise to the expected average West German monthly pension level of 1,100 deutsche marks.[62]

East German Prime Minister de Maizière had made clear that this was the type of offer his government wanted. There would have to be a coexistence "for the next months," he said, of planned and market economies; his government's motto was, "As much market as possible and as much state as necessary."[63] Intensive negotiations continued over the next weeks between the two German governments, and by May 13 a draft treaty for economic unification was completed. Although the treaty covered most issues, it left unresolved such difficult ones as the allotment of private property and the agricultural and industrial restructuring of East Germany. These issues were to be treated in separate negotiations, to begin after economic unification, planned for July 2, 1990.[64]

The West German government announced it would establish a $70 billion fund to carry out its obligations under a Treaty of Economic Unification.[65] On May 18 Chancellor Kohl and Prime Minister de Maizière, representing two German governments, signed a treaty to unite the two economies in a single social-market economy. Kohl called this "a first decisive step on the path to unity."[66] On June 21 both parliaments approved the Treaty of Economic Unification, which would take effect on July 2, 1990.

As a corollary, once economic unification took effect, there would be no more resettlement funds for East Germans coming into West Germany. Neither would there be any further continuation of the social services, housing, employment, and social insurance benefits that had hitherto been provided for the hundreds of thousands who had left East Germany. As Kohl had said to the people of East Germany immediately after the March 18 election,

> The citizens of East Germany . . . want a social market economy—and soon. They clearly rejected any successors to the Communist party. . . . My message in this hour is: Stay home, help in your communities, in your factories, in your offices, together with us to build this wonderful land. We will help you.[67]

Kohl's strategy of moving forward on reunification step by step was working—but for some weeks the West German Social Democratic party almost derailed economic unification. Throughout the winter and spring of 1990, leaders of the SPD had charged that Kohl was rushing German reunification. Kohl contended there was a need to move quickly because Gorbachev's agreement on reunification was fundamental and it was uncertain how long he would remain in power in the Soviet Union. At a leadership meeting in late May 1990, the SPD decided to oppose the Treaty of Economic Unification. Even though the East German SPD had approved it and asked the West German SPD not to oppose it, the West German SPD preferred to negotiate for better protection for East German workers and industries.[68] The Social Democrats controlled the West German Bundesrat, the upper house of the legislature, and so their negative vote could delay passage of the treaty. After some weeks of strong opposition from within the party, however, Oskar Lafontaine was persuaded to withdraw from his initial decision and the SPD accepted the Treaty of Economic Unification.

The International Dimension. Following the East German elections, the tempo of international diplomacy on German unification increased markedly. There were meetings among Western leaders, bilateral Western-Soviet disscussions, NATO meetings, European Community meetings, U.S.-Soviet negotiations at the level of foreign ministers, and a a U.S.-Soviet summit at the end of May 1990.

There were two rounds of two-plus-four meetings among the two German states and the four World War II Allies, the United States, the United Kingdom, France, and the Soviet Union. By June 1990 these talks were known as the "five versus one," since all states except the Soviet Union held the view that a reunified Germany should be in NATO. The newly elected governments of Czechoslovakia and Hungary also joined the East German government in endorsing a reunified Germany's membership in NATO.

On the one side, the Soviet Union proposed a formula to obtain a significant payment from West Germany in exchange for permitting reunification and withdrawing Soviet troops. The ultimate aim of the Soviet proposal was the neutralization of Germany and the dismantling of NATO. On the other side, Germany and its Atlantic Alliance Allies sought to ensure that a reunified Germany could remain in NATO and to prevent the Soviet Union from extracting unreasonable payments from West Germany if possible.

In the explicit and implicit negotiations held between April and June 1990, the Soviet position shifted in form but not in substance. On April 5 the Soviets said they would no longer insist that a unified Germany be militarily neutral, but they still would not accept a reunified Germany in NATO.[69] Both Germany and the United States immediately rejected this formulation, insisting that a reunified Germany should be able to remain in NATO.[70] On April 18 the Soviet Union sent East German Prime Minister de Maizière a letter specifically opposing a process of quick unification. Days later de Maizière met with Gorbachev in Moscow and told him personally that the East German government believed a reunified Germany should be part of the NATO security alliance, as neutrality was "no solution" for a united Germany; "We don't want to be a buffer zone," he said.[71] De Maizière offered to press for changes in NATO force structures and strategies, however, to reduce any threat to the Soviet Union.

For his part, Kohl pursued an active, multifaceted diplomatic strategy. To assure France and the other European states that a unified Germany intended to remain a part of democratic Europe, Kohl joined with President Mitterrand on April 20 to propose that the European Community move toward greater political unity and a common foreign policy by 1993. This joint French-German proposal would require a sharp acceleration in the pace of European integration planned for 1992. For France it represented an assurance that a reunited Germany would remain closely involved in cooperative Western institutions. A spokesman for the French foreign ministry made it clear that it was not a substitute for NATO, however: "For us the Alliance is absolutely essential."[72] While the French and German foreign ministers formally proposed this plan to an EC meeting, Presidents Mitterrand and Bush discussed the same issues in the United States. Mitterrand wanted assurance that the United States understood the French and German view of the long-term political and security arrangements for Europe. When Bush concluded the meeting he noted that both France and Germany were committed to including a united Germany in the Atlantic Alliance.[73]

The French-German proposals were presented to the leaders of the twelve EC countries at their regular meeting on April 28, 1989, in Ireland. Prime Minister Thatcher of the United Kingdom had reservations and asked, "What does political union mean?" She agreed, though, that the foreign ministers of the European Community should draw up a detailed program of union for future consideration.[74] These issues were discussed further at the meeting of the foreign ministers on May 19, 1990, and at the regularly scheduled meeting of the EC heads of government on June 24–25, 1990. It was decided that by the end of 1990 the EC leaders would begin negotiations for greater political union by 1993. Kohl intended this joint French-German initiative both to reduce the likelihood that France would work against German reunification in the two-plus-four negotiations and to anchor Germany further in the institutions of democratic Europe.

To prepare for the first round of two-plus-four negotiations, NATO foreign ministers met in early May 1990. They decided to hold a summit meeting in early July to discuss ways of transforming NATO into an organization for greater political cooperation while retaining its military purpose. The NATO foreign ministers also recommended halting development of new short-range nuclear weapons and opening negotiations with the Soviet Union to eliminate existing nuclear weapon systems. They agreed to the Soviet proposal to temporarily keep Soviet troops in East Germany after German reunification was accepted.[75]

On the eve of the first round of two-plus-four talks, held in Bonn on May 5–6, the Soviet Union again proposed that NATO and the Warsaw Pact be abolished. Soviet Foreign Minister Shevardnadze said Germany should become "a testing ground" for new forms of East-West security cooperation after its reunification. This meant a militarily "nonaligned" Germany, which would join both alliances for a transition period and thereby become "a place where [the alliances] would be gradually dissolved," to be replaced by "all-European security arrangements."[76] The United States and West Germany immediately rejected this proposal. Then at the May 1990 two-plus-four talks Shevardnadze went on to suggest that the 380,000 Soviet troops or a significant portion thereof might remain in a reunited Germany until 1995 or 1997.[77]

Alternatively, Shevardnadze proposed, if no agreement could be reached on Germany joining both alliances then Germany could move forward on reunification with the issues of foreign troops and military alliances postponed for negotiations over the next several years. This approach was sharply rejected by Kohl, who called it Soviet "negotiation poker" and a potentially "fatal development" in the effort of a reunited Germany to regain full sovereignty.[78]

At the thirty-fifth anniversary of the Warsaw Pact Treaty on May 13, 1990, Soviet Defense Minister Dmitri Yazov and the Soviet general commanding the Warsaw Pact both asserted that the alliance was not in decline, as the West perceived. They reiterated that a united Germany could not be included in NATO.[79] The democratically elected East German and Hungarian leadership, however, had already said that a united Germany should be in NATO. Even before the elections, in the March 1990 Warsaw Pact meeting, the foreign ministers of Czechoslovakia and Poland had opposed the Soviet position and endorsed the membership of a united Germany in NATO.[80] The process of liberalization in four of the six Eastern European countries was leaving the Soviet Union isolated on the question of NATO membership for a reunified Germany.

The next opportunity for progress on the German issue would be the U.S.-Soviet summit meeting, May 30–June 3, 1990. In mid-May Secretary of State Baker visited Moscow to negotiate with Shevardnadze and Gorbachev on strategic arms reduction and other U.S.-Soviet issues. The United States made a number of concessions to Soviet positions, which had hardened considerably since earlier in 1990. The United States also refrained from taking any action against Soviet coercive measures to end the Lithuanian struggle for independence. The United States provided a number of new opportunities for trade as well, and it relaxed restrictions on the export of high technology to Eastern Europe and to the Soviet Union. These conciliatory gestures were further enhanced by the May 23 meeting of the NATO defense ministers, who decided to lower the readiness of some NATO military units and to explore a West German proposal to form multinational units.[81] They urged the Soviet Union to make greater progress on the conventional-forces-in-Europe negotiations, to bring Soviet force numbers below the threshold level believed capable of a surprise attack.[82]

Chancellor Kohl agreed that Germany would pay about $750 million a year for at least five years to the Soviet Union, in reimbursment for the cost of their continuing troop deployments in East Germany. The estimated 380,000 Soviet forces in East Germany included more than 6,500 tanks, 5,000 rocket launchers, and 850 aircraft and helicopters on nineteen airfields. After making this concession to the Soviet Union, Kohl visited President Bush in Washington just before the U.S.-Soviet summit.[83]

Another example of an effort made to reassure the Soviet Union was West German Foreign Minister Genscher's meeting with Shevardnadze on May 23 in Geneva. At this fourth round of 1990 Soviet-German ministerial discussions, Genscher reportedly arrived with a package of concessions West Germany was willing to offer the Soviet Union in exchange for its approval of German unification and membership in NATO. Those concessions included Kohl's offer of payment for the continued stationing of Soviet troops in East Germany, new bank credits, new economic aid for the Soviet Union from West Germany and other NATO countries, and West Germany's assumption of East Germany's contracts to supply the Soviets with uranium to power their nuclear plants. The West Germans would have to buy the uranium on the world market, since most East German uranium mines would be closed because of dangerous radioactivity. Perhaps the most important concession was West Germany's promise to urge the NATO Alliance to revise its strategy of "flexible response." Under this military doctrine, NATO would use both conventional and nuclear weapons, if needed, to halt an attack from the East. Genscher proposed that NATO use only conventional weapons, unless the East first used nuclear weapons in an attack.[84]

Nevertheless, on the eve of the May 1990 U.S.-Soviet summit meeting, Gorbachev issued a warning over the intentions of the West to have a unified Germany remain in NATO. He said the Soviet Union had the right to maintain its troops in East Germany under the agreement signed with the three Western Allies at the end of World War II. He added that the Soviet Union "will remain where it is now with its group of troops" if a reunified Germany joins NATO.[85] Gorbachev also emphasized a theme he would present to Bush—that the West would certainly oppose a reunified Germany's joining the Soviet-led Warsaw Pact, and therefore the West should sympathize with the Soviet Union's opposition to a reunified Germany in NATO.

Gorbachev made these statements just after concluding several hours of meetings with French President François Mitterrand. He suggested that, like France, a reunified Germany could remain a political member of NATO but not participate in its integrated military command. Gorbachev also endorsed Mitterrand's proposal for the creation of Pan-European institutions to act as political bridges between East and West. West Germany immediately rejected this Soviet proposal, but West German Defense Minister Gerhard Stoltenberg noted the positive significance of the fact that "the Soviet president is now beginning to concern himself in public with the prerequisites for [German] NATO membership.[86]

From Kohl's point of view, however, this Soviet proposal was an apparent repetition of French cooperation with the Soviet Union on approaches that would be unacceptable to West Germany, despite the joint French-German initiatives of the preceding months. It must have raised concerns about the future. The French foreign minister, Ronald Dumas, undoubtedly added to these concerns by stating after Gorbachev's May 1990 comments that "the request concerning the security of the Soviet Union is in my view legitimate. It is the duty of the West to address this concern. If we do not find a proper solution within a reasonable period of time there is a threat of crisis or tension between East and West."[87]

At the conclusion of his meeting with the prime minister of Canada the day before arriving in Washington, D.C., for his third visit to the United States, Gorbachev said the following about the West's insistence on a unified Germany's membership in NATO: "The West hasn't done much thinking, an old record that keeps playing the same note again and again. They try to dictate and this will not suit us."[88] Apparently as a result of Gorbachev's persuasiveness, Prime Minister Mulroney of Canada seemed to tilt toward the Soviet position; he remarked that an "inadvertent insensitivity to the feelings of the Soviet Union" had entered Allied thinking. Mulroney urged that the Atlantic Alliance consider ways to be more "accommodating" to Soviet concerns about Germany.[89]

The spring 1990 U.S.–Soviet summit took place in an atmosphere of great cordiality. The United States stood by the concessions it had made on the strategic-arms-reduction issues and on the transfer of high technology to the Soviet Union. It added the important concession of an opportunity for the Soviet Union to have most-favored-nation trading status with the United States. This was contingent only on the Soviet Parliament's codifying a policy change permitting the emigration of those Soviet citizens, including those who are Jewish, who sought to leave.

There were reports of intensive discussions on German issues, including U.S.–Soviet consideration of possible limitations on German military strength. The United States, though, demanded that there be no limits imposed exclusively on a sovereign, united Germany. As one senior U.S. official put it, "The Germans are paranoid about singularity and about being set out somehow. . . . That's why you know you don't talk about limits on the Germans, you talk about a Conventional Forces Europe agreement in which everyone would be limited . . . [including] the Germans."[90]

At the end of the U.S.–Soviet summit, the statements issued by the two leaders showed there had been no change in the position of either side on Germany.[91] Following the summit Gorbachev traveled to several American states, giving a speech in California that included a conciliatory-sounding argument for the end of both alliances in Europe:

> Until now, alliances have been built on a selective, and in fact discriminatory basis. They were based on setting countries against each other. They divided countries and peoples much more than they united them. This system was perfected during the years of the cold war, producing the twin antipodes of the North Atlantic Alliance and the Warsaw Pact. But we are approaching a time when the very principles of alliance-building should become different. It should mean unity to create conditions for a life for every human being, protect the environment, combat hunger, diseases, drug addiction, and ignorance.[92]

Following this speech the Soviet Union announced it would withdraw some of its short-range nuclear weapons from Central Europe, "in order to create favorable conditions" for further negotiations on Germany and European security issues. The United States pointed out that the proposed withdrawals accounted for only 60 of about 14,000 Soviet tactical nuclear missile launchers in Central Europe and about 1,500 of its estimated 8,000 nuclear warheads.[93]

The U.S. Nine-Point Approach. After the U.S.–Soviet summit to end the stalemate on Germany, the United States proposed a nine-point approach. These "nine assurances" to the Soviet Union included:

• A united Germany would reaffirm its commitment not to develop nuclear, chemical, or biological weapons.

• After the conclusion of a first conventional-forces-reduction treaty—then under negotiation in Vienna—the NATO Allies would be prepared to move toward negotiating a second agreement to reduce the manpower of national armies, including those of a united Germany.

• NATO would be prepared to speed up the pace of negotiations to limit short-range nuclear weapons in Europe.

• There would be a guarantee not only of the Polish border with Germany but also of the Soviet border with Poland—legitimizing territory Stalin removed from Poland.

• No NATO forces would be stationed in the territory of the former East Germany.

- Soviet troops would be allowed to remain in East Germany for a transitional period, with expenses paid by the German government.
- NATO would review and revise its military doctrine and deployments to make them less threatening to the Soviet Union.
- The NATO countries would support the institutionalization and expansion of the thirty-five-nation Conference on Security and Co-operation in Europe.
- The Atlantic Alliance would approve German economic assistance to the Soviet Union, including payments for its German-based military forces and their housing once they returned to the Soviet Union, commercial lending, trade, and other commercial arrangements.[94]

U.S. Secretary of State Baker stated that the European Community, the Conference on Security and Cooperation in Europe, and NATO all "must now play a greater role in deepening and broadening European unity"; but he added that

> we must ensure that these organizations continue to complement and reinforce one another. NATO will continue to serve as the indispensable guarantor of peace—and therefore the ultimate guardian of democracy and prosperity. As President Bush stressed with President Gorbachev . . . we believe NATO will remain a cornerstone of both military security and political legitimacy in the new Europe.[95]

The seven members of the Warsaw Pact met in Moscow on June 7, and having pronounced an end to the idea that the West is "an ideological enemy," they appointed a special commission to draw up proposals to change the "character, functions, and activities" of their organization.[96] The declaration of the Warsaw Pact members echoed the Soviet approach and called for "the formation of a new all-European security system"; but the newly elected democratic president of Hungary, Josef Antal, publicly called for the dissolution of the Warsaw Pact within one year. Meeting in Scotland on the following day, the foreign ministers of the sixteen NATO countries declared they "extend to the Soviet Union and to all other European countries the hand of friendship and cooperation."[97] The NATO foreign ministers went on to say that they were determined to "seize the historic opportunities resulting from the profound changes in Europe to help build a new peaceful order."[98]

Economic Concessions. After the U.S.-Soviet summit, Warsaw Pact, and NATO meetings, Chancellor Kohl and East German Prime Minister de Maizière each met with President Bush in Washington, on

June 8 and 11 respectively. Bush repeated his view that "a united Germany and NATO will not be threatening to the Soviet Union," and Chancellor Kohl said "things are moving and in a good direction."[99] To maintain his strategy of keeping the momentum toward de facto unification Kohl now moved on two fronts. With apparent U.S. and NATO approval, he began to offer the Soviet Union the specific economic benefits that Genscher and Shevardnadze had discussed in May. German commerical banks offered a $3 billion credit to the Soviet Union, to be guaranteed by the German government. Kohl and Mitterrand jointly urged that the European Community also provide substantial economic assistance to the Soviet Union. They made this proposal some days before the June 26–27 meeting in Ireland of the EC heads of state.[100] At that meeting the European Community agreed in principle to provide significant Western economic assistance to the Soviet Union, but it did not commit its twelve member-countries to specific amounts. Kohl's official spokesman then revealed that in the February 1990 Kohl-Gorbachev discussions and in subsequent telephone conversations, Western aid to the Soviet Union had been discussed as an exchange for Soviet permission to reunify.[101]

For many years political negotiations between East and West Germany were facilitated by giving the East Germans payment in hard currency, credits, and scarce goods or technology. By one informed estimate, West German payments to the Honecker regime amounted to billions of dollars annually. The intent was to promote a more open relationship and travel to West Germany for millions of visiting East Germans.[102] Kohl and the EC, supported by Bush stood ready to provide the Soviet Union with billions to persuade it to accept both reunification and German membership in NATO. With the EC endorsement in hand, Kohl could expect the July 1990 NATO summit also to endorse this approach, and the seven industrial democracies, including Japan, to consider large-scale economic aid to the Soviet Union at their summit meeting later in July 1990.

Political Relations. Having achieved U.S. and Western endorsement for the international dimension of his strategy for achieving irreversible unification, Kohl moved beyond economic unification to pursue the second aspect of his domestic strategy: political relations with East Germany. Since 1953 West Germany celebrated a "day of unification" on June 17, to symbolize the hope that East Germans would not again be crushed as they had been by Soviet forces on June 17, 1953. On that date in 1990, Chancellor Kohl attended a dramatic debate in the East German Parliament, where members of the Christian Democratic majority unexpectedly proposed that the Parliament immediately approve a process of political unification with West Germany.

The proposal called for reconstituting the five pre–World War II states that had existed in the territory of what had become East Germany, and then permitting each state to accept West German sovereignty under Article 23 of the West German constitution. By a vote of 267 to 92, with 7 abstentions, the East German Parliament sent the motion to committee—thereby postponing a decision, but keeping the possibility open. Chancellor Kohl received a standing ovation from the East German members of Parliament, and after the vote he said, "German unity is coming. It will come soon."[103] This event demonstrated that the East German Parliament had the legal authority and capacity to bring about the accession of East Germany into West Germany. It was a way of telling the Soviet Union that if the East German Parliament completed its vote, the only way to reverse such an action would be by the direct use of coercion or military force.

Thus, the June 17, 1990, debate and test-vote in the East German Parliament was clearly intended to signal to the Soviet Union that following economic unification on July 2, 1990, both German governments were ready to advance toward political unification, irrespective of Soviet views. Days later Kohl suggested the possibility of holding the first all-German elections in more than fifty years, in December 1990.[104] Shortly thereafter the West German government released details of an approach to complete political unification by holding democratic all-German elections on December 9, 1990. The West German Social Democrats pronounced such a quick approach to unity "not acceptable," contending that a number of issues required time to work out. One of these issues was the difference in electoral systems. In West Germany, unless a party gets more than 5 percent of the vote, it cannot win any seats in Parliament—since the West German population was more than three times that of East Germany, this would disadvantage small East German parties. The June 1990 announcement of a blueprint for political unification was nevertheless made by the Kohl government, to put further pressure on the Soviet Union.[105]

Two-Plus-Four Talks. All this occurred in preparation for the second round of two-plus-four negotiations on Germany, scheduled for June 22, 1990, in East Berlin. How would the Soviet Union respond to Germany's direct offer of extensive economic support, to the cordiality of the U.S.–Soviet summit, to the symbolism of NATO's June 1990

111

declarations of cooperation, and to the nine-point U.S. proposal to reassure the Soviet Union? Speaking to the Soviet Parliament on June 12, Gorbachev reiterated his call for "dual membership" for a unified Germany in NATO and the Warsaw Pact, but he made one important change. He said that "united Germany could declare that for this transition period it would honor all obligations it inherits from the Federal Republic of Germany and from the German Democratic Republic. The *Bundeswher* [West German armed forces] would as before be subordinate to NATO, and the East German troops would be subordinate to the government of the new Germany." Gorbachev also said he had told President Bush that "the American presence in Europe, since it fulfills a certain role in maintaining stability, is an element of the strategic situation, and does not represent a problem for us."[106] The West German government called Gorbachev's remarks "fundamentally positive," but it rejected the idea of a united Germany continuing in both alliances.[107] And the Soviet minister of defense, speaking a few days after Gorbachev, emphasized that the Soviet Union would agree to a unified Germany only if it joined a collective European security system that replaced NATO and the Warsaw Pact.[108]

At the June 22, 1990, meeting of the two-plus-four foreign ministers, Shevardnadze presented a detailed paper that set forth the Soviet position. It called for a "transition period" of three to five years, during which the four Allied powers would "limit the strength of Germany's armed forces," revamp their structure to make sure they are "rendered incapable for offensive operations," enforce a "ban on the resurgence of Nazi political ideology," and require "the preservation of memorials commemorating those who were killed in the fight against fascism."[109] Shevardnadze said furthermore that the Soviet Union wanted evidence of NATO's intention to transform itself into more of a political alliance. He called for the four powers to reduce their troops in Germany to "token contingents" or withdraw them completely. Shevardnadze's proposal also called for the four powers to remove all their troops from Berlin within six months after German reunification, although the 380,000 Soviet troops would remain in the former East Germany.[110]

In essence, the Soviet proposal harked back to the Stalin letter of 1952. It represented virtually all the Soviet foreign policy objectives pursued during the previous forty years with respect to West Germany: demilitarization, controls over German armed forces, de facto neutralization, withdrawal of Western military forces from Germany, and, implicitly, the end of NATO as a military alliance. It opened the way for direct Soviet interference in the internal affairs of a unified

Germany by proposing that the four powers retain for some years the authority to crush what any one of them, including the Soviet Union alone, might perceive as a "resurgence of Nazi political ideology." U.S. Secretary of State Baker rejected the Soviet proposal immediately and publicly, saying it "would restrict German sovereignty for some years" and calling such restriction unacceptable to the West. A united Germany, in Baker's view, should not be "singularized or discriminated against."[111] The British and West German foreign ministers made similar comments.

Summary. During the fall and winter of 1989 the people of Eastern Europe began the process of unraveling their long-established Communist regimes and of moving toward democracy and constitutional government. During the spring and summer of 1990 political liberalization moved forward in Czechoslovakia, Hungary, Poland, and East Germany, although it was checked in Romania and Bulgaria. From September 1989 to June 1990 nearly 800,000 people fled from East Germany to West Germany, and the peoples and leaders of both Germanys made a series of fateful decisions that virtually guaranteed their peaceful reunification in freedom and democracy. The Soviet Union, however, remained determined that a united Germany not belong to the Atlantic Alliance as it existed in 1990, a political and military coalition to deter both coercion and direct attack. As spring turned to summer in 1990, the two Germanys moved toward de facto unification; but the future of a united Germany and Europe remained under the shadow of uncertainty regarding the design of the new international political order.

PART THREE
Alternative Futures

7
Reunification and Continuing Commitment to the Atlantic Alliance

When the de facto economic and social unification of two Germanys took place in July 1990, both the United States and the Soviet Union were determined to structure a new political order in Europe, each according to its own interests. The United States and its Allies in the Atlantic Alliance wanted full membership for a unified Germany in a North Atlantic Treaty Organization that, while changed to reflect the perception of a lower Soviet threat, retained enough military forces to deter or defeat any Soviet military coercion. The Soviet Union wanted either a reunified Germany to belong ultimately to no alliance, or the Atlantic Alliance and the Warsaw Pact both to be dissolved in the context of a new, all-European collective security system, or the Atlantic Alliance itself to change so substantively that it no longer functioned as a genuine military coalition, providing immediate and practical military protection to its members.

The Soviet Union might also consider itself successful if NATO becomes so much weaker militarily than the remaining Soviet forces that its capacity to deter Soviet coercion would be qualitatively lower, even with German membership. The withdrawal of a large portion of U.S. forces from Europe could create such a diminished Atlantic Alliance. The removal of most or all of the nuclear weapons supporting current NATO deployments in Germany would further undermine it, as would very sharp reductions in the total NATO forces facing the Soviet Union.

History will reveal which of these two alternatives emerges from the next years of transitional international politics. It is evident, however, that the outcome will depend on the comparative skill of the United States and the Western coalition on one side and the Soviet Union on the other side, in pursuing their international objectives.

117

This chapter analyzes the means by which the United States and its Western allies might succeed in bringing about a reunified Germany that remains a full ally in a militarily effective NATO and the possible implications of such a result. The next chapter examines the course the Soviet Union might pursue to gain its objective, the de facto neutralization of a reunified Germany, and the implications of such an outcome for world politics.

Criteria for an Effectual NATO. After the March 1990 elections in East Germany, the governments of West Germany, the United States, and other members of the Atlantic Alliance became convinced that reunification was possible and probable. They therefore became more determined that a reunified Germany should remain a full member of the Atlantic Alliance. As President Bush said in February 1990, "We share a common belief that a unified Germany should remain a full member of the North Atlantic Treaty Organization, including participation in its military structure."[1]

Full membership in an Atlantic Alliance capable of providing military protection to its members, if necessary, against the armed forces of the Soviet Union implies the following:

• that an integrated military command continues to exist, and that a reunified Germany is a member of that command

• that the combined NATO troop presence is kept at a level capable of defending against nonnuclear attack through conventional means alone

• that a logistical reinforcement network is maintained so that the United States and other countries can send forces to the sites of any potential or actual attack

• that European-based nuclear weapons are available to the Atlantic Alliance, to deter or respond to their use by the Soviet Union, including response as a "last resort" if a massive conventional invasion appears to be succeeding

• that strategic nuclear weapons are available to deter the use of Soviet strategic weapons for coercion or attack.

The Soviet Union has made it clear that it seeks the fading out of NATO, the de facto neutrality of Germany, or the weakening of the Atlantic Alliance in Europe to the degree that it is militarily no match for the remaining Soviet forces (see chapter 6). This analysis will assume the criteria listed above for a militarily effective Atlantic Alliance in discussing a reunified Germany as one of its members.

Internal and International Dimensions

Just as the process of moving toward Germany's de facto unification had both an internal and an international dimension, the post-July 1990 process of unification also had two dimensions. Both Germanys and the Western Alliance countries were committed to a reunified Germany's continued, full membership in NATO. In early July 1990, only days after economic and social unification began, the governments of East and West Germany began negotiations in East Berlin to establish a timetable for achieving full political unification by December 1990. Several issues faced the two friendly and cooperating German governments, including: when and how all-German elections would be conducted, whether as part of the scheduled December 2, 1990, national elections, or shortly after those; whether the capital of a united Germany should be Bonn or Berlin; and the merger of the countries' legal systems. The prime minister of East Germany, Lothar de Maizière, called the opening day of those talks , July 6, 1990, "an historic day on the path to German unity."[2]

The Christian Democratic-Social Democratic coalition government in East Germany decided that political reunification should occur before the end of 1990, through the accession of the five East German states to West Germany, as provided for in Article 23 of the West German constitution. Thus the timing and pace of political unification would be entirely within the formal authority of the two Germanys. And they had decided to move forward internally even before having a guarantee of how the international arrangements would be decided in the continuing two-plus-four negotiations. According to the plan of political unification through accession, as the five states of East Germany became part of the Federal Republic of Germany they would assume that nation's obligations and rights of membership in international institutions. These institutions included the United Nations, the European Community, and the Atlantic Alliance. This could mean that the only way for the Soviet Union to stop this from occurring might be through coercion of one type or another or by threats to prolong the stay of its 380,000 troops on German territory, even beyond the five to seven years the Soviets proposed in the June 1990 two-plus-four talks.

During two decades of efforts at détente with the Communist regime in East Germany, successive West German governments had found monetary payments in hard currency to be an effective means of obtaining important political and humanitarian concessions. As discussed earlier, the West German government offered substantial economic benefits to the Soviet Union during the spring of 1990, guaranteed them $3 billion in untied bank loans, spoke up for economic aid at the June 1990 EC meeting, and urged the July 1990 Houston economic summit of seven industrial democracies to provide the Soviets with $15 billion in economic aid. All the while West Germany continued to proffer its own additional aid.

At the July 1990 summit of NATO leaders in London, President Bush's comment on possible German plans for economic and technological assistance to the Soviets was this: "If the Germans decide they're going to do that, that's their business."[3] This remark signaled a significant change in the U.S. position, formerly an effort to withhold economic aid from the West until the Soviet Union reduced its military expenditures and its massive support for such hostile regimes as those of Cuba, Libya, Syria, Iraq, and North Korea. Bush's statement provided an opening for the German government to use its substantial economic resources to persuade the Soviet Union to permit a reunified Germany's membership in NATO. Given the economic crisis facing the Soviets in 1990, German economic aid proposals were likely to have an important impact on Soviet decisions.

After reportedly strenuous internal debate, the German government also took a decisive military step as another concession to the Soviet Union in exchange for permitting a reunified Germany's membership in the Atlantic Alliance. At the July 1990 NATO summit, Chancellor Kohl departed from the previous German position of rejecting any European arms-reduction agreement singling out Germany for limitations on its forces. He proposed that NATO offer a future "commitment . . . concerning the manpower levels of the unified Germany."[4] After a first agreement on conventional forces in Europe were signed, Kohl suggested that Germany would be willing to allow a second conventional-forces-in-Europe agreement that set a specific numerical ceiling on the military forces of a unified Germany. Of an estimated 540,000 West and East German troops at the time of the July 1990 NATO summit, 490,000 being West German, the West German government was reportedly prepared for cuts of 25 to 35 percent. Such cuts would bring the final estimated totals to 350,000–400,000, all but 50,000 being stationed in West Germany and the remainder in the former East Germany. Though still above the limit of 200,000 proposed by Shevarnadze in June 1990, this West German proposal indicated a willingness to reduce German troops in order to persuade the Soviet leadership to permit the new Germany to remain in the Atlantic Alliance.

The German approach, then, was both to maintain internal political momentum toward unification within the Atlantic Alliance and to offer the Soviets economic incentives and limits on German forces. The Atlantic Alliance approach complemented it, the United States and West Germany taking the lead. This was visible at the NATO summit meeting held in London on July 5–6, 1990. After two days of intensive debate among the sixteen heads of government, the "London Declaration on a Transformed North Atlantic Alliance" was formally issued. It represented the culmination of consultations among members of the Atlantic Alliance and the European Community, who had for months sought ways to reduce the perceived threat to the Soviet Union while still retaining the means needed to assure a military deterrent.

The London Declaration stated,

> As our Alliance enters its fifth decade it must continue to provide for the common defense. Yet our Alliance must be even more an agent of change. It can help build the structures of a more united continent.[5]

The London Declaration closely followed the proposal sent to NATO leaders by President Bush. It reflected ideas Bush had discussed with Gorbachev at the May–June Washington summit and proposals that the U.S. secretaries of state and defense had made to the Atlantic Alliance in previous months.

Among the most important of the conclusions and proposals offered by the London Declaration of the Atlantic Alliance were the following:

• "Europe has entered a new, promising era. Central and Eastern Europe is liberating itself. The Soviet Union has embarked on the long journey toward a free society.

• "The North Atlantic Alliance has been the most successful defensive alliance in history. As our Alliance enters its fifth decade and looks ahead to a new century, it must continue to provide for the common defense. This Alliance has done much to bring about the new Europe.

• "The unification of Germany means that the division of Europe is also being overcome. A united Germany in the Atlantic Alliance of free democracies and as part of the growing political and economic integration of the European Community will be an indispensable factor of stability which is needed in the heart of Europe.

• "The member states of the North Atlantic Alliance propose to the member states of the Warsaw Treaty Organization a joint declaration in which we solemnly state that we are no longer adversaries and reaffirm our intention to refrain from threat or use of force

121

against the territorial integrity or political independence of any state. . . .

• "We put the highest priority on completing this year the first treaty to reduce and limit conventional armed forces in Europe, along with the completion of a meaningful confidence-and-security-building-measures package. . . . We propose that once a CFE [Conventional Forces Europe arms reduction] treaty is signed, follow-up talks should begin with the same membership and mandate with the goal of building on the current agreement with additional measures including measures to limit manpower in Europe . . . [including] the manpower levels of a unified Germany."[6]

The NATO leadership invited Gorbachev to speak to a meeting of the full NATO membership, and they asked each member of the Warsaw Pact to sign an individual nonaggression pact with NATO and to appoint liaison personnel to remain at NATO headquarters on a continuing basis. On the practical, military level, the London Declaration said that "as Soviet troops leave Eastern Europe and a treaty limiting conventional armed forces is implemented, the Alliance's integrated force structure and its strategy will change fundamentally. . . ." Among the changes would be smaller and restructured active-duty forces, which would be highly mobile; a scaling back in the readiness of active units; and a greater reliance on the ability to "build up larger forces if and when these might be needed."[7]

Most important was the change concerning nuclear weapons. The United States proposed altering the doctrine of "flexible response," which since 1967 had authorized the Atlantic Alliance to use nuclear weapons against even a nonnuclear attack if it seemed to threaten a breakthrough. Relegating nuclear weapons now to a "last resort" measure, the London Declaration stated:

> To keep the peace, the Alliance must maintain for the foreseeable future an appropriate mix of nuclear and conventional forces based in Europe and kept up-to-date when necessary. But as a defensive Alliance, NATO has always stressed that none of its weapons will ever be used except in self-defense and that we seek the lowest and most stable level of nuclear forces needed to secure the prevention of war.[8]

This statement on nuclear doctrine was matched by the pledge that U.S. nuclear artillery shells would be withdrawn from Europe if the Soviets made corresponding withdrawals of their nuclear artillery. Concerning the use of nuclear weapons as a last resort, however,

President Mitterrand said, "We do not share the concept of last resort"; France would not feel bound by the NATO decision in the use of its national nuclear forces.[9]

In an important gesture toward the Soviet Union's strong interest in expanding and strengthening the Conference on Security and Cooperation in Europe (CSCE), the London Declaration said:

> The Conference on Security and Cooperation in Europe should become more prominent in Europe's future, bringing together the countries of Europe and North America. We support a CSCE Summit later this year in Paris which would include the signature of a CFE Agreement and would set new standards for the establishment and preservation of free societies. It should endorse, inter alia:
> - CSCE principles on the right to free and fair elections
> - CSCE commitments to respect and uphold the rule of law
> - CSCE guidelines for enhancing economic cooperation based on the development of a free and competitive market economy
> - CSCE cooperation on environmental protection[10]

The London Declaration also proposed a specific "CSCE Summit in Paris to decide how the CSCE can be institutionalized to provide a forum for wider political dialogue in a more united Europe."

Taken together, the actions of the two German governments and the sixteen leaders of the Atlantic Alliance offered the Soviet Union a comprehensive set of political, military, and economic incentives for permitting the unification of Germany within the Atlantic Alliance. The July 1990 London Declaration made it clear that NATO was willing to reduce significantly the level of its military forces and to reduce the level of its nuclear weapons, in exchange for substantial withdrawals of Soviet forces from Eastern Europe and the signing of a treaty on conventional arms reductions in Europe. The Alliance leaders proposed that following the London Declaration, significant progress should be made on the European-arms-reductions and confidence-building negotiations and treaties should be signed. Then the Soviet desire to expand the Conference on Security and Cooperation in Europe could be met through a conference that would institutionalize measures to build relationships among the European states. The two Germanys could move forward on their treaty on political unification, and following the first CFE Treaty, lower limits could be negotiated on the united Germany's armed forces. Germany could provide significant economic benefits to the Soviet Union in addition to those offered by other Atlantic Alliance members.

In return for this sequence of opportunities and benefits, the Soviet Union would agree to withdraw its military forces from Eastern Europe and to accept a unified Germany's full membership in the Atlantic Alliance. The Soviet reaction to the London Declaration in July 1990 was favorable. According to Soviet Foreign Minister Shevardnadze,

> In London it was declared that the West extends its hand to the East. For our part, we are ready to extend our hand toward them.[11]

The official Soviet statement about the London Declaration said that while its proposals "should be corroborated by specific deeds," it was nevertheless certain that "the decisions adopted move in the right direction and pave the way to a safe future for the entire European continent."[12] The Soviet reaction also emphasized that they had taken the initiative on a number of issues that NATO now accepted in principle, such as regular meetings between NATO and Warsaw Pact states "to discuss military doctrines."

By the time of the London Declaration, the Soviet Union had already signed agreements to withdraw all its military forces from Hungary (65,000), Czechoslovakia (70,000), and Poland (40,000) by the summer of 1991, though relatively few had left to date. Clearly the newly elected governments in Hungary and Czechoslovakia wanted the Soviet troops to leave on an accelerated basis; by the spring of 1990 Hungary was openly discussing its wish to leave the Warsaw Pact. This state of affairs, along with the fact that three Eastern European governments had stated their support for continued German membership in NATO, added further momentum to the process—a momentum fueled even from within the Warsaw Pact.

Neither the NATO summit nor the Houston economic summit in July 1990 brought decisions to accept the West German-French proposal for a $15 billion economic aid program for the Soviet Union. The U.S. again urged that the Soviet Union reduce its military expenditures and its military and economic subsidies to hostile foreign states. There was a general undertone of Western dissatisfaction with the tough conditions the Soviets had proposed at the June 1990 two-plus-four meeting. In mid-July 1990, when Chancellor Kohl made his second journey of the year to the Soviet Union to discuss unification with President Gorbachev, West Germany made it clear that there would be no further concessions or economic benefits until the Soviets consented to allow a unified Germany to remain in NATO.[13]

After two days of discussions, the Soviet and German leaders jointly announced a new treaty defining Soviet-German political,

124

economic, military, scientific, and cultural relations. In exchange for this the Soviet Union was renouncing any restrictions on Germany's future sovereignty, including its right to join the NATO alliance.[14] Gorbachev said, "We are leaving one epoch in international relations and entering another period, I think, of strong, prolonged peace."[15] Kohl also noted, "We could not have reached this agreement without the context in which the visit took place. . . . In recent months we've had tens of summit meetings at which all these burning questions touching on the fundamental changes in Europe were discussed." Kohl also made it clear that a reunited Germany would remain in NATO, and Gorbachev commented: "Whether we want it or not, the day will come when the reality will be that a united Germany is in NATO, and if that is its choice then it will still make formal arrangements to cooperate with the Soviet Union and that is to our advantage."[16]

Among the specific commitments announced in the Kohl-Gorbachev meeting were the following:

• A unified Germany would not produce, hold, or command atomic, biological, or chemical weapons; it would remain a party to the Nonproliferation Treaty.

• The future German army would be limited to 370,000—a reduction from the 667,000 for the combined forces of West and East Germany 494,000 and 173,000 (pre-October 1989 total), respectively.

• Soviet troops would be permitted to remain on the former East German territory for a three-to-four-year transition period, and Germany would pay the costs; U.S., French, and British troops would be invited by Germany to remain in West Berlin until all Soviet troops were gone from Germany.

• No NATO troops, nuclear weapons, or German troops under NATO command would be deployed on former East German territory during the transition, or, perhaps, afterward.

• Germany would provide economic benefits to the Soviet Union which were not publicly specified, but which would probably include additional German purchases of Soviet oil and gas in exchange for hard currency; German credits; direct financial aid; and the possibility of substantial transfers of technology and capital investment to the Soviet Union.

Except for the unknown dimension of potential German economic benefits for the Soviet Union, all of these conditions fell within the terms of the nine assurances offered by President Bush in June 1990 and the terms of NATO's London Declaration. For this reason the reaction was uniformly positive from the leaders of the Atlantic

Alliance countries. Further confirmation of approval came at the July 17, 1990, meeting of the two-plus-four foreign ministers, where both Germanys formally assured the Polish foreign minister that a reunified Germany would seek no changes in its borders.[17]

Looking to the immediate future, Kohl said the Soviet Union had formally agreed to conclude the two-plus-four discussions in time for the planned November 1990 CSCE conference to endorse German reunification.[18] That in turn would permit Kohl and de Maizière to move ahead with plans for all German elections in December 1990. See table 7–1 for an overview of these events.

Although this represented a historically important success for the Kohl-Bush-NATO strategy, it did not necessarily mean that Soviet long-term objectives toward Germany had changed. With a significant portion of the 380,000 Soviet troops in East Germany slated to remain until the end of 1994, the Soviets could undoubtedly calculate on using them as a bargaining lever, to ensure that the unified German government took no actions contrary to Soviet interests. Since a unified Germany would obviously not be fully independent until the unwanted Soviet troops were actually gone, the Soviet Union might seek to trade faster withdrawal for the removal of U.S. and other NATO troops on West German territory. In Germany the SPD is likely to seek the removal of foreign troops, and even a CDU-CSU–FDP coalition government might in the future be persuaded to go along with such an exchange.

The Soviets might also calculate that as the CSCE process became institutionalized year by year, a number of member states could gradually move away from the Atlantic Alliance, which in time would wither away. In addition, by having permitted a unified Germany to be in the Atlantic Alliance but promised to reduce a significant part of its forces in Europe, the Soviet Union could expect NATO's net military strength to decline significantly. One German observer has written about the urge toward "competitive disarmament" within NATO, in the absence of a perceived military threat from the Soviet Union.[19]

Perhaps another reason for the Soviet Union's acquiescence in the formal membership of reunified Germany in NATO is the knowledge that the massive Soviet strategic nuclear forces ensure that it will remain the most militarily powerful country in Europe. In February 1990 the U.S. Department of Defense reported that the Soviet Union had 2,952 strategic nuclear delivery vehicles, with a total of 13,322 hydrogen bombs on those missiles and bombers. The United States had 1,899 missiles and bombers, armed with 12,570 hydrogen bombs.[20] Even if a strategic-arms-reduction treaty between the United

TABLE 7–1: The Road to Reunification of Germany
within the Atlantic Alliance, 1990

July 2, 1990—East Germany adopts West Germany's currency and economic and social system.

July 5–6, 1990—NATO heads of government meet in London and issue the London Declaration on a Transformed North Atlantic Alliance. The document declares the cold war over, promises no first use of force under any circumstances, declares nuclear weapons a "last resort," and expresses willingness to sign a nonaggression pact with the Warsaw Pact and all of its members.

July 6, 1990—East Germany and West Germany begin negotiations to establish a timetable and framework for full unification by December 1990, to include all-German elections on December 2, 1990.

July 9–11, 1990—At the Houston economic summit of the seven leading industrial democracies, Germany and France propose $15 billion in economic aid to the Soviet Union. The representatives commission a study of potential economic aid to the Soviet Union.

July 14, 1990—NATO Secretary General Manfred Woerner meets with Gorbachev in Moscow to deliver the London Declaration and to invite Gorbachev to address NATO in Brussels. Gorbachev accepts.

July 15–16, 1990—Kohl meets with Gorbachev in the Soviet Union to persuade him to allow a united Germany to be a member of NATO. Gorbachev agrees, in the context of limits on German armaments and a promised German-Soviet treaty to include unspecified levels of German economic and technical aid.

July 17, 1990—The two-plus-four talks held in Paris, with Poland as an additional participant, codify the existing German borders as permanent.

August 1990—East and West Germany complete a treaty on political unification.

September 12, 1990—Two-plus-four talks lead to the signing of the Treaty on the Final Settlement with Respect to Germany, which restores German sovereignty and defines the international aspects of German reunification.

September 1990—Elections are held in the five reconstituted East German states, allowing them to complete the process of accession to West Germany under Article 23 of its constitution.

October 3, 1990—German reunification is completed.

November 9, 1990—Gorbachev visits Kohl for the formal signing of German-Soviet treaties.

November 19–21, 1990—Paris CSCE conference endorses: German reunification; the signing of a treaty to reduce conventional forces in Europe (CFE); and the Declaration of Paris to expand CSCE functions and establish several CSCE entities.

December 2, 1990—German national elections scheduled and held as an all-German election.

December 13–14, 1990—The European Community met to discuss future steps toward political unity and foreign policy cooperation.

Source: Author.

States and the Soviet Union gradually cuts these forces by 40 percent, this massive nuclear superiority over European states means that "the Soviet Union will . . . [have] plentiful nuclear options against Europe that no amount of disarmament can suppress."[21] Further, the Soviet Union will retain a large portion of its conventional armed forces, estimated at 4.5 million in 1990. These alone would constitute a significant coercive threat from the Soviet perspective.

In summary, the Soviet Union may have been moved to accept a reunified Germany's membership in NATO by the symbolic and practical concessions Germany and the Atlantic Alliance offered, by anticipated tangible economic rewards, and by its confidence in its own military superiority, both in conventional and nuclear weapons, enabling it to act decisively if its basic interests were threatened. A further reason might be the Soviet perception that this course would be most likely to bring about a desirably altered Atlantic Alliance. Over the years the Alliance could change from an effective military deterrent into a loose political coalition, in a Western Europe that could grow unaccustomed to serious efforts at maintaining military self-defense. In the Soviet view this could lead to Western Europe's becoming separated from the United States in any real military sense. Thus, in line with the Soviet strategy of "removing the image of the enemy," permitting a reunified Germany to remain in NATO might be part of a continuing Soviet effort to bring about the de facto neutralization of Germany, as we will examine in chapter 8. First, however, it is important to outline some of the possible effects that can result from a reunified Germany's remaining in NATO.

Implications of a Reunified Germany's Membership in NATO

This discussion will consider seven possible consequences of effective NATO membership for a united Germany in an effective NATO. First, remaining in the Atlantic Alliance will further strengthen German democratic institutions at a time of transition, as a new international order is formed in Europe and 16 million individuals who have lived under Communist dictatorship are absorbed.

In March 1990 the East Germans voted for freedom; 84 percent voted against the Communist regime that had been in power for forty-five years. Like many people who have experienced Soviet methods, of course, millions of East German adults are likely to retain a fear of the Soviet Union and a fear of what might happen should the Soviet leadership change its views on having permitted political liberalization to occur in Eastern Europe. The shared democratic values of the Atlantic Alliance, its entirely defensive character, its success in preventing war for more than four decades, and its role as the shield behind which the political and economic institutions of Western Europe could develop all constitute what the Christian Democrats have called "the European roof" under which unification could take place. Continuing membership in the Atlantic Alliance will give all the major political parties in Germany an added sense of confidence about the future, permitting Germany to deal with any possible changes for the worse in Soviet policy. That confidence will create and reinforce the positive expectations within which German democracy can continue to develop. As the astute German observer Josef Joffe has written:

> The reassuring career of the Bonn Republic cannot be divorced from the ultra-stable European order . . . built in and around Germany. . . . In historical terms the postwar order was 'just right': it protected Germany against others and against itself; it pulled the sting of Russian as well as of German power; and it achieved all this not by imposition and discrimination but by community and integration. Paranoid nationalism cannot fester when safety is reassured within so cozy a framework.[22]

Given the German-Soviet treaty and the new dimensions of that bilateral relationship, Germany's continued membership in the Atlantic Alliance will be all the more necessary to avoid misunderstandings in the West—especially as the institutions of a new Europe evolve and are tested by time.

Effects on the European Community. A second consequence of Germany's continued membership in the Atlantic Alliance might be improved political cohesion in the European Community. The economic integration of 1992 and the political transformation of Europe make the early 1990s a time of transition for the European Community in its relations with the rest of the world. By remaining in the Atlantic Alliance, in which eleven of the twelve EC members also participate, Germany is far more likely to coordinate its foreign and security policies effectively with the European Community—at least in matters directly involving Europe.

Conversely, a Germany no longer in the Atlantic Alliance could perceive of itself as swinging back and forth, between its interests in the East and those in the West—precisely the kind of swing politics that proved so disastrous for Germany and for Europe in the past. Undoubtedly the need to guard against this perception accounts in part for Chancellor Kohl's joining President Mitterrand in 1990 to propose greater coordination of foreign policy within the European Community. This was important to assure France, Germany's closest European partner, as well as the other members of the European Community, and to embed further a reunified Germany in Western Europe.

Peace in Europe. Third, Germany's remaining in the Atlantic Alliance might significantly increase the probability of further peaceful evolution in Europe—even if Soviet policy should change for the worse. As a member of NATO Germany can contribute its resources, its political presence, the physical space of its territory, and its reduced but significant military forces to ensure the maintenance of a military deterrent against Soviet coercion or attack. Such a credible military deterrent could prevent any potential Soviet miscalculation that might lead to a campaign of coercion against Germany or any other NATO country. Without Germany many West European countries might feel defenseless.

Political and Economic Support. A Germany remaining in NATO will be far more able to provide political and economic support to prodemocratic governments and groups in Eastern Europe. Germany would then have the confidence to increase its involvement in Eastern Europe, not only in commercial terms—something that is likely to happen in any case—but also to use its immense post–World War II political experience, resources, and democratic legitimacy to help build and strengthen genuinely democratic institutions in the East European countries. Despite obstacles, the people of Poland, Hungary, and Czechoslovakia might be able to achieve full political democracy in the next years. And it may well be that Germany could also play a major role in the more difficult and extended process of reinforcing democratic and free-market institutions in Yugoslavia, Bulgaria, Romania, and perhaps even Albania.

If Germany should withdraw from the Atlantic Alliance it might be much more diffident in its support of democratic leaders and institutions—many of whom would be in conflict with Soviet foreign policy objectives. Virtually all such institutions would be in competition with Soviet-supported national Communist parties and the remaining hard-core networks of secret police, military, and party personnel working directly with the Soviet Union. In the vortex of complex, often hidden struggle that will mark East European transitions in the 1990s, a Germany not protected and reinforced by NATO might proceed with far less confidence, vigor, and positive effect in the cause of helping to build the institutions of political democracy.

Free-Market Institutions. The same principle applies to the development of free-market economic institutions in Eastern Europe. Germany's growing commercial relationship with Eastern Europe is certain, but this relationship need not necessarily include German concern with market institutions. Those groups within Eastern Europe seeking the expansion of free-market institutions will be allied with those seeking democracy, and Germany can have an enormously constructive impact in furthering both goals. It is the explicit intention of the Atlantic Alliance, as expressed in the London Declaration of July 1990, that the Conference on Security and Cooperation in Europe should further both goals. As a member of the Atlantic Alliance with the political confidence and resolution to act diligently, Germany would do far more than it would as an unattached neutral country, keeping one eye carefully alert for signs of Soviet displeasure.

The U.S. Presence. With Germany in the Atlantic Alliance, the United States is far more likely to continue to maintain a significant military presence in Western Europe. That fact in itself would contribute to the maintenance of peace, stability, and deterrence during the transitional years. If Germany became neutral it would almost certainly request that the United States and all other Atlantic Alliance members withdraw virtually all their forces from its territory. Far more than might be perceived at present, the departure of those 420,000 Allied troops—especially the U.S. forces, returning across the Atlantic Ocean—would weaken the European capacity to maintain a credible deterrent and would separate the United States politically and militarily from the Atlantic Alliance. The number of U.S. and Allied forces stationed in Germany might be considerably reduced even with Germany in NATO, as a result of future arms reduction agreements, but Germany's participation in the Atlantic Alliance will provide American political leaders with an important basis for maintaining a significant political and military commitment to Europe.

Resistance to Soviet Pressure. The Soviet Union evidently intends to extract a considerable price from Germany in return for acquiescence to Germany's NATO membership and for the promised withdrawal of Soviet forces. Chancellor Kohl's government understands that there is a broad consensus among German political leaders for a policy of expanded Soviet-German economic relations—one that will involve Germany's giving the Soviet Union economic and technological assistance for some years. If Germany were not in the Atlantic

131

Alliance, the degree of Soviet extraction of German resources would likely be far greater than otherwise.

As long as Germany is a member of NATO, it will be better able to refuse those Soviet "requests" for money or technology that go beyond what German leaders consider reasonable. This refusal might in turn have the constructive effect of preventing the Soviet leadership from using German economic and technological resources as a substitute for internal Soviet economic and political reforms, which could foster pluralism and improve the Soviet standard of living and economy over the long term. It will also reduce the likelihood that German resources and technology would provide the Soviet Union with a dangerous margin of military superiority.

Security for Germany, Security from Germany. As the distinguished scholar Wolfram Hanrieder has written, NATO provides "security for Germany, and security from Germany."[23] The countries of Eastern Europe are more likely to welcome close relations with a NATO-anchored Germany than with a neutral Germany, which they might perceive as attempting to build its own "bloc" of neutral states between East and West. Further, German membership in NATO would reassure all of Europe that Germany had virtually no reason to seek nuclear weapons. Both perceptions would contribute to stability in Europe.

The evolution toward democracy in Eastern Europe, the ensuing reunification of Germany, and the Soviet decision to allow a reunited Germany to remain in the Atlantic Alliance have all been enormously beneficial events. They contribute to the cause of democracy and peace in Europe. These events represent a major triumph of Western values, institutions, and current leadership. If Germany remains a full member of a militarily effective NATO until the Soviet Union itself makes a full transition to genuine democracy, the prospects for peace and peaceful evolution in Eastern Europe will greatly increase, and the level of armaments in Europe will decrease. This outcome is possible but another possible outcome must also be examined.

8
Reunification and de Facto Neutralization

During the twentieth century Germany and the Soviet Union—the two major continental powers of Europe—fought each other in two world wars. They also concluded many surprising, often sudden agreements, such as the Rapallo Pact for Economic Cooperation in 1922, the Hitler-Stalin Alliance in 1939, the 1990 agreements on reunification in NATO, and a German-Soviet cooperation. The lesson taught by contemporary history is that German-Soviet relations are complex, are of vital interest to both countries, are subject to surprising shifts, and have a major impact on world affairs.

For Stalin, one such surprise was Hitler's decision in June 1941 to break the 1939 agreements and invade the Soviet Union. The resulting war led to the deaths in the Soviet Union of "at least 7 million men in battle and a further 7 million civilians."[1] Further, of 5.2 million Soviet troops captured under German control, it is estimated that about 3.3 million died "by neglect or murder at German hands."[2] In the same war Germany lost 4 million soldiers and 600,000 civilians, killed with most of the German fatalities on the Eastern Front in battles with the Soviet Union.[3]

That history explains why each of these two countries since the end of World War II has made its relationship with the other a major focus of its foreign policy. The reunification of Germany has made the bilateral relationship even more important for both countries. As one German scholar has noted, after World War II the Soviet Union held that

> Germany had to be impeded from ever again being able to threaten the Soviet Union militarily and that there were two alternative ways of attaining this goal: A Germany that was autonomous but more or less dependent on the Soviet Union, or a separate Communist state carved out by the division of Germany.[4]

For the next forty-five years a major purpose of Soviet foreign policy was first to prevent and then to reverse the rearmament of Germany and its inclusion in a military alliance with the United States and West European countries. As the dramatic events of 1989 unfolded in Europe, the Soviet Union at first opposed the approaching reunification of Germany and its membership in NATO. It later acceded to the momentum of political events, however, agreeing that reunification could occur, and subsequently agreeing that a reunified Germany could remain a member of NATO.

The issue might end here; but it is possible that the July 1990 Soviet decision to trade German membership in NATO for a comprehensive German-Soviet agreement on cooperation was a tactical concession, reflecting no change in the Soviet intention to bring about the de facto neutralization of Germany and the dismantling of NATO. For that reason it is worth exploring how the Soviet Union might seek to achieve this objective and the implications of such a development.

Soviet Policy toward Postwar Germany

In December 1941 German tank divisions were within sight of Moscow; much of the Soviet Union had been overrun, and the Soviet government had been evacuated to a distant city beyond the Ural Mountains. The Soviet capacity for long-range strategic thinking about Germany is illustrated by the following vignette, related by William Hyland, a former senior U.S. government official. Stalin was receiving Anthony Eden, foreign minister of Great Britain, the new Soviet ally in that black moment of December 1941:

> One might think that Stalin would have been preoccupied with obtaining military assistance or stimulating any desperate scheme to relieve the pressure on his front. Yet the conversations primarily concerned Russia's postwar ambitions. Stalin presented draft treaties for a military alliance and for postwar political cooperation. In addition he had a secret protocol in which the British would agree to recognize new western boundaries for the USSR. As for Germany, Stalin's scheme was simple: Germany would be dismembered into rump states. . . . [There would be] a transfer of [German] territory to Poland. The USSR would collect substantial reparations [from Germany].[5]

After the war Stalin partially carried out his plans, annexing territory from Poland and compensating Poland with territory annexed from Germany. The Soviet Union also collected billions in reparations from occupied Germany, including reparations from the new Communist state of East Germany until 1954, along with occupation costs, paid by East Germany until 1959.[6]

The Soviet Union's various stratagems of pressures and diplomatic maneuvering in the late 1940s—including the blockade of Berlin—were unsuccessful in preventing the establishment of West Germany and later in preventing West German rearmament and membership in NATO. It is worth recalling, however, that one of the Soviet efforts to prevent German rearmament and military integration with a Western alliance was Stalin's 1952 offer of a reunified, neutral, demilitarized Germany with free elections. Another was the 1954 Soviet proposal for the establishment of a Conference on Security and Cooperation in Europe, which was to include all the European powers but to exclude the United States.[7]

The post-Stalin Soviet leadership initially tried a diplomacy of normalization with the West. Soviet troops were withdrawn from Austria, which was permitted to become fully independent as a neutral state. The Soviets participated in the Geneva Summit of 1955 and took the initiative to open diplomatic relations with West Germany after it joined NATO. This policy was followed in the late 1950s by a diplomacy of coercion—including the Soviet ultimatums about Berlin, the building of the Berlin Wall, and the nuclear confrontation over the 1962 emplacement of Soviet missiles and hydrogen weapons in Cuba. The post-Khrushchev leader, Brezhnev, then returned to a diplomacy of normalization. As Hyland relates,

> In 1965–1967 the Soviets began to emphasize a European security conference, which would have as its starting point the dissolution of military blocs. As a subsidiary theme, there was a Soviet attempt to exclude the United States from participation.[8]

A member of the German parliament and scholar of Soviet issues, Hans Huyn, points out that in 1981 it was Brezhnev and not Gorbachev who began talking about "a common European home."[9] Defectors from European Communist regimes have shown evidence that since the 1960s "the Soviets had developed a mechanism for running the Warsaw Pact as a military alliance through Comecon [the economic organization] so the Warsaw Pact could be 'dissolved' without altering capabilities."[10] In 1984 a defector from the Soviet KGB, Anatole Golitsyn, published a book revealing that in the early 1980s Soviet strategic plans included the intention to reduce sharply the perception of a Soviet or Communist threat among the Western Europeans, as a means of achieving the neutralization of Germany.[11]

Soon after Gorbachev was named by the Politburo as the new

leader of the Soviet Communist party in March 1985, he made the diplomatic proposals that evolved into the new era of détente, marked by U.S.-Soviet summit meetings in every year from 1985 to 1990. In 1985 Gorbachev proposed a moratorium on the Soviet deployment of additional intermediate-range nuclear-armed missiles targeted against Western Europe and a halt to the testing of nuclear weapons. In 1986 he wrote to a leader in the British Labor party that if the United Kingdom dismantled all its nuclear weapons and removed the U.S. nuclear bases, the Soviet Union would no longer regard it as a nuclear target.[12] In that year Gorbachev also proposed a worldwide ban on all nuclear weapons to take effect in the year 2000—one of the main themes discussed in the 1986 U.S.-Soviet summit, held in Iceland. In June 1987 the United States proposed a "global double zero option" for the complete elimination of both types of intermediate-range nuclear missiles from Europe. By December 1987 an agreement to bring this about was signed by the United States and the Soviet Union at a summit meeting in Washington, D.C.

From the Soviet point of view two important interests were served by this agreement. First, it eliminated what Soviet sources described as "the potential capability of the U.S.A. to create for us at any moment an extremely uncomfortable military threat," meaning nuclear-armed missiles that could reach Soviet targets in ten minutes.[13] Politically, the Soviet Union perceived the treaty as weakening the "military presence of the U.S.A. in its . . . positions both in Europe and Asia," a Soviet advantage that "corresponds to our military and political interests."[14] Dr. Gerhardt Wettig, a German scholar who studies the Soviet Union, notes that after the INF treaty was signed Gorbachev emphasized that it provided a start for "the next stage of struggle for disarmament and peace, including ideological struggle that would be carried on within Western societies."[15] The Soviets believed that the effect of the 1987 INF treaty would be the "devaluation of American nuclear guarantees" for Western Europe, including Germany. They contended that in time the consequence would be to put "the question before the West European politicians what value the [North Atlantic] bloc still had under these conditions."[16] Therefore, the elimination of NATO was part of the Soviet motivation for concluding this agreement.

The former U.S. Ambassador to France (1981–1985), Evan G. Galbraith, held this perspective on Soviet thinking and pointed out the potential political risks of the 1987 INF agreement. Writing in May 1987, some months before the final agreement was concluded, Ambassador Galbraith said:

U.S. nuclear missiles [in] West Germany . . . serve to reinforce the will of the German people to defend themselves.
Without these weapons their determination will erode. The
supposed protection offered by U.S.-based strategic forces is
not enough. Few Europeans believe that the U.S. President
would let go a salvo of U.S.-based strategic nuclear missiles—thus provoking the almost certain destruction of
American cities—solely in defense of Western Europe.[17]

Galbraith went on to write that "to give up East Germany in exchange
for a neutral Central Europe and decimated NATO is not a bad deal
for a strategic thinker like Gorbachev. . . . Don't be surprised if they
offer the reunification of Germany—that is, a denuclearized, largely
demilitarized, neutral Germany."[18]

By 1988 Gorbachev's proposed internal reform efforts, glasnost
and perestroika, were widely believed in by most people in the West.
Western perceptions of a fundamental change in Soviet foreign policy
objectives were reinforced both by the Soviet decision to remove most
of its combat forces from Afghanistan by early 1989 and by Soviet
participation in the agreement signed among Cuba, Angola, and
South Africa, concerning the conflict between the pro-Soviet regime
in Angola and the anti-Communist armed resistance movement.[19]
Glasnost was extended to military issues, to include Soviet proposals
for expanded negotiations on confidence-building measures in Europe and Soviet invitations to U.S. military leaders to visit formerly
sensitive military facilities in the Soviet Union. After the chairman of
the U.S. joint chiefs of staff, Admiral William Crowe, visited the
Soviet Union in 1989, he returned saying they are "not my enemy.
. . . Soviets are a great deal like Americans." This led Gorbachev to
comment, "Admiral Crowe's visit to this country in our military
facilities demonstrates that we're moving from the notion of enemy
to the notion of partner."[20]

Gorbachev's leading adviser on the United States had said explicitly in 1987 that the Soviet Union "would remove the image of the
enemy" in the West. In December 1988 Gorbachev gave the dramatic
promise at the United Nations to make unilateral Soviet military
reductions of 500,000 men, out of a force approximating 4.5 million.
This promise, combined with the beginning of liberalization in Poland
in the spring of 1989 and U.S.–Soviet détente, established a spirit of
positive expectations and warm enthusiasm when Gorbachev paid a
state visit to Germany in June 1989.

From the summer of 1989 to the summer of 1990 momentous,
beneficial changes occurred in Eastern Europe. They could not have
occurred had the Soviet Union decided to prevent the unraveling of

Communist regimes with whatever level of force might be necessary. The NATO leaders' London Declaration of July 1990 thereupon formally declared the Soviet Union no longer to be an enemy and made a number of changes intended to highlight NATO's defensive character and reduce its military capabilities, especially German-based conventional and nuclear forces. And throughout this dramatic time, the Soviet leadership constantly repeated that it sought the replacement of both alliances by a new European collective security arrangement.

The de facto neutralization of Germany would be a large step toward this Soviet objective and might be achieved in any of three ways. First, a reunified Germany could formally leave NATO at a later date. Second, a reunified Germany might remain associated with NATO but no longer function as a member of the military command; it might perhaps request that all or most of the 420,000 deployed foreign NATO forces leave German territory. Third, NATO itself might change to the point that it no longer posed a credible military deterrent to Soviet coercion or attack. This could occur in a number of ways, including large-scale unilateral reductions in existing forces, redeployments of forces, the removal of all or nearly all European-based nuclear weapons, and the end of a realistic military doctrine and operational command for conducting an effective defense in the event of crisis or proximate threat. It is certainly within the capability of Soviet statecraft simultaneously to pursue all three methods of neutralizing Germany and NATO.

Given the international political context following the events of July 1990—German economic reunification, the NATO London Declaration, and the Soviet-German agreement on reunification—a logical approach for the Soviet Union would be to seek the de facto neutralization of Germany by coordinating its actions to encourage existing trends in four arenas: in Germany; in diplomacy among the NATO countries, especially France; in the United States; and in Eastern Europe.

The New Germany

The central role of Germany in the military structure of NATO is illustrated by a few facts. In 1988 nearly 1 million NATO forces were stationed on German territory—495,000 from West Germany and about 425,000 from six Allied countries. The former West Germany alone held more than 4,000 military installations for the NATO forces, and during the late 1980s more than 1 million air sorties were flown each year in German air space and 5,000 military exercises were conducted on German territory to maintain NATO readiness.[21]

138

Having obtained reaffirmation of West Germany's pledge not to acquire nuclear, biological, or chemical weapons, the Soviet Union will likely pursue the removal of Allied nuclear weapons from German territory in its bilateral dealings with the German government and public. Both the Soviet and German political leaders know that public opinion polls suggest denuclearization is very much desired by most of the German population.

In future negotiations concerning the timing of the withdrawal of 380,000 Soviet troops from formerly East German territory, the Soviet Union might well link the pace of withdrawal to additional political, economic, or military concessions from Germany—for example, that Germany reduce the size of its combined armed forces below the agreed upon level of 367,000. As the Soviet government knows, in February 1990 a leading West German Social Democrat had said "security partnership means . . . reduction of the *Bundeswehr* [army] to 240,000 . . . [,] disarmament by 50 percent in the conventional field, drastic reduction of long- and medium-range arsenals . . . [, and] finally, dissolution of the military blocs."[22] The Kohl government had already announced its plans to reduce the West German Army to 400,000 and to make further cuts, but the FDP, the coalition partner of the CDU-CSU, said in late 1989 that it wanted the West German armed forces reduced to no more than 350,000.[23] The Soviet Union may well use the leverage of its troop pullout to encourage both the full denuclearization of German territory and the increasing self-demilitarization of a reunified Germany.

It is also quite possible that the Soviet Union could seek some type of parity between the withdrawal of its troops from the former East German territory and the withdrawal of U.S. and other NATO forces from the former West German territory. Political momentum for the removal of foreign NATO troops could gain force from a German perception of Soviet reasonableness in permitting Germany to remain in NATO and cooperation in the context of the 1990 German-Soviet treaty. Such a view has long been held by the SPD, the Greens, and elements of the FDP. After all, in the postunification context many Germans would argue there is no longer any Soviet threat. If the combination of internal political trends and Soviet persuasiveness were to lead the reunified German government to denuclearize, to further reduce its armed forces, and to remove all or nearly all NATO troops—including virtually all the U.S. troops—the cumulative result could be the de facto neutralization of Germany, even if it were to continue as a member of NATO.

From the Soviet point of view, even though the SPD lost the December 1990 German elections, that important party's views, expressed in Parliament, in public discussion, and in the national media, will provide an opportunity to encourage German self-demilitarization. If the Soviet Union can continue to maintain the image of not being a military threat, it will expect that many in the SPD will continue pressing for the de facto substitution of membership in a European collective security arrangement such as CSCE for reliance on NATO. Even before the events of 1989–1990, the SPD was moving in that direction—contending that it is the most realistic way to maintain peace. After the Soviets' reasonableness in 1990, the SPD could argue that the success of German reunification and the unraveling of communism in Eastern Europe render a security alliance no longer necessary and the collective security approach the best guarantee for a future of peace.

The "antinuclear left" dominated the German SPD during the 1980s. As early as 1982 its leader and candidate for chancellor in the 1990 election, Oskar Lafontaine, called for the withdrawal of the Federal Republic from the military part of NATO, declaring at the SPD party congress that year, "I find it unbearable that the American president alone can decide on the use of nuclear weapons in our country."[24] Although the SPD did not win the December 1990 elections, it received, along with the Green party, 37 percent of the vote, and therefore could act as a strong pressure-group for denuclearization, demilitarization, and the distancing of Germany from NATO. Given the tendency of an important sector of the Free Democratic party to share these perspectives, the Soviet Union could well calculate that even though the CDU-CSU–FDP coalition continues as the government of Germany, it could find itself compelled to make a series of decisions and concessions on security issues that would in effect bring about German neutralization in the next years.

The Soviet-German agreement permits Soviet forces to remain on East German territory until the end of 1994. Augmenting that presence, the large Soviet diplomatic, commercial, and intelligence contingent in Germany—both open and covert—might attempt to supplement Soviet conventional diplomacy through a series of direct actions intended to bring about the removal of all foreign NATO forces, especially American, from Germany at the request of the reunified German government. The initial reluctance of some NATO Allies to welcome German unity, especially former British Prime Minister Thatcher's, and the comments from some in NATO countries about the need to "keep Germany down" could all be used to create a sense of antagonism between Germany and other NATO members. Real or fabricated hostile remarks about Germany might be exploited to create the impression in Germany that remaining in the Alliance is an expression of submission and inferiority rather than of independence and sovereignty.

The Soviet Union has the capacity to use agents of influence in Germany to mount political action campaigns intended to create a national mood favoring a European security arrangement, and opposing the "anachronism" of NATO. It might also use such direct means as provoking hostile incidents between German civilians and U.S. forces in a systematic strategy to achieve its objective. Taken together, the strong positions evolved by the antinuclear left of the SPD's 1980s leadership and the Soviet capacity to reach German public opinion directly may in the end have a significant impact—perhaps even more in the aftermath of the 1991 war to counter Iraq's aggression against Kuwait.

As an illustration of how the SPD views Germany and NATO, consider this remark made in March 1990 by Horst Ehmke, a leading SPD member of the German parliament: "You cannot shift the border line of NATO to the East and at the same time say we will not take advantage of what is happening in Eastern Europe. . . ." Ehmke went on to contend that after reunification Germany would leave NATO, and "NATO and the Warsaw Pact would both be replaced by a new security system."[25]

France and Other NATO Members

The German intention to cut back its military forces is likely to be reinforced by the actions of other prominent NATO members. Even before the dramatic events of 1989, many NATO countries had concluded that the Gorbachev-led Soviet Union and Warsaw Pact were much less threatening, and they announced budget cuts or freezes. These countries included Denmark (a three-year defense spending freeze was announced in March 1989); Canada (defense cuts were announced for 1989–1994); Italy (defense spending was frozen until the year 2000, with the army reduced by 35,000 in 1989–1990); the Netherlands (budget cuts and military personnel are to be reduced by 15 percent by 1997); the United Kingdom (budget cuts were made in 1990); and the United States (cuts planned for the 1991–1995 period by the Bush administration include two army divisions, two aircraft carrier battle groups, fifty-two other naval ships, and 20 percent cuts in the size of the marine corps and the army).[26] Except for Turkey and France, virtually all NATO member-countries reduced their armed forces in 1990.

By the early 1990s the strategic arsenal of France is to include 600 submarine-launched nuclear warheads.[27] France also has its own tactical nuclear missiles, the Pluton and the Hades, the latter with a range of 250 miles. Logically, it would be in France's national interest to keep a reunified Germany in NATO and maintain close French-German bilateral political and security cooperation. It would also be in France's interest to reassure Germany in the new Europe by extending its nuclear protection to a reunified Germany. Certainly the Kohl government made every effort in 1990 to deepen and encourage bilateral cooperation with France—for example, taking a number of joint diplomatic initiatives related to the further political integration of the European Community. It is quite possible, then, that France will remain a steadfast advocate of a reunified Germany's continued full membership in an effective NATO.

The Soviet Union, however, may well attempt to move France away from this position. During the entire post–World War II era, the Soviets gave special attention to establishing a distinctive bilateral relationship with France in an effort to split the Atlantic Alliance and to play upon France's latent fear of Germany before and after its rearmament.

In the 1960s, General de Gaulle, as president of France, proposed a "Europe from the Atlantic to the Urals." This proposal included the Soviet Union but excluded the United States. Since France was not willing to rely on the nuclear protection of the United States, de Gaulle sped up the creation of France's independent nuclear force and in 1966 withdrew from the joint military command of NATO and required the NATO military headquarters to move out of French territory. In December 1989 the Soviet effort to continue a special relationship with France was evident in the statement by French President Mitterrand, following his meeting with Gorbachev in the Soviet Union, agreeing that German reunification was proceeding too quickly.[28]

In February 1990 French Foreign Minister Ronald Dumas derided U.S. support for the continued existence of NATO as "anachronistic."[29] Dumas reflected the conventional leftist view in the governing French Socialist party, which largely agrees with the view of the left wing of the German SPD—that the time has come for an all-European security system, not necessarily including the United States.[30] Gorbachev and the Soviet leaders will undoubtedly seek to entice France with a vision of its growing influence in a new post-NATO Europe, from which most American military forces would have withdrawn.

In the next years, a French government might perhaps conclude that if Germany no longer felt protected by U.S. nuclear weapons in Europe—either because the U.S. strategic guarantee was no longer credible or because of de facto German neutrality—then the only source of nuclear protection would be France. Such a Realpolitik perspective might suggest that Germany, separated from the American nuclear guarantee by the weakening or elimination of NATO, would depend on the French nuclear deterrent for its security and therefore might be far less of a competitive problem to France— politically and economically, in the European Community and in Eastern Europe. Such thinking could lead some in France to welcome the evolution of events in the direction of Germany's following the French example: leaving the NATO military command and permitting few Allied forces or weapons on its territory.

The United States

A recurrent theme of Soviet diplomacy in the Gorbachev years was that the United States and the West must take specific steps to reduce the Soviet Union's fear of Western and specifically German military power. This thinking was not new. As Hyland has written, during the 1950s and the 1960s the Soviet Union succeeded in creating the perception among many Western leaders that "if they could satisfy Soviet security interests, the unification of Germany could then be settled."[31] The July 1990 London Declaration of the NATO leadership represented a significant effort to accommodate perceived Soviet security concerns. NATO's acceptance of a ceiling on German military forces and other such accommodating steps most likely will in turn be used by those within Germany seeking denuclearization, demilitarization, and the removal of U.S. troops.

The Soviet use of civility in its relations with NATO, Germany, and the United States may well be one aspect of its maneuvering to encourage precisely this kind of evolution, away from military preparedness, toward the self-demilitarization of Germany and NATO as a whole. When the Soviet Union accepted the offer of the Bush administration in February 1990 to limit U.S. and Soviet forces on the central front to 195,000 each, it well understood that this would mean moving its forces back several hundred miles from their current deployments, while 200,000 or more American troops would move 3,000 miles across an ocean. The Soviet leadership probably assumed that once 200,000 U.S. forces had left Germany pursuant to this joint agreement, the political effect within Germany would be to accelerate the process of demilitarization. This disengagement process would help maintain a benign image in Western Europe while the Soviets continued to herald a CSCE collective security agreement as the new approach to guaranteeing peace and security in Europe.

An important internal dynamic in U.S. politics could also accel-

143

erate the process of U.S. troop withdrawal from Europe. After nearly a decade of larger-than-usual federal budget deficits, and facing hundreds of billions of dollars in additional federal financial obligations because of the savings and loan disaster of the 1980s, President Bush changed course in mid-1990 and agreed to raise taxes to reduce the larger-than-expected budget deficit. Then the deployment of 540,000 U.S. combat forces to the Persian Gulf and the war of 1991 all further increased the expected federal budget deficits and provided another reason to reduce the U.S. troop presence in Europe.

In the aftermath of the Persian Gulf war and the perception of a sharply lower military threat in Europe, there will be significant political pressures for redeploying troops from the Persian Gulf to the United States rather than to Europe. And in the political-fiscal context of the early 1990s, both major political parties will have strong incentives to limit future military spending—to avoid cuts in social programs and to keep the tax increases as low as possible. Both political parties would prefer to reduce U.S. forces and eliminate bases abroad, including in Germany, rather than eliminate bases in the United States. When they are combined, Soviet reasonableness in the 1990 agreement on German reunification within NATO, the November 1990 accord to reduce conventional weapons in Europe, and these budget considerations add up to a context for possible large-scale reductions of U.S. forces in Europe, especially Germany.

Beginning in 1971, Senator Mike Mansfield, a leading Democrat, annually submitted a congressional resolution requiring the withdrawal of a significant portion of U.S. troops based in Europe. He maintained that European countries had recovered economically and were perfectly capable of providing for their own defense, and that it was time for the United States to stop subsidizing the wealthy nations of democratic Europe. Starting in the 1980s, such American conservative commentators as Irving Kristol joined this call for large-scale withdrawals of U.S. forces from Europe. None of these proposals had much prospect until the unraveling of communism in Eastern Europe in 1989 redefined the debate over defense-spending in the United States. In April 1990 Senator Sam Nunn, chairman of the Senate Armed Services Committee and the leading spokesman on military issues for the Democratic majority in the United States Senate, proposed that the United States reduce its troop strength in Europe from 305,000 to between 75,000 and 100,000 in the early 1990s.[32] In making this proposal Senator Nunn said,

> The question today is not whether we reduce military spending; that is inevitable. The question is whether we reduce

military spending pursuant to a sensible military strategy that meets the threats of today and tomorrow.[33]

Since the United States would need 30,000–40,000 military personnel to maintain a significant portion of existing facilities in NATO countries other than Germany, the implications of Senator Nunn's proposal were that the U.S. military presence in Germany would be reduced to about 40,000.

In June 1990 Congresswoman Pat Schroeder, a member of the Democratic majority on the House Armed Services Committee, proposed even sharper cuts. After pointing out that 250,000 U.S. soldiers in Germany were accompanied by 220,000 dependents and employed 125,000 civilians at enormous cost, Congresswoman Schroeder proposed that the United States change its approach in the defense of Europe to one of maintaining a military-logistics infrastructure for rapid reinforcement should the need arise, but cutting back troops in Europe to 50,000.[34] Assuming that much of the U.S. air, naval, and other military infrastructure were maintained in the other NATO countries, this proposal would leave the U.S. troop presence in Germany in the range of 10,000.

Since President Bush himself proposed a cut of 100,000 U.S. troops in January 1990, the Democratic leadership in Congress can argue that the Republican administration has acknowledged the reduced military threat and the only question remaining is, how deeply to cut. NATO's London Declaration of July 1990 that the Warsaw Pact is no longer an enemy and the formal dissolution of the Warsaw Pact in 1991 might well provide the Democratic congressional leadership with further arguments for deep cuts in U.S. forces based in Europe, especially in Germany.

Although some will argue for reducing U.S. troops deployed in Germany and Europe because of a perceived reduction in threat and a need to save scarce budget dollars, others in the United States will call for more equitable burden sharing, contending that

> Western Europe is as rich as the United States; the Common Market has the men, money and resources to defend itself from any invasion Moscow could mount. It's time she did so. . . . Our Founding Fathers warned against international 'entangling alliances.' Our present ruler seems determined to entangle us forever in Europe's endless conflicts and recurring quarrels.[35]

Another conservative commentator notes that in view of the defense cuts many European NATO countries have already made without consulting NATO or the United States, it is time for "the United States

. . . to devolve its responsibilities for European security to the West Europeans. By doing so, American taxpayers who had shouldered the bulk of the NATO defense burden during the cold war, will finally reap the benefits of their investment."[36]

These similar prescriptions for large-scale U.S. troop withdrawals from Europe come from elements of the left, center, and right of the U.S. political spectrum. Therefore, the European and the Soviet leadership may decide it is likely that the United States will significantly reduce its forces in Europe, especially Germany. It is further evident that many U.S. legislators would find it politically more palatable for the United States to reduce its armed forces abroad rather than close additional military bases and facilities at home. The contemporary U.S. geopolitical perspective concerning the diminished Soviet threat to Europe is likely to combine with the efforts of those in favor of lower military expenditures to reduce U.S. forces in Europe and Germany. Such reductions are likely in turn to reinforce the views of those Germans who favor further self-demilitarization and a shift away from NATO and the United States, toward a Europe-wide collective security agreement under CSCE auspices. Over the next years, these perspectives—in the United States and in Germany—could mutually reinforce each other.

The 1991 Persian Gulf war opened another dimension of distance between Germany and the United States and between Germany and other key NATO countries, such as Turkey. Enforcing a UN Security Council resolution, the United States led a coalition to reverse Iraq's conquest and annexation of Kuwait. Much of the German left opposed the war and organized massive demonstrations of protest, involving tens and even hundreds of thousands of persons in Bonn and other major German cities. A leading Protestant clergyman, Bishop Gottfried Forck, supported the protests and caught the mood of the German left when he said, "Saddam Hussein committed a great injustice when he invaded Kuwait. But that did not justify an attack on Iraq. An injustice was met with *an even greater injustice*" (emphasis added).[37] Although initially German demonstrators sought to distinguish between opposition to the war and opposition to the United States, as the conflict went on and the casualties mounted— military and civilian on both sides—the two views became more intertwined.

At the same time, questions arose about the level of German governmental support for actions taken partly in defense of German direct interests; Germany was one of many countries with a high energy-dependence on the Persian Gulf and an interest in deterring future aggression there. Following reunification, during the months-long military buildup in the gulf, Germany decided not to send combat forces outside the NATO area. An unspoken view was that many NATO leaders sympathized with this view—German combat forces could best contribute to the alliance by remaining in Germany and maintaining deterrence there. This approach seemed sensible, in view of German history—both because of the fears that might be evoked abroad by images of German military action in foreign lands and because of the strong pacifist sentiment within Germany, which might react to combat abroad with a massive campaign for total German disarmament.

As a large, wealthy state, however, Germany was expected to make a significant financial contribution—and its initial outlay was viewed as meager. On January 29, 1991, two weeks after hostilities began, Chancellor Kohl pledged $5.5 billion in financial support and described this action as "proof beyond words that we support the United Nations resolutions."[38] Germany also contributed some 8,000 soldiers and some aircraft toward NATO reinforcement of Turkey, which faced the possibility of Iraqi retaliation for permitting its airfields to be used for staging combat missions against Iraq.

Some German political leaders, however, publicly questioned whether Germany would be obligated to help NATO-ally Turkey if it were attacked by Iraq. The NATO secretary general, Manfred Woerner, himself a former German minister of defense, explicitly stated that any attack upon Turkey would be viewed by all sixteen NATO members as an attack upon all. The German government also took a firm position, but the questions raised within Germany led the president of Turkey to say, "I think Germany has become so rich it has completely lost its fighting spirit."[39] A report in February 1991 indicated that 61 of 800 German soldiers assigned to NATO duties in Turkey had refused to carry out their orders, and in 1990, 21,000 Germans had refused the military draft and applied for the status of conscientious objectors. The same report indicated that the German minister of defense, Gerhard Stoltenberg, agreed that antiwar sentiment was strong among part of the population; he added, "We have a lot of work to do to explain to the German people why the alliance [against Iraq] is justified."[40]

The extensive military preparations made by Iraq with Soviet- and Western-supplied materiel and weapons raised another uncomfortable question for Germany. At the end of January 1991, an analysis produced for the U.S. Senate's Committee on Foreign Relations indicated that 110 German corporations had sold to Iraq materials and equipment for the production of weapons of mass destruction.[41] This number exceeded that of any other Western country—in

147

the United Kingdom there were thirty-six corporations, in France, twenty-two, in the United States, twenty-two. The sales involved an array of nuclear, chemical, biological, and missile technologies that went beyond the range sold by any other country as well. The threat posed by these weapons to American and other anti-Iraq coalition troops produced a potential for recriminations against Germany by the NATO nations that sustained casualties in the war.

Eastern Europe

Among the new governments of Eastern Europe, Poland, Hungary, and Czechoslovakia clearly sought an end to their military commitments under the Warsaw Pact. East Germany, of course, left the pact a few days before reunification in 1990. At the same time each of these governments, aware of the lessons of history (1956, 1968), realized that any unilateral withdrawal from the Warsaw Pact could bring serious problems from the powerful Soviet Union. During 1990 the Soviets sought to maintain the structure and obligations of the Warsaw Pact, both to preserve their own influence in Eastern Europe and to have a bargaining tool—to be able to exchange the dismantling of the Warsaw Pact for the dissolution or diminution of NATO.

But in 1991 the Soviet Union formally dissolved the Warsaw Pact. The Soviet Union indicated its intention to maintain bilateral military lines, however, with each of the former pact countries, and it continues its efforts to have the Conference on Security and Cooperation in Europe establish an international mechanism to replace the NATO alliance. The Soviet Union also urged the governments of Eastern Europe to present this case in Western Europe. The Soviets probably assumed that if elected, democratic governments are seen to favor the dismantling of both military alliance systems and express this view to the leaders of Western Europe and the United States, then the Soviet objective of replacing NATO with an all-European security system would be advanced. Czechoslovakian president Havel's visit to NATO headquarters in March 1991, however, illustrated otherwise. The leaders of Poland, Hungary, and Czechoslovakia have not only praised NATO—in Havel's words, a "democratic, defensive alliance"; they have urged that it remain intact and suggested they might ilke to join it at some time in the near future.

An extensive U.S. government analysis written in 1990 following the unraveling of the East European Communist regimes points out that most of the new governments are reducing military spending and the size of their military forces. Further, this analysis concludes that newly elected East European governments will "want a role in a new European-wide collective security structure . . . which would replace military commitments to the Warsaw Pact. In the meantime they will try to diminish the Pact's role as a military alliance and foster Soviet interest in transforming it into a regional caucus for policy information sharing with little or no executive authority."[42]

The Soviets can employ a number of means to pressure the East European governments to take this position if necessary. Although the Soviets agreed to withdraw their military forces from Hungary, Czechoslovakia, and Poland by July 1991, they have subsequently been setting conditions on those troop withdrawals, such as requiring large cash payments for vacated Soviet military facilities. Repeated Soviet demands for these payments, months after withdrawal agreements were reached, may well suggest to Eastern Europeans that the Soviet Union will make final troop withdrawals conditional on the achievement of progress in replacing NATO.[43]

The decades-old, Soviet-led and -managed economic trading system with the former Warsaw Pact countries provides another source of Soviet leverage on Eastern Europe. During the 1980s the Warsaw Pact countries averaged more than 50 percent of their trade with the Soviet Union, ranging from Romania, obtaining 46 percent of its imports from the Soviets, to Czechoslovakia, obtaining 72 percent; see table 8-1. By mid-1990 the East European countries still conducted about 40 percent of their total trade with the Soviet Union—Bulgaria being the most dependent, Romania the least.[44] But in the vital energy sector the East European countries imported from the Soviets about 25 percent of their total energy consumption and many of the raw materials needed for industrial production (see tables 8-2 and 8-3). As Roger Robinson, an expert on Soviet economic and financial strategy, has pointed out, "The inordinate reliance of the [East European] countries on Soviet energy supplies . . . constitutes a strategically significant . . . risk" for Eastern Europe.[45] His analysis concludes that the total market value of oil and gas imports from the Soviet Union to Eastern Europe is nearly $15 billion annually.[46]

Eastern Europe's dependence on Soviet supplies is further increased because "there is a large investment and fixed infrastructure for natural gas imports from the Soviet Union, and the largest indigenous source of energy in Eastern Europe, coal supplies, has had a devastating environmental impact."[47] Eastern Europe is thus likely to "come under growing domestic and international pressure to reduce that consumption." To put in context the potential Soviet energy leverage on Eastern Europe, an analysis by the Center for Security Policy notes that the 1973–1974 Arab oil embargo of various

TABLE 8–1
WARSAW PACT PRINCIPAL TRADING PARTNERS, 1986
(in billions of U.S. dollars)

	USSR–Warsaw Pact	USSR		Warsaw Pact		EC	
	%	$	%	$	%	$	%
			Imports				
Bulgaria[a]	71	9.7	63	1.2	8	N.A.	N.A.
Czechoslovakia	72	10.7	44	6.6	28	2.2	10
East Germany[b]	52	11.2	41	3.1	11	N.A.	N.A.
Hungary	48	2.8	29	1.9	19	2.4	25
Poland	46	3.2	29	1.9	17	2.2	19
Romania[c]	46	4.0	38	0.9	8	N.A.	N.A.
USSR	—	—	—	38.6	43	10.1	11
Warsaw Pact average	55.8	6.9	40.6	7.7	19.1	4.2	16.2
			Exports				
Bulgaria[a]	69	8.7	62	1.1	7	N.A.	N.A.
Czechoslovakia	75	10.0	43	7.4	32	1.9	8
East Germany[b]	50	10.1	37	3.6	13	N.A.	N.A.
Hungary	50	31.3	33	1.7	17	1.9	20
Poland	39	2.9	24	1.8	15	2.6	21
Romania[c]	34	3.4	27	0.9	7	N.A.	N.A.
USSR	—	—	—	51.1	53	12.8	13
Warsaw Pact average	52.8	11.1	37.7	9.7	20.6	4.8	16

N.A. = not applicable
a. Warsaw Pact figures exclude Romania and East Germany.
b. Warsaw Pact figures exclude Bulgaria and Romania.
c. Warsaw Pact figures exclude Bulgaria and East Germany.
SOURCES: *The United Nations International Trade Statistics Yearbook*, vol. 1, 1987; *The 1989 Information Please Almanac*, 42nd edition (New York: Houghton Mifflin Company, 1989).

industrial democracies affected only "5 percent of consumption, yet the economic impact of that cutoff was massive and adverse—even on economies far more robust than any in Eastern Europe. . . ."[48]

The Soviet decision in the spring of 1990 to cut off energy supplies to Lithuania, an effort to coerce that country's Parliament to rescind its declaration of independence, illustrates the willingness of the Gorbachev regime to use energy supplies for its political pur-

TABLE 8-2

EAST EUROPEAN RELIANCE ON ENERGY IMPORTS, 1988

(quadrillions of BTUs)

	Energy Production	Energy Consumption	Total Energy Imports	Import Share of Consumption (percent)
Bulgaria	0.65	1.49	0.84	56
Czechoslovakia	2.22	3.26	1.04	32
East Germany	2.93	4.00	1.07	27
Hungary	0.80	1.20	0.40	33
Poland	6.24	6.57	0.33	5
Romania	2.76	3.30	0.54	16
Total	15.60	19.82	4.22	21[a]

a. Total represents weighted average for all six countries.
SOURCE: Energy Information Administration, *International Energy Annual 1988* (Washington, D.C.: Government Printing Office, 1989).

TABLE 8-3

ENERGY IMPORTS FROM THE USSR AS A SHARE OF TOTAL ENERGY IMPORTS, 1970-1977

(percent)

	1970	1975	1977
Bulgaria	86	93	93
Czechoslovakia	80	86	85
East Germany	66	79	80
Hungary	66	73	82
Poland	87	75	75
Romania	19	13	9
Total[a]	73	76	76

a. Total represents weighted averages for all six countries.
SOURCE: U.S. National Foreign Assessment Center, *Energy Supplies in Eastern Europe: A Statistical Compilation* (Washington, D.C.: December 1979).

poses. In November 1989, as the transition in Eastern Europe was gaining momentum and moving beyond mere changes in Communist leadership, a key adviser to Gorbachev said,

> The Warsaw Pact is still in force—and can be used as a political weapon. . . . The same is true of raw materials which we supply to East European countries (all of which depend on the Soviet Union for energy supplies). The new opposition forces have to take this into account.[49]

151

A U.S. government analysis in May 1990 points out that the Soviets increasingly will want to receive hard currency for their oil and gas exports to Eastern Europe—rather than the "substandard heavy machinery and equipment Eastern Europe has specialized in making. . . ."[50] Further, it finds that Eastern Europe wants to be "less vulnerable to disruptions in the Soviet economy and to the threat of a politically motivated energy shut-off." The sharp increase in world oil prices (from about $20 a barrel to $34 a barrel) following Iraq's invasion of Kuwait in the summer of 1990 also increased Soviet energy leverage over Eastern Europe. This may not persist, however, as oil prices decline in the wake of Iraq's expulsion from Kuwait.

For the near future, Soviet means of influence on the East European countries will include diplomacy, the bilateral arrangements replacing the Warsaw Pact's commitments, the presence of Soviet troops in Eastern Europe, the economic and energy dependence of Eastern Europe, the looming shadow of overwhelming Soviet military power, and Soviet covert links with its former national Communist allies. This power need not ever be used in order to have a great impact on neutral countries with no more means of self-defense than Lithuania had when it suspended its declaration of independence. The strength of the Soviet drive for the de facto neutralization of Germany is visible not only in the pattern of its actions over the past forty years but in the statements and actions of the Gorbachev regime as well.

The Soviet Union has demonstrated a capacity for international action to accomplish many—but by no means all—of its strategic objectives. Using a strategy that can blend normalization, political action, and implicit coercion, it may seek to bring about the de facto neutralization of Germany by intensifying or fomenting useful trends within Germany, within other NATO members, including France and the United States, or by means of coalition-building and political persuasion—using even the East European countries that the West wants to help. The objective is to have an all-European security conference as a substitute for NATO as the best means of preserving peace in the future.

Notably, Jeane Kirkpatrick, the former U.S. Ambassador to the United Nations and a seasoned analyst of international politics, has concluded that in the new Europe "a meaningful long-term role for NATO will not survive . . . if present trends in the Soviet Union continue." One of the important reasons she points to is the philosophy of President Mitterrand of France, whose "own quasi-Gaullist vision of a stable Europe without the blocs coincides with Gorbachev's in some crucial ways. They also share a barely articulated desire to reduce the role of the United States and NATO in Europe and to enhance the CSCE."[51] It is therefore important to consider the possible consequences of the de facto neutralization of Germany.

Consequences of the de Facto Neutralization of Germany

For those who believe the foreign policy of the Soviet Union in the 1990s will be marked only by a desire to establish cooperative relations based on sovereignty and reciprocity with other nations, the de facto neutralization of Germany could appear to provide an opportunity for further détente in Europe. The same would be true for those who view the Soviet Union in the 1990s as being too overcome by internal economic, social, and political problems to carry on a strategically aimed foreign policy. Indeed there are reports that some German leaders fear the Soviet Union will feel "defeated" by the unraveling of communism in East Germany and Eastern Europe and favor giving it special consideration so that it will not develop a "Versailles complex" of resentment after this defeat. These views of the Soviet Union as a nation transformed by Gorbachev into a benign power or one incapable of hostile, purposeful international actions are held by many Westerners—by both liberals and conservatives, including leaders. They would lead to the expectation that few if any negative consequences would follow de facto neutralization.

Some Westerners who do not share this optimistic outlook about the Soviet Union and who believe an effective NATO alliance must continue until the Soviet Union has made a complete transformation to political democracy nevertheless believe NATO could continue to be militarily effective even if Germany were neutral. As one German author puts it, the Atlantic Alliance would simply be "centered on America's traditional allies, France, Britain . . . holding the balance against a diminished and remote Soviet Union."[52] Others might point out that NATO existed without Germany or its military from 1949 to 1955, a time of serious threat from the Soviet Union. Such a reassuring historical observation, however, ignores the fact that during those years the United States had overwhelming strategic nuclear superiority over the Soviet Union. Furthermore, the United States was then able to use the territory of West Germany for NATO military purposes—something that would no longer be possible if a reunified Germany were neutral.

It is worth examining how much the NATO–Warsaw Pact or NATO–Soviet military balance as it existed before implementation of the 1990 Conventional Forces in Europe agreement might be altered by the de facto neutralization of Germany (see table 8–4). In May

153

TABLE 8–4

NATIONAL FORCES AND FOREIGN TROOPS DEPLOYED IN NATO AND
WARSAW PACT COUNTRIES, 1989

In NATO Countries			In Warsaw Pact Countries		
	National	Foreign		National	Foreign[a]
Belgium	92,400	3,100	Bulgaria	117,500	0
Canada	89,000	0	Czechoslovakia	199,700	70,000
Denmark	31,600	0	Ger. Dem. Rep.	173,100	380,000
France	466,300	0	Hungary	68,000	65,000
Fed. Rep. of			Poland	412,000	40,000
Ger.	494,300	401,000[b]	Romania	171,000	0
Greece	208,500	3,300	USSR	4,258,000	0
Iceland	0	3,100			
Italy	390,000	15,000			
Luxembourg	800	0			
Netherlands	103,600	2,800			
Norway	34,100	c			
Portugal	75,300	3,800			
Spain	285,000	8,600			
Turkey	650,900	4,900			
U. K.	311,650	27,900			
United States	2,124,900	0			
Totals	5,358,350[d]	473,500	Totals	5,399,300[e]	555,000

N.A. = not applicable.
a. Only includes Soviet ground forces.
b. Troop breakdown: Belgium—26,600; Canada—7,100; France—52,700;
   Netherlands—5,700; U.K.—69,700; U.S.—239,200.
c. Prepositioned equipment for 1 U.S. Marine Expeditionary Brigade.
d. Total does not include reserve forces of 8,277,500 troops.
e. Total does not include reserve forces of 7,527,000 troops.
SOURCE: International Institute for Strategic Studies, *The Military Balance
1989–1990* (New York: Brassey's, Autumn 1989).

1990 the NATO–Warsaw Pact balance in Europe indicated a total troop
strength of 2.9 million for NATO versus 3.5 million for the Warsaw
Pact; 24,000 tanks for NATO versus 48,000 tanks; 18,000 artillery for
NATO versus 36,000; and 6,000 combat aircraft versus 12,000.

To consider the case of a neutral Germany we must subtract the
current number of West German combat forces from the NATO
ledger. We could also reasonably assume that 200,000 fewer U.S.
combat forces would be available to NATO in Europe. Assuming that
the United States would leave its military equipment in Europe,
prepositioned to support NATO, and that the other NATO forces
would remain approximately as they were in 1990, the NATO that
remained after the neutralization of Germany would have a man-

power strength in Europe of about 2.2 million. The Soviet Union would have 2.7 million (or 3.5 million if one includes the former Warsaw Pact countries). The tank strength of this residual NATO would be about 19,000, compared with 32,000 for the Soviet Union alone or 45,000 if one included former Warsaw Pact countries; artillery, 17,000, compared with 27,000 for the Soviet Union, 35,000 inclusively; and combat aircraft, 5,000 for the residual NATO, compared with 5,000 for the Soviet Union and 12,000 inclusively. In 1990 the former Warsaw Pact countries other than the Soviet Union accounted for only about 800,000 of the 3.5 million inclusive figure.

Whatever the political intentions of the new leadership in the East European countries, it is reasonable to assume that the Soviet Union might seek to preserve the Warsaw Pact as an entity even after the neutralization of Germany; in this way it can trade the formal disbanding of the Warsaw Pact for the disbanding of NATO. Although the formal command structures of the East European national military forces may well continue to run directly to the Soviet general staff as long as the Warsaw Pact is in existence, the dramatic political changes of 1989–1990 sharply reduced the reliability of most Warsaw Pact national armies. It is therefore appropriate to compare the residual NATO balance with the Soviet Union alone.

Clearly, the military balance in Europe would move against the residual NATO after the de facto neutralization of Germany. Assuming that the U.S. strategic arsenal remains committed to the defense of NATO, however, and thereby deters any Soviet coercive use of its enormous offensive strategic nuclear arsenal, this projection would suggest that the residual NATO could still mount a defensive effort. This case would be even more likely if the neutralization of Germany led to more assertive Soviet international conduct, resulting in a French decision to rejoin the NATO military command.

More likely in such a case, however, would be a French effort to form a special bilateral political-military relationship that would protect a reunified Germany with French nuclear weapons. Reportedly Mitterrand has alluded to the necessity of including Germany "in discussions and decisions 'on the use of our weapons.' "[53]

After the NATO–London Declaration the French minister of defense sought a 4 percent increase in military spending, offering the following explanation: "There is a giant vacuum opening in the center of Europe as the Soviet Empire collapses and American withdrawals from a reunited Germany begin."[54]

As noted above, such French perspectives might be precisely what the Soviet Union will use to facilitate the neutralization of Germany. The Soviets will seek to encourage the image of a future

Europe without an American presence through NATO, bound together in an all-European security arrangement, in which Germany and France have a special bilateral relationship with each other *and* with the Soviet Union that increases French influence and ensures French predominance among the West European countries.

Although a militarily neutral Germany would remain a member of the European Community and other West European institutions, clearly it would develop a deeper cooperative relationship with the Soviet Union and the countries of Eastern Europe in the next years. Already in 1990 West Germany was the largest Western trading partner with Eastern Europe. The expanded relationship between a democratic, reunified Germany and Eastern Europe could have many beneficial consequences, such as promoting the growth of democratic and market-oriented institutions, and moving the East European countries away from dependence on the Soviet Union and toward closer relations with the West. If Germany were neutral, however, it is more likely to be hesitant in building democratic institutions, as the Soviet Union might discreetly object to such activities as interfering in the affairs of countries that border it. Germany's relationship would then be almost entirely commercial, which might create an atmosphere of competition between Germany and a number of other Western countries—especially France.

In the longer term, Henry Kissinger suggested:

> An Austrian-type neutral solution for Germany would create a single bloc from the French-German border to the Polish-Soviet border of states with similar international status and therefore propelled toward joint diplomacy. Surely there is no better formula for eventual German hegemony over central Europe or a long term German-Russian conflict.[55]

Professor Stanley Hoffmann concluded that a neutral Germany might be "tempted again to be a freewheeling major player, subject to fits of insecurity because of real or imagined threats from the east or west."[56] Describing the situation earlier in the century of a Germany positioned between East and West, Kissinger summarized the dangers that emerged from that era of independent security politics: Germany's effort "to manage simultaneously all dangers—real or imagined" in turn "threatened each of Germany's neighbors sufficiently to bring about precisely the coalitions that its first chancellor, Otto von Bismarck, described as Germany's nightmare."[57]

Germany in the 1990s faces two types of potential hazard: in the East, the Soviet Union might try to coerce ever more resources from a reunited Germany; and in the West, suspicions and resentment of a reunited Germany's independent foreign policy might erode the bonds of the European Community and other recently established institutions. If Germany remains democratic and a member of the EC and other West European political institutions, however, even a neutral Germany has no reason to repeat the mistakes that sparked two world wars in this century. The risk will be present in the minds of all, of course, both in Germany and abroad.

The Soviet Union intends to control that risk by ensuring that a neutral Germany is virtually demilitarized and therefore incapable of posing any serious military threat, irrespective of its diplomacy and international political actions.

Soviet-German Economic Relations—Cooperation to Compulsion

At their meeting in July 1990 the leaders of the seven major industrial democracies received a letter from Gorbachev requesting significant economic and technical assistance:

> The Soviet leadership is looking for new possibilities to supplement the internal transformations through financial and economic support from outside. Perhaps it would be possible to talk about working out long term agreements on large scale credit and cooperation over investments which would be a serious factor in stabilization and transition to the market economy.[58]

On July 15–16, 1990, Chancellor Kohl visited Gorbachev in the Soviet Union for their second round of direct negotiations on German reunification. In return for Gorbachev's permission for a reunified Germany to remain in NATO, Kohl assured Gorbachev that Germany and France would continue seeking $15 billion in direct assistance for the Soviet Union from the industrial democracies. He further assured him that Germany would sharply increase its purchase of Soviet oil and natural gas for hard currency, would permit private companies to undertake large-scale, long-term building operations in the Soviet Union, and would expand technical assistance to the Soviet Union. Kohl promised to meet all East German state enterprise commitments to the Soviet Union, to consider additional aid and investment, to limit German armed forces, and to ensure there would be no nuclear, biological, or chemical weapons in the German arsenal.[59] These large promises were supplemented by Germany's agreement to provide $8 billion in costs for the maintenance and removal of Soviet forces in Germany, and the Soviets clearly plan to seek even more help from Germany.

As the Soviet-German relationship deepens and as Soviet economic needs grow it is likely that the Soviet Union would demand even greater—perhaps far greater—economic and technical help. Further, some German businesses would be interested in the Soviet market; the German government would be interested in maintaining a cordial relationship with its powerful eastern neighbor; and German trade unions, strongly linked to the SPD, would be likely to welcome this cordiality, for political-ideological reasons. A steady increase in German economic and technical support for the Soviet Union would therefore be probable in the absence of any countervailing forces.

The more this German-Soviet economic relationship would grow, the more impetus would come from within Germany to continue and expand it. The larger the cumulative Soviet debt to Germany, the more critical it would be to German bankers to maintain a relationship that could some day permit some repayment. The larger the German industrial investment in the Soviet Union, the more the German business sector would press for continually expanding credits and subsidies. The more the German governmental and political leaders would assure the public of the wisdom of this course, the more those leaders would feel the need to continue. The greater the German dependence on Soviet oil and gas imports, the greater the potential leverage of the Soviet Union. All of these eventualities could occur during the early 1990s, while a large proportion of the 380,000 Soviet troops still remain on formerly East German territory. The Soviet Union could perhaps extract additional economic benefits from a Germany anxious to have the Soviet forces gone, as the price for accelerating or even complying with the previously agreed upon schedule of troop withdrawals.

From the Soviet point of view, one progression of events could be as follows: first, consensual economic cooperation with Germany; next, expanded German economic aid to the Soviet Union, driven in part by German interest groups that seek to maintain good relations in order to protect their financial and political interests; finally, a form of perhaps subtle and disguised political dominance over a militarily weak Germany, permitting the Soviet Union to demand and receive as much economic and technical assistance as it wants from Germany.

If Germany were to resist the subtle transition from cooperation with the Soviet Union to political-economic subordination, the Soviets might use secret, coercive, and persuasive threats. A Soviet citizen ostensibly not part of the government might, for example, meet with senior German officials and warn of a risk that various Soviet-allied states in the Middle East might start sending more terrorist groups into Germany. Germans would recall the sharp increase in terrorism

that followed Germany's request in 1977 that NATO deploy intermediate-range nuclear missiles to balance Soviet nuclear deployments.

A neutral Germany is likely to be even more vulnerable to Soviet
political action and Soviet covert measures, which in turn could mean
a series of public protests by disciplined activist groups favoring more
help for the Soviet Union. Ultimately, a neutral Germany attempting
to resist Soviet requests for increased aid would be faced with the
overwhelming military power of the Soviet Union, brandished privately but effectively, since a neutral Germany would be incapable of
resisting military coercion. As Ambassador Evan Galbraith wrote in
1989, in the context of German neutrality the Soviet Union would be
able to "call up their [German] bankers and industrial 'partners' . . .
and tell them what the current Soviet needs are and what additional
items and amounts will be required tomorrow."[60]

"All-European Security" and Soviet Dominance

If Germany does experience a shift from cooperation to compulsion
in its relations with the Soviet Union, would it later be able to return
to NATO, or to seek bilateral military agreements with the United
States or France, or to seek agreements with a combination of Western
nuclear powers for protection? This is certainly possible, but unlikely.
The world would not remain the same after the neutralization of
Germany.

Germany itself would probably experience the first few years of
neutrality as an advantageous, perhaps even euphoric time of peaceful hopes and new, close relations with the Soviet Union, along with
continued close relations in the European Community, and with the
West. In that context it is highly likely that Germany and France
together would move diligently to bring about the all-European
security system so long sought by the Soviet Union. This plan was
accepted in principle at the July 1990 NATO summit and was clearly
expressed in its London Declaration. Gorbachev said in May 1990
that:

> NATO is associated with the cold war—but as an organiza-
> tion designed from the start to be hostile to the Soviet Union,
> as a force that whipped up the arms race and the danger of
> war. Regardless of what is being said about NATO now, for
> us it is a symbol of the past, a dangerous and confrontational
> past, and we will never agree to assign it a leading role in
> building a new Europe. I want us to be understood correctly
> on this.[61]

The events that could lead to the de facto neutralization itself
could also add momentum to the substitution of the Conference on

Security and Cooperation in Europe for the NATO alliance as a means of providing security in Europe. By the time Germany might realize that it was becoming subordinate to the Soviet Union, NATO might still exist, but it would be much weaker. By the time Germany might decide to return to a military alliance with the West it would be viewed with some suspicion—perhaps even hostility—for having become neutral and for having vastly aided the Soviet Union. Germany would undoubtedly be blamed for providing tens of billions of dollars in money and technology to the Soviet Union and thus contributing to its increased military strength. Once Germany had been neutral but later regretted its neutrality, fearing the consequences, it is uncertain whether any Western nuclear armed power could be willing to take the risks involved in extending its nuclear protection to Germany—and the Soviet regime would be very assertive in seeking to prevent any German return to NATO or other form of alliance with a Western nuclear power.

If the Soviet Union maintains the present style of pursuing its strategic objectives, it is also likely in this scenario to deepen the West's perception of it as posing no military threat. German concerns about subordination to Soviet economic demands could therefore be viewed as alarmist, not credible, or a matter of money rather than of freedom or security. If Germany were to attempt to appeal to the all-European security system through the institutions of CSCE, it would discover what most of the history of the United Nations and the League of Nations has shown about collective security systems—they do not function well when needed against very powerful aggressor nations. As Henry Kissinger observed about the replacement of the NATO Alliance by the CSCE,

> No arrangement would be more likely to create conditions in which one nation can dominate. For if everyone is allied with everybody, nobody has a special relationship with anybody. It is the ideal circumstance for the most ruthless seeking to isolate potential victims.[62]

The stage would then be set for the Soviet Union to achieve the objective described by Lev Navrozov, a former Soviet citizen now writing on Soviet affairs in the United States:

> To Finlandize Eastern Europe in exchange for the Finlandization of Western Europe, which means unlimited Soviet access to West European science and technology and that means the chess-like peaceful checkmate of the United States, for the latter will be unable to compete with the Soviet Union's irreversible [military] supremacy resulting

from the combination of its manpower and space and West Europe's financial and technological resources.[63]

Evan Galbraith, a former U.S. ambassador to France, concluded that once Germany had been neutralized and substantially demilitarized, "most of continental Europe will fall defenseless into line. France will be isolated . . . [,] Europe will feed the big bear to keep him outside the door. The Soviet Union will have created a coprosperity sphere without having fired a shot."[64]

Gorbachev speaks frequently of Soviet "new thinking" in foreign policy and the need to ensure that "the global political process could be demilitarized."[65] Certainly the new style of Soviet diplomacy is warranted by the strategic objectives of removing the U.S. military presence from Europe, creating a neutral Germany, ending the functioning Atlantic Alliance, and obtaining significant economic and technological aid from Germany and, later, much of Western Europe.

One further possibility should be considered among this range of possible consequences. According to one British observer, if Germany became neutral "it would then become a choice between nuclear predominance over Europe by even the diminished Soviet Union and Germany going nuclear."[66] Germany certainly possesses the technical means to manufacture nuclear weapons and to do so quickly. A significant consensus among German leadership groups is unlikely, however, concerning any open or clandestine attempt to acquire nuclear weapons. If such an attempt were made, the Soviet Union, the United States, or a European country would probably detect it at an early stage. Any effort to obtain nuclear, chemical, or biological weapons would contravene German agreements made since 1954, so it is probable that the major powers would act immediately to terminate and dismantle any German nuclear weapons program. An independent German nuclear deterrent is therefore unlikely to be a consequence of the neutralization of Germany.

Summary. The possible consequences of German neutrality range from relatively benign to extremely dangerous from the perspective of the West and of the United States. The transition from Soviet-German cooperation to German economic subordination to the Soviets is not inevitable, and even in the context of German neutrality it is potentially preventable; nevertheless it is possible and probable, given the desperate Soviet need for Western financial and technological support. A reunited Germany with an annual GNP in the range of $2 trillion could initially provide billions of dollars annually to the Soviet Union, and ultimately many tens of billions. Those resources

161

could translate into Soviet military strength and innovations that could cost the West hundreds of billions of dollars to counter. Should the Soviet Union transform dominance over Germany into dominance over Western Europe in the context of the all-European security institutions, the interests of the United States and the free world would be dramatically set back. This outcome is possible, though not inevitable; it is one of the many reasons why the United States has a strong interest in maintaining a reunited Germany as a military as well as political member of the Atlantic Alliance. After a discussion of conceptual insights and hypotheses about the future suggested by the historic transitions of 1989–1990 (chapter 9), the final chapter will examine how this interest might be supported. It also proposes an institutional framework to build on the constructive opportunities of the current era of transition in Germany, in Europe, and in U.S.–European relations.

PART FOUR
Conclusion

9

The East European and German Transformations— Conceptual Perspectives

The history of the world is none other than the progress of the consciousness of freedom.
—GEORG WILHELM FRIEDRICH HEGEL

In a recent conceptualization of international relations, James N. Rosenau, an eminent scholar in the field, defines the contemporary era as one of turbulence. He writes that "tensions and changes . . . ensue when the structures and processes that normally sustain world politics are unsettled and appear to be undergoing rearrangement. [These turbulent conditions] develop rapidly . . . [,] sustained by the complexity and dynamism of diverse actors whose goals and activities are inextricably linked to each other and facilitated by technologies that transmit information almost instantaneously [and] tend to be marked by quick responses, insistent demands, temporary coalitions, and policy reversals."[1]

Although written before the onset of the historic transformations in Eastern Europe and Germany in 1989–1990, the description of turbulence can certainly be applied to those events. This chapter will explore from a conceptual perspective the causes of these transformations and, by reflecting on these momentous events, will suggest insights about the nature of political and international change. Those insights will be used as a foundation for suggesting hypotheses about the future implications of these two transformations.

The Disintegration of Communism in Eastern Europe

It was not the convergence of impersonal, "historical forces" that caused the breakdown of Communist regimes. Nor were these events the result of Gorbachev's intentions. Gorbachev's efforts to limit the changes of 1989–1990 and his cooperation in the repression of self-

165

determination in the Baltics and other Soviet republics in 1990–1991 show that the East European events went beyond his expectations of reform communism. This evidence is strong—even though it was Gorbachev who, starting in 1987, added an international dimension to his perestroika and glasnost by openly telling East European leaders and peoples that all Communist states had sovereign rights and should find their "own way to socialism."[2]

Nor did these events occur as the result of a Western plan to build up an infrastructure of opposition groups that could one day coalesce into a peaceful popular insurrection. Certainly the existence of the West—as a group of free, prosperous, and peaceful states— was a moral and political beacon of immense importance, and the information available though Western electronic media—including Radio Free Europe and Radio Liberty—played an important role in bringing information about events inside Eastern Europe. But the states of the free world were not direct, causal agents. In fact, the Western leaders seemed at first surprised by the mass repudiations of the Communist regimes in 1989 and then reticent, concerned that any responsive action might provide Soviet hardline elements with a reason for intervention to maintain the Communist power structure.

Nor were the events of 1989–1990 simply the inevitable, if unanticipated, next stage in a process of political modernization or development. No reasonable theory describes a probable, or automatic structural historical progression from dictatorship to democracy.[3] Nor is such a model suggested retroactively by those events or by the modern history of states, as more than 100 of 163 socioeconomically disparate sovereign states have remained dictatorships for decades.

The analytic approach that best describes these dramatic events is the "choice-oriented perspective" proposed by Henry Nau, which "emphasizes the role of national (or human) purpose and policy choices" in world affairs.[4] The choices made by three distinct groups —the peoples of the East European countries, the Communist elites in control of those regimes, and the Soviet leadership—produced the net changes when they interacted with each other in the context of turbulence.

Rosenau's concept of bifurcation is also useful for understanding the process that occurred:

> The state centric system now coexists with an equally powerful though more decentralized, multi-centric system. Although these two worlds of world politics have overlapping elements and concerns, their norms, structures, and processes tend to be mutually exclusive.[5]

From this perspective, we see that the peoples of Eastern Europe used the political resources available to them—words, symbols, organizations, and demonstrations—to attain their goals of democracy, an opening to the market economy, and independence. At the same time, the states of Eastern Europe and the Soviet Union, from their "state-centric" vantage point, sought ways to combine modest reform with the maintenance of ultimate control in Communist hands.

West Germany, as has been noted, used moral arguments and, most likely, financial incentives to persuade East European regimes to permit East Germans seeking asylum to travel to West Germany. But all other Western states were virtually absent from the state-centric arena. The decisions of 1989 were made by and among the Communist regimes, acting without disturbance from any Western pressures or threats.

This absence reflected the continuing importance and reality of balance-of-power politics in East-West state relations. In 1953, 1956, and 1968, the Soviet Union used military force to suppress popular movements for freedom. Unwilling to risk war with the Soviet Union the West had taken no military action to deter or counter the Soviet use of force in Eastern Europe. This policy did not change in 1989, as everyone, including the peoples seeking freedom, understood.

And yet there was a new level of Western media and public attention to the events in Eastern Europe, beginning with the drama of the spring 1989 negotiations between the Polish regime and the Solidarity opposition, and continuing with Poland's elections, the first free, albeit limited elections held by a Communist regime. They were held in June 1989—on the same day that the Chinese Communist regime brutally crushed the peaceful prodemocracy movement in Tiananmen Square. The spring 1989 visit of President Bush to Germany, Poland, and Hungary, with his moving and prophetic words expressing the vision of one Europe "whole and free," provided important symbolic support for the aspirations soon to be dramatically revealed by the peoples of Eastern Europe.

As the momentum of events increased in the summer and autumn of 1989, the rapid expansion of Western media coverage and Western public interest served as an informal political endorsement that emboldened the opposition in Eastern Europe. The media in Western Europe had given sharply increased attention to Eastern Europe in the spring of 1989, as two events coincided there: the drama of a massive vote against communism in the Polish elections in June and the opening of the Hungarian border with Austria in May. When the border was opened, hundreds and then thousands of young adults from East Germany—many in families, with young children, and most with their own automobiles—escaped to freedom in West Germany. Both events demonstrated for the people of Eastern and Western Europe what they had long suspected but could not previously know for certain—that the overwhelming majority of the population rejected the Communist systems of Poland and East Germany.

Then, in late August 1989, the flow of East Germans seeking refuge in the West increased to a torrent and produced scenes of joy on the evening television news, as those who succeeded were warmly welcomed in West Germany.[6] At the same time, Europe—East and West—was moved by the inauguration of the Solidarity-led government of Tadeusz Mazowiecki in Poland, virtually on the fiftieth anniversary of the August 23, 1939, Hitler-Stalin pact. West European television played newsreel footage tracing the dark days from this totalitarian entente to the beginning of World War II, on September 1, 1939. In the Soviet Union, glasnost had produced official commissions that denounced the Hitler-Stalin pact and the coordinated invasion of Poland it had set in motion, and that admitted the Stalin regime was responsible for the killing of 14,000 captured Polish army officers. Also shown on West European television was the mass protest by hundreds of thousands of citizens of the three Baltic republics—Lithuania, Latvia, and Estonia—who joined hands to form a 600-mile-long human chain across their republics, to protest their absorption by the Soviet Union as a result of the Hitler-Stalin pact.

These events and images set the stage for a cycle of peaceful demonstrations for freedom that grew steadily in East Germany during September and October of 1989. An estimated 85 percent of East Germans could receive West German television programs, and one observer coined the term "telerevolution" for the events of 1989. In his words,

> Television reached out and touched a Central European audience of millions. . . . Television viewers . . . shared the same feelings as the students, intellectuals, trade unionists, and just ordinary people of Leipzig, Dresden, and Prague. Their level of emotional involvement, increased so instantaneously by television, moved them to share the feelings . . . and more significantly to participate in revolutionary change themselves.[7]

The Hopes of Individuals. While the Brezhnev-era gerontocracies ruling the East European regimes tried to tread their way between the public protests and their perceptions of Soviet pressure for some

168

degree of opening and reform, the Western governments watched. The ever larger popular demonstrations and ever more evocative images in Eastern Europe fulfilled Rosenau's model of the second world of international politics (the decentralized, multicentric system alongside that of states). The actions of those citizens—not states— reflected the transformation in one of Rosenau's three parameters of international politics—that at the level of individuals, where "the analytic skills of individuals have increased to a point where they now play a different and significant role in world politics. . . . People are more able and ready to question authority." And among the five forces he believes have made this an era of large-scale change and transition, two were significant in the East European events:

> The dynamics of technology, particularly those associated with the microelectronic revolution that have made social, economic, and political distances so much shorter, the move- ment of ideas, pictures, currencies and information so much faster . . . [; and] the skills and orientations of the world's adults . . . [;] today's persons in the street are no longer as uninvolved, ignorant, and manipulable with respect to world affairs as were their forebears.[8]

The nineteenth-century observer of political institutions, Alexis de Tocqueville, wrote that "the most dangerous time for a bad government is when it starts to reform itself." As a corollary, he concluded that revolts were most likely to occur not when people were most repressed, but rather when a growing prospect appeared for opening up a formerly closed system. This idea was expanded upon in Crane Brinton's classic comparative study of revolutions, *The Anatomy of Revolution*,[9] and it led to the concept of a political-oppor- tunity model to explain social mobilization on a large scale. Sidney Tarrow identified four factors, derived from his synthesis of the literature on social mobilization in Western societies, which he asso- ciated with "the onset of a wave of mobilization . . . as a collective response to generally expanding political opportunities":

• "Levels of access to institutional participation have begun to open up"; the Solidarity negotiations, Polish elections, and Solidarity- led government would be examples.

• "Political alignments are in disarray and new realignments have not yet been formed." This observation can be applied to the unset- tling effects for the Brezhnev-era Communist leaders in East Ger- many, Czechoslovakia, and Bulgaria, who were perceived as out-of- step and out-of-favor with Gorbachev and with their own Communist successor-generation—as well as with the majority of the population.

169

- "There are major conflicts within the political elite that challengers can take advantage of." There were very visible differences between the reform Communist factions and the hard-line dominant factions within several of the countries.
- "Challengers are offered the help of influential allies from within or outside the system." The major religious institutions were very important as allies in Poland and East Germany. To some unknowable extent, the outpouring of Western public and media interest, along with the objective and credible reporting of Radio Free Europe, could also be viewed as support for the democratic opposition.[10]

The Moral and Political Genesis of Self-Emancipation in Eastern Europe

The literature on the political functioning of international and national systems offers valuable insights, but the moral-political dimension must also be explored in answering a crucial question: Why were thousands and then hundreds of thousands of people ready to risk injury, imprisonment, or even death to confront the Communist regimes in the autumn of 1989?

The answer has four elements: the inward decisions already made by many to seek freedom and truth using only peaceful means; the example of vibrant, successful democracy that the West offered; the perceived opportunities created by the divisions within, and miscalculations by, the Communist elites; and the increasing confidence and loss of fear as each success occurred. Each of these elements will be considered in turn.

It was a tragedy for the peoples of Eastern Europe that at the end of World War II—despite the promises of "free and unfettered elections" made at the 1945 Yalta summit—they went from German-Nazi occupation to Soviet-backed Communist rule. In Poland, Hungary, Czechoslovakia, and East Germany repeated but unsuccessful resistance efforts were made against the Communist regimes, involving mass demonstrations. Usually these efforts met with some concessions and with repression, through the secret police. When the rule of the pro-Soviet Communist elites seemed threatened, however, Soviet combat forces were used directly against the people, as happened in East Germany (1953), in Hungary (1956), and in Czechoslovakia (1968). After the military intervention in Czechoslovakia, the Soviet regime proclaimed its intention to use any means necessary—including force—to preserve what it considered to be the essential elements of Communist authority. This proclamation became known as the Brezhnev doctrine.

Undoubtedly, it was the crushing of a reform Communist government in 1968—despite Czechoslovakia's promises to remain loyal to the Warsaw Pact military alliance—and the inaction of the West that led the peoples of Eastern Europe to the conclusion that there would be no rescue from the West or through the use of force. But submission to the regimes did not imply consent to their world view. The quest for individual liberty continued to take new forms during the next two decades.

The flowering of U.S.–Soviet détente and West German *ostpolitik* in the early 1970s led to the Helsinki Final Act of 1975, cosigned by the members of NATO and the Warsaw Pact and by eleven other European states. It committed these nations to the acceptance of current borders, progress on security issues, and the observance of a broad range of human rights. These commitments reinforced a tendency within the opposition elements of the East European countries to focus on the expansion of personal authenticity, individual autonomy, and civic institutions not under state or Communist party control—rather than on efforts to change political structures. The historian Gale Stokes has termed this an era of "retreat from politics," of a search for a means to "live as if one were a free person," even though the demoralizing events of 1968 left the Communist regimes in power and led them all to become more repressive.[11]

A Communist concession designed to reduce mass protests in 1956 permitted a major institution in one Communist country to sustain a virtually autonomous existence. In the words of Adam Michnik, the Catholic church in Poland

> was actually the first to provide definite proof that it was possible to be an independent institution in a totalitarian state environment, and the church itself demonstrated the first type of antitotalitarian action. . . . On the one hand, they built a church, a building to which people could come to meet God, and on the other hand, they built the real community that develops around the task of building a church.[12]

Michnik was one of the cofounders in 1976 of the Workers Defense Committee (WDC) in Poland, which evolved into the Solidarity movement in 1980. Describing the evolution of the WDC, Michnik wrote:

> The ethos of the WDC . . . was the rejection of violence. The WDC program was simple: to reconstruct the civic community, to build its institutions, to revive all of the spheres that had died under the Communist regime. . . . The WDC

wanted to prove that it is possible to challenge force and deception, to reject force, consciously choosing conflict without force, and to reject deceit by speaking the truth. . . . The WDC [leadership] . . . declared publicly that they were organizing as a workers aid institution, they called on public opinion for assistance and solidarity, and finally they signed the declaration . . . , giving their addresses and telephone numbers. They issued a challenge to the Communist bureaucracy, saying "You signed the Helsinki declaration on human rights, and we want to and will make practical, political use of your signature."[13]

The Polish example was followed in 1977 by the establishment of Charter 77 in Czechoslovakia, which defined itself as a "free, informal community of people united by a willingness to strive for individual and collective human rights. . . . It was not an organization and not intended as the basis for oppositional political activity, and it would obey the laws of the country and wanted the regime also to follow its own laws."[14]

In a 1978 essay entitled "The Power of the Powerless," Vaclav Havel offered an evocative literary expression of this quest for freedom. He said the totalitarian state embodied "lies" and that individuals could affirm truth.

Because the regime is captive to its own lies, it must falsify everything. It falsifies the past, it falsifies the present, it falsifies the future. . . . Individuals must not believe all these mystifications, but they must behave as though they did. . . . They must live within a lie. . . . Living within the lie can constitute the system only if it is universal. . . . Therefore everyone who steps out of line *denies it in principle and threatens it in its entirety* [Havel's emphasis].[15]

In these words Havel identified the brittleness of the regimes while also offering a vision that would be realized eleven years later: "Are not these informal, nonbureaucratic, dynamic, and open communities that comprise the 'parallel polis' a kind of rudimentary prefiguration, a symbolic model of those more meaningful 'postdemocratic' political structures that might become the foundation of a better society?" During the next decade, 1978 to 1988, in effect this transformation occurred, as Poland's Solidarity movement led the way to what Brzezinski has termed the "self-emancipation" of Poland first, and much of Eastern Europe afterward.[16]

In 1979 the Soviet Union invaded Afghanistan, Soviet-backed Vietnam invaded Communist-ruled Cambodia, and widespread revelations began to surface about the mass murder and brutality that had characterized rule by the Communist Khmer Rouge.[17] In that same year, 1979, as the mass-terror phase of Communist rule was visible in the newest additions to the Soviet camp, the Polish pope of the Catholic church visited his homeland and received an enormous outpouring of public enthusiasm, showing the people and the Communist regime that decades of indoctrination had failed. Solidarity was founded in 1980, grew within a year to a membership of 10 million, and was recognized by the regime as a legal institution by summer 1981.

The Soviet regime was deeply concerned that the combination of the Solidarity workers movement and the religious enthusiasm in predominantly Catholic Eastern Europe sparked by the Polish pope could threaten communism in the entire region. The Soviet Union threatened to invade Poland if it failed to control Solidarity and was most likely the instigator of the failed assassination attempt on Pope John Paul II in May 1981.[18] Solidarity was suppressed by the Polish regime in December 1981. But it survived as an underground organization.

Despite repression, small, courageous groups of Eastern Europeans seeking democracy endured—often with help from religious institutions. Gorbachev assumed power in 1985 and proclaimed his reformist agenda in 1986, which "not only inspired greater hope in Eastern Europe but provided the opposition with convenient tactical legitimation. In that context Poles took the lead in generating a wider coalition of East European democratic opponents to the existing Soviet-type systems."[19] This effort included the establishment of a regional journal of opposition to Communist rule, beginning in 1986, and beginning in 1987, joint meetings among opposition groups from various East European countries. By 1988 hundreds of opponents to Communist and Soviet rule in Poland, Hungary, Czechoslovakia, and East Germany, had signed joint statements. It was "the first time since Stalin's imposition of regional hegemony that a joint East European opposition to Soviet rule was able to coalesce and express itself openly."[20] These events marked the gradual evolution of the East European opposition, back to a concern with politics and political institutions. By 1989 the focus of their political aspirations had become the attainment of democracy.

The Existence of the European-Atlantic Democracies

Just across the artificial division of Europe, the peoples of Eastern Europe could see and contrast life in the democratic world with the history of failure and tragedy produced by both fascism and communism. The Eastern Europeans recognized that existing democracies are not perfect human societies. Havel, visiting as the president of Czechoslovakia, told the U.S. Congress in 1990,

> As long as people are people, democracy in the full sense of the word will be no more than an ideal. . . . It can never be fully attained. . . . You have thousands of problems of all kinds, as other countries do. But you will have one great advantage: you have been approaching democracy uninterruptedly for more than 200 years.[21]

But with each passing decade of the contemporary era, it has become increasingly clear that the democracies of the world do ensure civil liberties for their citizens, do function through a competitive, pluralistic political process open to all, and can provide mixed economies that result in economic well-being for most and social help for those in need. The democracies have been a model also because of their demonstrated ability to evolve together in peace and to reconcile with such previous enemies as Germany and Japan. This evolution of a norm of peaceful relations among all democratic countries, both within the European-Atlantic relationship and worldwide, has contrasted with the coercive Soviet hegemony in Eastern Europe and with the pre–World War II pattern.

Although they have been peaceful, however, the democracies have not been pacifist. The ability and willingness of the European-Atlantic democracies to establish a defensive alliance and to maintain the levels of strategic and conventional military forces needed to ensure their independent survival have been critical to their role as models for the future of Eastern Europe. Indeed, the multiple dimensions of democratic success—freedom, prosperity, cooperative international relations, and survival against heavily armed totalitarian powers—have produced what Henry Nau called "this convergence of view in the postwar world" in favor of democracy on an ever wider scale.[22]

The balance of power and the implicit threat of Soviet military counteraction stopped the democracies from preventing the repressive use of Soviet force in Eastern Europe. Nevertheless, the democracies have had direct internal effects in the region, not only by their example but also as a result of trade, aid, tourism, media, and other forms of relations. The East European Communist regimes sought and obtained billions in Western economic aid and credits, starting with détente and *ostpolitik* in the early 1970s, and this aid made them more careful in their methods and in the extent of their repression— if only to avoid jeopardizing current or future economic benefits from the West. At the same time, millions of tourists visiting from the West over the years provided firsthand glimpses of the contrast in circumstances—and the tourists were free to leave, while few of the East's citizens could visit or travel to the West.

Also important were the moral encouragement and practical support for some of the opposition organizations, which came from citizens and leaders of the democracies. Most significant, perhaps, was the role of the U.S. trade-union federation, the AFL-CIO, in providing both types of help for the Solidarity movement in Poland. Once the United States established the autonomous but publicly funded National Endowment for Democracy in 1984, it provided aid for Solidarity and other prodemocratic groups in Eastern Europe and in other dictatorships of the left and of the right. By one account, as of 1987 this assistance had made it possible for several hundred books to be published secretly each year in Poland and for several hundred "independent journals . . . , from local bulletins to serious literary, philosophical, and political periodicals," to be published free of censorship each year.[23]

Brzezinski points out that by 1988 "the traditional Communist control over domestic communications was disintegrating" not only because of such parallel publishing and such Western broadcast media as Radio Free Europe, but also because an estimated 1.4 million videocassette recorders had by then made possible the "dissemination of uncensored films, political discussions, and dissident platforms." As late as 1988, on the eve of the unraveling, polls conducted in Western Europe among Eastern Europeans likely to support the regime—those with permission to travel to the West, and who intended to return to their countries—showed that "communism had the committed support of at most only about 15 percent of the population."[24] And this proved to foreshadow the massive popular rejection of the Communist parties in the free elections held in East Germany, Hungary, Czechoslovakia, and Poland in 1990.

Miscalculations of the Communist Elites and the Paradox of Dictatorship

In the late 1970s, partly to counter the visibly growing disaffection of the East European peoples and partly because of the Brezhnev-era military-buildup, the Soviet Union strengthened military integration with the Warsaw Pact armed forces. By the early 1980s it had imposed conditions for direct Soviet command of those forces without prior approval of the national Communist authorities. From the early 1980s on, including the Gorbachev years, the Soviet Union sought to

175

establish new, more extensive, direct economic links with Eastern Europe. These would include ties between entire production sectors and individual firms, in what Brzezinski concluded was "yet another Soviet design for gaining greater direct control over the region's economy," to benefit Moscow economically and to increase Soviet political control. This control would counter the effects of increasingly visible political and cultural pluralism among many of the peoples in Eastern Europe.[25]

The first miscalculation Gorbachev made was to underestimate the impact on the Eastern Europeans of the perestroika and glasnost campaigns he had launched in 1985 and 1986, intended to reinvigorate the Soviet system after twenty-one years of "stagnation" under Brezhnev. Gorbachev also overestimated the durability of the institutional structures keeping the national Communist regimes in control and subordinate to the Soviet Union. When Gorbachev inaugurated glasnost he sought to use the "creative intelligentsia" to bring pressure for reform on the recalcitrant apparat.[26] He did not take into account the cumulative, delegitimizing impact, either in Eastern Europe or the Soviet Union, of the cascade of revelations about Soviet repression, corruption, incompetence, and failure, past and present.

Nor did the Soviet leadership consider carefully or judge soberly the impact within the East European Communist parties of this cascade of Soviet anti-Brezhnev negative revelations in 1986, 1987, 1988, and 1989, exposing the crimes of an era in which the Brezhnev generation of leaders who still held power in Eastern Europe were also culpable. Such exposures obviously undermined the relationship between the Soviet and East European regimes and further reduced whatever public support those leaders still had; more importantly, Gorbachev's policies sharpened the intraparty division between the hard-line ruling gerontocracy and the reform Communists, most of whom were contemporaries of Gorbachev.

A third major miscalculation was Gorbachev's reported approval of the Jaruzelski regime's proposal to solve its economic problems by negotiating with Solidarity and by permitting it to compete in the limited but free elections of June 1989. Here it seems Gorbachev had learned the wrong lesson from his own experience with the limited and partially open March 1989 elections for a new Congress of People's Deputies as part of the Soviet governing system.

Gorbachev had added the "democratization" phase to perestroika in order to give himself more authority vis-à-vis the party apparatus, through the reinvigoration of the Soviet government institutions. As one observer noted, those March 1989 elections had produced "a resounding defeat not just for the apparat as Gorbachev wished, but for the party as an institution. For the first time in seventy years, the population had the possibility of saying no to official candidates and did so, at least in the large cities, on a major scale."[27] Nevertheless, Gorbachev attained the results he wanted from the new Congress of People's Deputies—it "elected" him president and chose a new Supreme Soviet that was "in effect, a consultative assembly rather than a genuine legislature . . . [and] would do his bidding."[28] As events showed, Gorbachev's approval of Jaruzelski's plan reflected a failure to understand the major differences between the degree of political experience and mobilization of the opposition in Poland and that in the Soviet Union as of the spring of 1989.

As one Solidarity leader noted in retrospect, "The Communist bureaucracy probably intended the Round Table [negotiations] as a kind of trap for Solidarity[,] perhaps . . . to gain legitimacy for its own authority . . . or to coopt some segments of the democratic opposition into the camp of the authorities." But this same Solidarity leader concluded that in fact the negotiations "paved the way for the rehabilitation of the people who opposed the military state . . . [and] made it possible for Poland to use elements of the Spanish route to democracy, a scenario in which the reform wing of the ruling camp could find a common language with the democratic opposition."[29]

Yet a fourth serious and ironic miscalculation emerged from the Jaruzelski-Solidarity entente in the summer and fall of 1989. Solidarity, the most active and organized of all opposition movements in the most restive Communist East European state, kept its commitments and did not challenge the Polish Communists' control of the bureaucracy, the military, or the secret police. (Only after the unraveling of communism and the elections in the other countries did Walesa, in the summer of 1990, begin pressing for fully free elections to choose a new president of Poland.) This "good behavior" of Solidarity probably reinforced the view of the Gorbachev faction—that the best response to the rising tide of protest in the fall of 1989 would be Soviet support for the reformist factions of the national Communist parties and Soviet help for their pushing aside of the Brezhnev-era leaders who had rigidly resisted perestroika in their own domains, as the hard-liners had done in the Soviet Union.

A fifth miscalculation was then made by Gorbachev and the reform Communists as the unraveling process began. They were initially overconfident that a series of concessions—travel opportunities, negotiations with opposition elements, incorporation of some opposition leaders in coalition regimes, promises of free elections at some future time—could stem the tide of oppositional protest and satisfy popular demands while halting well short of full democracy.

But the loosening of regime controls was followed by ever larger public protests demanding full democracy. The regimes sensed that unless they resorted to a massive use of force using Soviet troops or their own troops—which were under Soviet control to an extent unknown precisely to the civilian Communist elites—they could lose control and the elites could find themselves at great personal risk. Misguided by Soviet overconfidence that these challenges could be mastered by the reform Communists taking over Eastern Europe, the new regimes under pressure made a sixth miscalculation: they made even more concessions, thereby setting the stage for the free and fair elections in East Germany, Hungary, and Czechoslovakia that completed the unraveling of Communist rule.

This movement in a matter of weeks from overconfidence to unraveling illustrates a central paradox of all dictatorships. Years, and decades in the case of these Communist regimes, of rule that combines repression with the devious political penetration and manipulation of opposition elements serve to establish a sense of invulnerability among rulers. Barring the brief interlude of Communist rule in Hungary in 1919, the historical record showed that not one Communist regime had ever been removed from power before 1989, except as a result of external intervention (Grenada, 1983). Once people found the opportunity to reject these Communist regimes and to act effectively in the political contest without using violence—which would give the regimes a pretext for responding with overwhelming force—the regimes crumbled. As the insights of Tocqueville and Havel show, these regimes could not survive, once stripped of the lie of popular assent and of their will to use coercion. Paradoxically, dictatorships are both enduring and brittle. Once their elites begin to miscalculate, the momentum of popular hopes for greater freedoms can outpace their capacities to retain power.

The Loss of Fear and the Demonstrative Effect of Success

Although virtually no armed opposition had met the Communist seizures of power in Eastern Europe, more than 100,000 persons were executed during that process, and hundreds of thousands more were killed afterward or died in forced resettlement and in labor camps.[30] Then after the victorious Communist parties consolidated their power in the late 1940s using Stalinist brutality, Stalin in turn had tens of thousands of East European Communists executed or imprisoned.

After Stalin's death in 1953, Khrushchev's de-Stalinization speech, and internal reform initiatives ("the thaw") in 1956, tens of thousands were released from concentration camps and the repression lessened in both the Soviet Union and Eastern Europe. Yet in subsequent years, after each attempt at rebellion and each massive, prolonged protest in Eastern Europe, those deemed in any way guilty were punished by the Communist states by one means or another. These means ranged from execution to imprisonment to employment at menial work in remote villages; Dubcek was a janitor for twenty years. Every member of an opposition group in the 1970s and 1980s faced these risks and knew so.

They also knew that in June 1989, after ten years of liberalization in the economic arena, the Chinese Communist leadership brutally suppressed the peaceful witness for freedom in Tiananmen Square, killing thousands and then systematically rounding up, imprisoning, torturing, and in some cases executing those suspected of being prodemocracy organizers. In October 1989, Honecker explicitly threatened to do the same in East Germany.

But the Eastern Europeans perceived that Gorbachev did not want to use the Chinese methods and that he and the national Communist elites needed and wanted more, not less, Western aid, investment, and trade. They also knew that the Soviet army had been stalemated after ten years of combat in Afghanistan and that tens of thousands of Cuban and Vietnamese troops had failed to crush other anti-Communist armed resistance groups. Some believed that these facts might reduce the willingness of Soviet troops to risk combating resistance forces in Eastern Europe, which might well be supported by elements of the national armed forces.[31]

Honecker's removal and the decision of his reform Communist successors to use compromise rather than repression marked the end of fear and the acceleration of the tempo of political protest and effort by the opposition. In turn, the gathering success of those efforts in Germany, symbolized by the opening of the Berlin Wall on November 9, 1989, and by the euphoric reaction in both East and West Germany to that event, sparked a similar loss of fear in Czechoslovakia, leading in turn to the unraveling of that regime.

Also in the historical consciousness of East European opposition in Poland, Hungary, East Germany, and Czechoslovakia were the memories of past rebellions that had revealed—suddenly and definitively—those populations' overwhelming rejection of communism. As long as massive military force was not used against them, these memories of the past and the experiences of hundreds of thousands of people who publicly decided, in Havel's words, to "live within the truth" served to remove the fear that had prevented movement toward freedom.

German Reunification within NATO

The fundamental prerequisite for German reunification within NATO was the self-emancipation of the peoples in most of Eastern Europe, including East Germany, in 1989–1990. The tactics and strategy of the West German effort to attain this result were discussed earlier, in chapter 6; the purpose here is to examine this outcome from the perspective of the study of politics.

In contrast with the democratization process that involved the peoples of the East European states and the Communist elites in direct interaction, the German reunification issue involved those participants along with the states of the Atlantic Alliance, especially the United States, the United Kingdom, France, and West Germany. These four Western powers were involved in direct negotiations and bargaining with the Soviet Union and East Germany. The formal process for this bargaining was the series of two-plus-four talks among the four World War II victors and the two Germanys, which began in February 1990 and continued until reunification. At the same time there was bilateral bargaining at the state level, between the Soviet Union and each of the key Western states. At this level the Soviet Union sought to divide the West in pursuit of its objectives, which evolved from the attempt to use reunification as a means of ending West German participation in NATO to the attempt to extract a significant price, in security concessions and economic benefits, for permitting continued German membership in NATO.

It is important to understand that this international bargaining process took place within a balance of power framework. The Western states recognized Soviet military capabilities in Eastern Europe, including East Germany, and they acted on an understanding that these realities and the post–World War II agreements, although violated by the Soviet side in a number of important dimensions, gave the Soviet Union the right and the ability to decide when and whether there would be German reunification, and whether it would occur within NATO.

Holsti's construct of the "influence ladder" defines six tactics that states use to obtain their objectives: (1) persuasion; (2) the offer of rewards; (3) the granting of rewards; (4) the threat of punishment; (5) the infliction of nonviolent punishment; (6) the use of force.[32] The Western states used only the first three means; there was never any consideration of moving from incentives to threats against the Soviet Union in the bargaining process. This policy reflected the explicit Western recognition of power realities and the implicit understanding that no member of NATO, including West Germany, was willing to use the three additional means of obtaining objectives to challenge Soviet power over East Germany or Eastern Europe. The corollary of this implicit understanding among the NATO member-states was that in view of the balance of power, the only tactics that could be used were those linked with incentives for the Soviet Union. This policy may have significant implications in the future, if Soviet hard-line elements seek to use their 380,000-member combat force remaining on German territory or other means to extract further concessions in coercive ways.

The capabilities brought by the two sides to these negotiations were therefore highly asymmetric. The Soviet Union began with the premise of its military power—including its forces in East Germany—which would not be challenged in any way by the Western states. And the Soviet Union had a tradition of effective statecraft, as well as extensive experience in playing upon the interests and perceptions of Western powers (such as France) to bring about enough differences to avoid a solid diplomatic front. Gorbachev seemingly tried to do this in his December 1989 and spring 1990 bilateral meetings with President François Mitterrand.

But the Soviet Union also had significant economic needs, which the Gorbachev leadership believed could best be met by Western financial and technological assistance. On the Western side, after initial hesitation by the governments of Britain and France, the clear objectives of the West German government and the unequivocal backing President George Bush gave to Chancellor Helmut Kohl led to a solid, unified Western position in favor of German reunification, through a process of democratic choice and as a full member of NATO.

The clarity of West German objectives was succinctly expressed in Kohl's "Ten-Point Program for Overcoming the Division of Germany and Europe," presented to the West German Parliament on November 28, 1989—nineteen days after the opening of the Berlin Wall. In it Kohl quoted NATO endorsements for the reunification of Germany dating from 1967 and from the May 1989 NATO summit. Like the East European democratic opposition, he sought to portray Gorbachev as sympathetic to German aims. Excerpting from the Soviet-German statement made at the conclusion of Gorbachev's June 1989 visit to Bonn, Kohl quoted their affirmation of a "common European home," a favorite Gorbachev phrase of the period, which both leaders had said included "the realization of human rights . . . [and] unqualified respect for the integrity and security of each state. Each state has the right freely to choose its own political and social system."[33]

In addition to recognizing the need for clearly defined objectives, the West German government also understood the need to be effective simultaneously in three political arenas—because developments in one could affect any of the others. These three areas included relations with its allies, especially France and the United States; relations with the post-Honecker regimes in East Germany; and relations with the Soviet Union. The events suggest that West Germany's strategy was to be politically active in all three arenas in order to move the process forward as quickly as possible. As one respected analyst noted, "Any government that knows how to get where it wants to go has an advantage."[34] This West German clarity of purpose and strategy increased the capabilities of the Western coalition.

Also, West Germany was ready to be flexible in meeting Soviet concerns about the potential military power of a reunified Germany. In 1954, as part of the condition for West German rearmament, it had been required to forgo the development or possession of atomic, biological, or chemical weapons of mass destruction. The Kohl government did not hesitate to accept a continuation of this prohibition, and after some weeks of haggling it also accepted a ceiling on its forces above the one originally proposed by the Soviet side, but considerably below the numbers that would have resulted from a merger of the two German forces—370,000 as compared with 680,000.

The economic success and prosperity of West Germany was used as an argument to persuade the Soviet leadership that it could gain by agreeing to reunification with continued NATO membership. In the context of Germany's flexibility on the security issues, this argument was probably the decisive factor in persuading Gorbachev to agree. Kohl promised a total of about $15 billion in various payments and credits from Germany in the course of the negotiations leading to reunification. In addition Kohl promised undisclosed future levels of German economic and technological support for the Soviet Union, and he promised to urge other industrial democracies to be generous also.

In the negotiating process, therefore, the following Western capabilities were used successfully: West German clarity of objectives and strategy; firm support from its key allies, especially the United States; flexibility on the security issues; and a willingness to provide economic rewards in exchange for Soviet allowance of reunification within NATO.

Leaders were very important. Kohl exemplified a leader capable of "thinking of time in a stream," in the phrase of Neustadt and May, who can transcend the present and establish a clear idea of its links with the historical past and the desired future. Kohl also understood that while "the past has predictive value . . . what matters for the future in the present is departures from the past." He demonstrated his ability to undertake "continuous comparison, an almost constant oscillation from present to future to past and back," as he visualized the historical possibilities opened by the courage of the East German people's quest for liberation.[35]

At the same time, Kohl understood and explicitly accepted the validity of Germany's neighbors' historic fears. At the fiftieth anniversary of the start of World War II, on September 1, 1989, Kohl told the West German Parliament:

> Today we are filled with sorrow and with the sense of responsibility that the memory of World War II entails. Particular responsibility derives from the fact that the war was unleashed by the criminal regime that was in control of Germany then. . . . Keeping alive the memory of it is what we owe to the innocent victims, above all those of the Shoah, the unparalleled genocide of the European Jews, and the Poles, against whom Hitler waged a total war of enslavement and annihilation.[36]

Kohl's sense of the present explained his insistence on the need for Germany to remain in NATO, in the existing European Community, and in other democratic, integrating institutions. His sense of the future was evident in his program for German reunification, which called for a "common European identity" based on the "fundamental values of freedom, democracy, human rights, and self-determination" that would include all of Eastern Europe and even, someday, the Soviet Union.[37]

The roles of Kohl, Bush, Gorbachev, and other leaders in these events, as well as the importance of the bargaining competence of West Germany and its allies, all provide further support for Nau's "choice-oriented" analytic perspective. The Social Democratic leadership in West Germany continually opposed most of Kohl's initiatives; had the SPD been in office, the pace of events would have been far slower. In view of the resurgence of Soviet hard-liners in November 1990, the resignation of Shevardnadze as foreign minister in December 1990 (with his warning about the "return of dictatorship") and reported opposition to Soviet military violations of the 1990 Conventional Forces in Europe arms reduction agreement, the SPD leadership might well have missed the opportunity for reunification, or at least for reunification within NATO.

The decisions of individual citizens and of large groups of individuals were also an important causal factor in these events. First, hundreds of thousands of people voted against the East German Communist regime by fleeing to the West. Second, millions of West Germans willingly paid the human and financial costs of absorbing these immigrants and making them feel welcome. Third, small bands of opposition activists in East Germany kept the hope of greater freedom alive during years of repression. Fourth, hundreds of thousands joined them in the fall and winter of 1989. And finally, millions of East German voters constituted the 48 percent bloc that voted for the CDU-CSU–led coalition seeking the speedy reunification of Germany—in sharp contrast with the positions of the competing Social Democratic and Communist parties. That fateful choice and the selection of a grand coalition democratic government, which then worked closely with Kohl and West Germany in a common strategy, turned the two-plus-four talks into a "one vs. five process" and contributed to a momentum that moved the Soviet Union to accept the Western view on this major issue.

Implications for the Further Study of Politics

Some years ago a wise student of politics reminded us that political science demands a conscious effort to amass knowledge, and that this in turn required setting forth "impressions of a study in hypothetical terms that are susceptible to further exploration."[38] The unraveling of communism in Eastern Europe and the reunification of Germany are changes of historic significance, and this study has raised important questions about the future of German foreign policy. Therefore, this provides an opportunity to suggest a number of hypotheses that might be the basis for further investigation.

Such hypotheses will link independent variables with a dependent variable, which is "the international-relations behavior the researcher is seeking to comprehend and that is predicted to undergo change as conditions vary."[39] And we recall that "independent variables are all those factors that shape these behaviors and determine the variance."[40] This analysis will suggest a number of propositions that might be tested by future research, concerning the irreversibility of the changes in Eastern Europe, the implications of these changes for the future of other Communist regimes, and the factors that could either produce a neutral German foreign policy, or cause Germany to remain an active member of the Western alliance.

Irreversibility of the East European Changes. Speaking to a joint session of the U.S. Congress in February 1990, President Vaclav Havel of Czechoslovakia said the democratic opening in Eastern Europe "is,

I am firmly convinced, a historically irreversible process."[41] Many other political leaders, East and West, have made similar statements. In late 1990, however, the process of partial liberalization in the Soviet Union began to reverse itself as press freedoms and other forms of glasnost were restricted, hard-liners were appointed to key positions in internal security, and the Soviet regime's political cunning and violence thwarted the independence of Lithuania and the other Baltic republics.

In November 1990 the head of the Soviet KGB, Vladimir Kryuchkov, revealed the resurgence of the hard-line elements of the Soviet ruling elite when he said that the KGB would fight "with all the means" at their disposal "against . . . certain radical movements . . . masterminded by foreign support."[42] Brzezinski had written in 1988 that "a Soviet domestic crackdown would require some turning of the screws in Eastern Europe, even if [this fell] short of direct intervention."[43] After the reversal of glasnost in the Soviet Union and the crackdown on the Baltics in early 1991, a number of East European leaders expressed a renewed fear of Soviet power and how it might threaten their fragile progress. For example, the first deputy minister of interior of Czechoslovakia warned, after the Soviet use of force in Lithuania in January 1991, against "the state terrorism of Soviet forces which under certain circumstances could destabilize the situation in the former Communist countries."[44] All this suggests the following propositions:

• The transitions to democracy in Poland, Hungary, and Czechoslovakia will remain vulnerable to reversal through Soviet manipulation or direct intervention until the Soviet Union itself either is no longer ruled by the current Communist party, becomes a functioning democracy, or sharply reduces its military power.

• The reunification of Germany is irreversible, as long as it is protected and guaranteed by the membership of Germany in NATO.

Conditions for the Unraveling of Other Communist Regimes

Communist regimes continue to rule in Bulgaria, Romania, the Soviet Union, China, North Korea, Vietnam, Laos, Cuba, Ethiopia, Afghanistan, Angola, Mozambique, Cambodia, and other countries controlling almost 2 billion of this planet's population. In the last four of these named countries, armed insurgencies have fought for years and have not yet displaced the central Communist regimes—even though these armed struggles constitute evidence both of the hope of a significant portion of the population for an end to Communist rule and of external support for that purpose. Those armed efforts might well succeed if enough political, diplomatic, and military aid were provided, but to date the Soviet Union has been more effective in its support of pro-Soviet Communist regimes than those states have been in supporting their armed and unarmed opponents.

If a possibility develops, however, for the unraveling of Communist regimes in the coming years, without violence, in Romania, Bulgaria, the Soviet Union, and perhaps China and North Korea, then the following propositions may hold:

- The possibility for the replacement of Communist regimes without internal warfare may exist when four conditions are met: (1) there is a conscious and ever growing quest for freedom among the population; (2) the democracies maintain their civil liberties, peaceful relations, and strength; (3) there are divisions within the Communist elites, and these lead to miscalculations; (4) the populations begin to lose their fear of repression.

- The process of German reunification demonstrates that when a single national culture is divided between a Communist state and an economically successful democratic state—as in the cases of North and South Korea and of Communist China and the Republic of China—the cultural-historical ties add a strong dimension of credibility and attraction to the more pluralist political system for the people in the Communist state. The more democratic the pluralist state becomes, the stronger this attraction is likely to be and the greater its impact provided it can survive as an independent entity.

As actions taken to maintain Communist control in China since 1989 and in the Soviet Union since late 1990 demonstrate, it is likely that the Communist political elites have made similar observations and will seek to counter threats to their rule.

The Soviet Union, Germany, and the Future Foreign Policy of Germany

In the contemporary era, a new relationship has been established between the Soviet Union and Germany, a direct result of the events of 1989–1990. This book has analyzed how the long-term Western and German interests might be affected either constructively or destructively by the evolution of this relationship. A number of testable hypotheses can now be summarized:

- As long as its current Communist regime remains in power, the Soviet Union will attempt to use its relationship with Germany both to extract significant economic and technological benefits and to bring about a German shift toward de facto neutrality.

- Unless the German political leadership and government recognize this risk and act promptly to avert it, it is unlikely that another NATO member will fully understand the risk or attempt—in time—to counter it; friendly governments will assume no major problem exists if the Germans themselves seem unaware or unconcerned about such a drift toward neutralism.

- A gradual shift of Germany toward de facto neutralism could occur despite its leaders' current contrary intentions, as a result of the subtle but cumulative and converging impact of four factors: (1) domestic-interest-group and ideological politics, in combination with the well-documented phenomenon in democratic politics of those with a direct interest devoting far greater attention to the improvement of German-Soviet relations than the general public and disinterested leadership devotes to broad political effects—until the final stages of the process become dramatically visible; (2) the coherence of Soviet purposes in this matter under its current or future Communist leadership, along with the historical pattern of Soviet adaptation in its statecraft to new and unexpected circumstances; (3) the likelihood of a substantial reduction of the U.S. military (and therefore geopolitical) presence in Western Europe—especially in Germany; (4) the ambiguity of elements of the democratic left in a number of European countries, including Germany and France, and the prospect that France might miscalculate its interests.

- As long as Germany remains in NATO and NATO remains a viable defensive military alliance, the Soviet Union's means to attain its objectives in Europe will not include direct military coercion of Germany or any NATO member-state. They could well include, however, a variety of indirect coercion methods, such as support for terrorism and for internal political destabilization. This outcome would be even more probable if the Soviet Union should seek to restore Communist rule in all or some of the current transitional countries of Eastern Europe.

- The Soviet leadership can seriously miscalculate the effects of its decisions, as it did in the unraveling of communism in four East European countries. It might well do so in the case of its expanded relationship with Germany. If Germany continues as a democracy and a member of an effective NATO alliance, the new level of German-Soviet cooperation—provided it does not improve Soviet offensive military capabilities to any significant extent—might lead to further pressures inside the Soviet Union for internal liberalization. In the case of the former East Germany, "nearness" to a democratic Germany did in fact help to bring change.

187

The choice-oriented perspective on politics interprets the future of the European-Atlantic political system not as predetermined by existing forces of history, but rather as shaped by these forces and by the decisions of leaders and peoples in all its countries. The following chapter will offer perspectives on and suggestions for the policy decisions that would increase prospects for a future that strengthens peace and freedom.

10
Toward the New Europe

The task before us is to consolidate the fruits of this peaceful revolution and provide the architecture for continued peaceful change.

President George Bush, December 1989

In 1989 and 1990 the world witnessed two historic transformations. First, in Eastern Europe most existing Communist regimes unraveled, and those nations began to move toward political democracy and free market-oriented economies. Second, as part of this movement toward freedom, the people of East Germany fled westward by the hundreds of thousands. In March 1990 they voted against communism and for the peaceful reunification of Germany in freedom; this was achieved in October 1990 within the Atlantic Alliance.

If this process of building free institutions in Eastern Europe continues and succeeds, it will open enormous prospects for a new era of peaceful relations among all the democratic governments in Europe. It could add enormously to the momentum of constructive, liberalizing change in the Soviet Union. For decades the Soviet leadership feared and repressed political democracy in Eastern Europe, believing that if any East European country moved from Communist rule to democracy and free market-oriented economies the example would inspire like-minded Soviet citizens.

Two Possible Futures—In Summary

As was discussed in chapter 5, this process of liberalization in Eastern Europe began in April 1989 with the agreement of the Polish Communist regime to permit the Solidarity movement to compete in fair and free elections for a minority of the seats in the Parliament and for all the seats in a new (but powerless) national Senate. In late May 1989, on the eve of those promised free but limited elections, President Bush was in Germany, en route to Eastern Europe, and said:

> Our hopes run especially high, because the division of Europe is under siege, not by armies, but by the spread of

> ideas. . . . The momentum for freedom . . . comes from a single powerful idea—democracy. . . . For 40 years the world has waited for the cold war to end. And decade after decade, time after time, the flowering human spirit withered from the chill of conflict and oppression. And again the world waited. But the passion for freedom cannot be denied forever. The world has waited long enough. The time is right. Let Europe be whole and free."[1]

At the time these prophetic words were spoken, the division of Germany had symbolized since 1945 the division of Europe and the cold war. By the end of 1990 the peaceful reunification of Germany in freedom could well symbolize the capacity of the Atlantic community and the European states to bring about a Europe "whole and free." Whether this hope will be realized in the coming years will depend on the actions of the peoples and governments of all of the countries involved, including those of the United States, the Soviet Union, and Germany. Most important perhaps will be the foreign policy decisions made by the government of reunified Germany in the context of the transition to a new Europe.

It may well be a portent of the new era that Gorbachev was the first head of state to visit reunified Germany and the two countries signed a Treaty of Friendship and Cooperation on November 9, 1990—the first anniversary of the opening of the Berlin Wall. At the signing, Gorbachev declared, "The era of confrontation is over. The face of Europe and the world has changed"; Kohl called the Soviet-German agreement "an appeal to all citizens to play their part in the process of reconciliation."[2]

In this first major treaty concluded by the new Germany a symbolism derives from the two possible meanings of the crumbling of the Berlin Wall and Gorbachev's November 1990 visit. The East German leadership intended the opening of the Berlin Wall in 1989 to provide an outlet for those East Germans determined to leave, expecting this to reinforce their ability to continue in power; but the people of East Germany decided otherwise. Gorbachev hoped that his new and special relationship with Germany would provide major economic benefits to strengthen the Soviet Union and would ultimately lead to a relationship in which Germany would move toward de facto neutrality. Such a move would open the way for an end to the military aspect of the NATO alliance—a Soviet purpose and interest for decades, which Gorbachev reaffirmed in 1990. But it is quite possible that the people and government of a reunited Germany will decide otherwise and that the foreign policy of the new Germany may contribute to the "withering away" of the Soviet regime.[3] There are indeed two quite different foreign policies that Germany might pursue.

The two futures that may follow German reunification and the new relationships between Germany and the major powers were analyzed in chapters 7 and 8. The negative future would be one in which, despite the best intentions of the German leadership, the Soviet Union is able to manipulate its relationship with Germany, and the German people's own desire for peace, arms reduction, and denuclearization brings about the self-demilitarization of Germany, the removal of most U.S. and other Western troops from its soil, and its de facto neutralization. These results might stem from a political-economic process in which German economic aid for the Soviet Union is used—gradually and subtly—to bring about some degree of German political subordination to the Soviets on key international issues. Such subordination could occur because a growing number of German business, financial, and political groups could have an ever larger stake in maintaining good relations, and because of hidden Soviet manipulations using the repayment of its ever increasing debt, its troop withdrawals, and its covert networks.

As this subtle transformation occurred, the Soviet Union could continue to project the image of a reasonable and benign power in Europe. Simultaneously, German hopes for peace could lead Germany into strong advocacy of a European political process that in effect would gradually transform the NATO military alliance into a political coalition, or would lead to the dismantling of NATO and its substitution by the Conference on Security and Cooperation in Europe (CSCE) or some other collective security arrangements.

If such changes should occur before the Soviet Union itself were to become a genuine political democracy or were to reduce its massive military forces to pose no offensive threat, these changes would set the stage for greatly increased Soviet political influence in all of Europe. This could accomplish the decades-long Soviet foreign policy goal of removing the United States from the military alliance with Western Europe and could to a dangerous degree enable the Soviets to make political and economic requests of Western Europe that could not be refused.

In his letter to the leaders of the seven leading industrial democracies at their July 1980 summit meeting, Gorbachev expressed the Soviet need for large-scale economic and technological help from the West. By the end of 1990 the Soviets had obtained more than $33 billion in new financial commitments from the West, including $15 billion from Germany alone, $2.4 billion from the European Community, and $1 billion in credits from the U.S.—the first such aid since

1975.[4] It is in the Soviet interest to build the new Soviet-German relationship so as to provide an incentive for sharp reductions in the U.S. military presence in Europe and for the withering away of NATO as a military alliance. In such a new European political context, the Soviet Union would calculate it could obtain full access to Western Europe's money, technology, and production resources.

As was described in chapter 7, however, Germany's peaceful reunification in freedom carries the potential for an enormous positive historical opportunity. In this bright future, Germany would remain a member of a NATO alliance that retains a credible military deterrent against existing Soviet military capabilities. Further, the new, reunified Germany, while increasing its ties with the European Community, could also become an important source of political and practical support for transitions to democracy and to free market-oriented economies in Eastern Europe—and perhaps, ultimately, in the Soviet Union. In this positive future, the Soviet-German relationship could lead to a range of new personal and institutional relationships that serve to stimulate the liberalization of Soviet political and economic life.

At the October 28, 1990, meeting of the EC heads of government, German Chancellor Kohl and French President Mitterand demonstrated that their cooperation in the interests of bringing the European Community toward greater political and economic unity would continue after German reunification. Despite objections from the United Kingdom, the EC members, with France and Germany in the lead, agreed to move toward the establishment of a European central bank by 1994 and to "strengthen the identity of the Community and the coherence of its actions on the international scene."[5]

This French-German entente in the strengthening of the EC institutions—formally approved at the December 14–15, 1990, meeting of the European Community leaders—was the first major foreign policy action taken by Germany after reunification. In addition, Germany and France jointly proposed in December 1990 that the nine-member Western European Union—originally formed to coordinate the defense policies of European NATO members—be strengthened to provide the institutional basis for a common West European defense policy. They contended that such a "European pillar" would strengthen NATO and the European Community. At the same time, however, the EC heads of government reaffirmed that their closer cooperation in security and defense should "take into account the importance of maintaining and reinforcing existing links within the frameworks of the Atlantic Alliance."[6]

Both of these initiatives offered evidence of Chancellor Kohl's repeated promises, made during the months of international negotiations about reunification, that Germany intended to work toward closer political unity within the context of the European Community and that this would continue to guide German foreign policy after reunification. At the same time, since France also signed a new Treaty of Cooperation and Friendship with the Soviet Union in November 1990, this movement toward closer political and economic cooperation among the EC states illustrated that France and Germany shared the view that they could both reinforce the unity of the West and reach out to the East.[7]

One analysis of Mitterrand's purpose in signing the 1990 treaty with Moscow, however, suggested that he was seeking to establish "a new identity for his country in the vanguard of a European confederation. That goal was enshrined in a Treaty of Cooperation and Understanding with the Soviet Union."[8] If such a "European confederation" includes only genuine democracies, the effects would all be positive; but a "European confederation" that includes the Soviet Union and excludes such non-European powers as the United States and Canada could open the way to the military decoupling of the United States and Western Europe. Since there is a long history of French ambiguity about America's role in Europe, and since the United Kingdom is likely to be preoccupied by its differences on EC political-economic issues, it will most likely depend on the foreign policy of a reunified Germany to maintain a European focus on the continuing need for military alliance among the Atlantic democracies.

The peaceful reunification of Germany in freedom represented a major political success for the NATO alliance and for its basic premise that an armed coalition including the United States could deter Soviet military attack. Over time, according to the premise, this coalition and the political and economic accomplishments of the NATO countries would create additional pressure for freedom and independence throughout Eastern Europe, which the Communist regimes could not suppress forever. The beginning of the transitions to democracy in Poland, Hungary, and Czechoslovakia, along with the dismantling of the former East German army and the 1990 Treaty on Conventional Forces in Europe (CFE), provide an opportunity for future real reductions in the size and offensive capabilities of the conventional military forces facing Western Europe. This will be especially true when Soviet armed forces are withdrawn from Eastern Europe—promised by July 1991; when the 380,000 Soviet troops are withdrawn from the territory of former East Germany—promised by the end of 1994; and when all CFE reductions are implemented—promised by 1995.

If the democratizing East European countries reduce their national military forces with the end of the Warsaw Pact, the sum of these changes will open the way for significant reductions in NATO forces.

These potentially beneficial developments in the military realm have their counterpart in the prospect of Eastern political transformations aided by Germany and other leading democracies. As reunified Germany acts to help the citizens in its formerly Communist region to rebuild free civic institutions and market-oriented economic practices, the peoples and governments of Eastern Europe can benefit from the example. Further, since 1964 the Federal Republic of Germany has made important contributions to the building of democratic institutions in many countries through political development foundations affiliated with each of its major political parties. As a result, Germany has accumulated vast experience in encouraging the building of democratic institutions in transitional settings, and it will have the opportunity to apply the lessons of this experience to Eastern Europe in the 1990s.

In addition, Germany is likely to provide significant economic assistance and to be a major source for investment funds and trade for most of Eastern Europe. Taken together, the political development and economic aspects of Germany's involvement with Eastern Europe might make significant contributions to the prospects for democracy's success throughout that region. Further, the likely political and economic revitalization of the former Communist region of Germany could add importantly to the appeal of democratic and market institutions, not only in Eastern Europe, but also ultimately the Soviet Union.

The risks and positive opportunities for the new Germany in Europe were well summarized by Horst Teltschik, for many years director of Chancellor Kohl's foreign policy staff. Noting that Kohl was the first Western political leader to propose the "institutionalization of the CSCE process" and endorse the need to create a "pan-European peace order with cross-alliance security structures," Teltschik wrote in 1990 that these new approaches and the closer German-Soviet relationship are only possible in the context of German "friendship with the United States and anchorage in the Atlantic Alliance, on the one hand, and . . . close ties with France and integration in the European Community on the other . . . [as] the two decisive pillars of German foreign policy."[9]

The Results of the New Germany's First National Elections

The future international role of the new Germany will be shaped by the results of its first national election, held in December 1990. As we saw in chapter 6, following the opening of the Berlin Wall in November 1989 Chancellor Kohl and his CDU-CSU-FDP coalition government took the lead in promoting reunification with continued NATO membership. Kohl never wavered from this course, holding firmly to the fundamentals of his position at every stage of negotiations with the Soviets—although in 1990 Germany paid more than $15 billion to help persuade the Soviet Union to permit reunification.

By contrast, in 1989 the major opposition party, the Social Democrats (SPD), were slow to understand that the reunification opportunity they had given up as forever lost in the early 1980s was now beckoning on the horizon. Even after the SPD endorsed reunification in December 1989, however—weeks after the Berlin Wall was opened—it maintained a somewhat ambiguous stance both in East and West Germany. The SPD constantly maintained that Kohl's government and political coalition were moving too quickly and were not sufficiently concerned about the economic consequences for East Germany of rapid transition to a market economy.

The East German voters in the region most supportive of the SPD before Nazi rule gave the party only 22 percent of the vote in the March 1990 elections. They voted overwhelmingly for the parties affiliated with the West German CDU-CSU, the Alliance for Germany, received 48 percent of the vote.[10]

Instead of learning a lesson from this defeat, the SPD questioned, initially opposed, and even threatened to use its veto power in the Federal Council (Bundesrat) to prevent the economic unification of both Germanys in July 1990—even though Chancellor Kohl and Lothar de Mazière, the freely elected East German prime minister, had agreed upon it. The SPD did not carry out its threat, but throughout the reunification process it continued to support unification ambiguously while constantly raising questions about its pace, terms, and cost.

From the time the Berlin Wall fell in November 1989, the unification of Germany became the most important political issue for 70 to 90 percent of the German people—a phenomenon that continued right through the final unification, nearly a year later. The SPD had been ahead in the opinion polls for the December 1990 German national election—before the unification process gained momentum. But once this momentum began in the spring of 1990, Chancellor Kohl became the preferred candidate of ever larger proportions of German voters, and support for SPD leader Oskar LaFontaine as a possible chancellor declined steadily from May 1990.

Chancellor Kohl and his foreign minister, Hans-Dietrich Genscher, understood the historic opportunity facing Germany: that reunifica-

TABLE 10–1

RESULTS OF THE DECEMBER 1990 GERMAN NATIONAL ELECTION

Party	National Vote (percent)	Bundestag Seats (of 656)
CDU/CSU	44	313
FDP	11	79
SPD	33	239
PDS (Communist)	2 (but 9 in former East)	17
Alliance '90	1 (but 4 in former East)	8

SOURCE: Marc Fisher, "Grateful Germans Vote to Keep Kohl," *Washington Post*, December 3, 1990.

tion was possible and that it was important for German reunification to proceed to the point of irreversibility before any possible change in Soviet leadership or policy might pose new obstacles to that opportunity. The German voters rewarded that historic foresight of the governing CDU-CSU–FDP political coalition with victory in the December 1990 national elections.

Taken together, the two coalition parties received 55 percent of the December 2, 1990, vote, with 44 percent going to the CDU-CSU and 11 percent going to the FDP. The Social Democratic party (SPD) saw its support decline to 33 percent—the lowest since 1957—and the Greens, a coalition of leftist groups concerned with environmental issues, failed to reach the 5 percent vote level required for representation in the Parliament. See table 10–1.

Both the SPD and the Greens had displayed ambivalence about German reunification, and this seems linked to their loss of popular support. The renamed Communist party of former East Germany, the party of Democratic Socialism (PDS), received 2 percent of the votes nationwide but 9 percent in the former East German regions—down from 16 percent in March 1990. Pursuant to an October 1990 decision of the German constitutional court, votes were counted separately in the former East Germany so that East German–based parties would have a chance for representation in Parliament if they received more than 5 percent in that region alone. This procedure helped a coalition of groups that had led dissent in the former Communist-ruled region, the Alliance '90 Coalition, to obtain eight seats in the Parliament. A small far-right party received only 2 percent of the vote nationwide and obtained no representation in the Parliament.

The similarity of election results in both parts of Germany was noted by Kohl: "This is a day of joy; I am particularly happy that the result in the former East Germany is almost identical to that in the west. This means that in all of Germany we are the ones trusted to take responsibility."[11] This consensus, along with the past and present political commitment of the CDU-CSU and FDP parties to a Germany closely tied to the European Community and Atlantic Alliance, increases the prospects for the positive future that can evolve from German reunification.

The political and economic resources of a reunified, democratic Germany firmly allied with the West in NATO and embedded in such institutions of Western Europe as the European Community can be a factor of extraordinary importance in leading the way toward the positive transformation of Eastern Europe and, perhaps, the Soviet Union. The question is, What international arrangements are more likely to reinforce the positive aspects—present and future—of German reunification? The answer depends on whether it is assumed that the hopeful events of 1989–1990 have already created a new Europe, or whether they are the opening phase of a complex, fragile, potentially reversible process of transition to a new Europe.

The Fragility of the East European Transitions

The starting point for examining the progress of transition in Eastern Europe must be the understanding that all large-scale political and economic changes toward freedom are likely to be intrinsically complex, fragile, and reversible. Politically, there has been enormous progress in Czechoslovakia, Hungary, and Poland, all of which held free and fair national elections in 1990, bringing to office governments representing the will of the population. Unfortunately the 1990 national elections in Bulgaria and Romania were neither free nor fair. Although the renamed Communist parties in Romania and Bulgaria permitted partial, limited openings, and democratic groups were able to organize and compete to some extent, the Communists used the power of the state and their party networks deriving from many decades of rule to ensure that democratic opposition would not win majorities in the voting process. In Yugoslavia, a country with a national Communist regime long independent of the Soviet Union and long marked by a comparative openness of travel and expression and by elements of a mixed economy, the year 1990 was one of intense conflict among ethnic groups and between prodemocratic and hard-line Communist groups. Although political transitions could be described as well under way in Poland, Hungary, and Czechoslovakia, they have only begun in Bulgaria and Romania, and they are marked by intense fragmentation and conflict in Yugoslavia.

197

From an economic point of view, all the transitional governments are moving toward greater reliance on markets rather than central state planning, and all these East European transitional governments are seeking Western assistance and investment. In 1990 the Soviet Union also proclaimed a transition to what it termed a "planned market economy," while clearly intending that the Communist regime retain ultimate control. The situation there remains comparable to the Chinese Communist regime opening its economy in significant ways for nearly a decade but, as its renewal of repression in June 1989 illustrates, determining that it would retain ultimate political power over the people.

The evidence of contemporary history concerning Communist regimes therefore indicates that although openness and movement toward market institutions and trade with market economies can be politically liberalizing, some Communist regimes will restrict the political consequences of such openings and retain power for themselves. The Bulgarian, Romanian, Yugoslavian, Soviet, and Chinese regimes, among others, illustrate this.

A long road still lies ahead, then, until all the countries of Eastern Europe make a transition to full political democracy. Threats to this transition come from many directions, and they include the intention of the Communist regimes in three of the six countries under discussion to retain political power while opening economically. But even in Poland, Hungary, and Czechoslovakia, a potential threat always lurks in the remaining hard-core apparatus of the Communist party, the bureaucracy, the secret police, and elements of the military.

Threats to national cohesion and democratic progress also derive from the revival and resurfacing of ethnic and national conflicts. Such conflicts are especially evident in Yugoslavia and are present also in the case of Hungarian minorities in Romania, in Slovak separatism, and in other issues repressed by the Communist regimes. Some of these ethnic conflicts, including reported anti-Semitism in several countries, could over time revive right-wing or nationalist extremism.

The largest threat looming over the transitional countries of Eastern Europe, however, is the risk that the Soviet leadership will resume the intent to dominate Eastern Europe. This threat became even more serious at the end of 1990 with the visible resurgence of the hard-line Soviet elements in the Communist party, the KGB, and the military. The Soviet decision in early 1991 to use military force—after months of political and economic coercion—against the efforts of Lithuania, Latvia, and Estonia to establish their independence led Andrei Kozyrev, the prodemocratic foreign minister of the Russian republic, to warn: "If the forces of darkness prevail in the Soviet

Union, Central Europe is next on their agenda."[12] Following the Soviet repression in the Baltics, the newly elected president of Poland and longtime leader of the Solidarity movement, Lech Walesa, warned of a future "deadly threat" from the Soviet Union, as the Soviets unilaterally delayed the expected date for withdrawal of their 40,000 combat troops from Poland. Originally promised for 1991, the proposed withdrawal was deferred until a time after Soviet forces would have left German territory—promised to occur by the end of 1994. And it is worth noting again that a senior official of the Havel government said in early 1991 after the Soviet repression in the Baltic republics, "the state terrorism of the Soviet Union . . . under certain circumstances could destabilize the situation in the former Communist countries" of Eastern Europe.[13] A similar foreboding was expressed by the American commentator William Safire.[14]

The East European countries know they are not presently and are unlikely in the future to be under NATO military protection. If the Soviet regime should decide that the democratization process in Eastern Europe is a threat and has to be reversed, it would likely attempt to do so first through covert alliance with the remaining hard-core Communist apparatus in each country, rather than by open threats or use of force.

But a variety of methods are open to a Soviet regime that might in the future intend to promote a Communist restoration in Eastern Europe. The optimistic effort at a transition from monarchy to republican government made in Europe in 1848, in which restoration of the monarchies followed a period of euphoria, stands as a historical lesson. Further, the political skill and the coercive and military potential of the Soviet Union make the possibility of Soviet-inspired Communist restoration a contingency to be considered seriously— especially as the demands in the Soviet Union for democracy and national autonomy appear increasingly to threaten the future of Soviet Communist elites and their hold on power.

The most visible danger to the transitional countries of Eastern Europe derives from the enormous economic difficulties that accompany the transition process. In every country the immediate short-run effects of the transition have included increased inflation and unemployment; for large numbers of working people transition has created enormous uncertainty about the future.

East European dependence on the Soviet Union for much of its energy supplies, along with Soviet insistence that starting in 1991 payment for energy and other Soviet exports must be made in hard (Western) currency, will sharply increase the intrinsic uncertainties of the large-scale transitions in economic institutions. Iraq's invasion of Kuwait in 1990 caused a sharp increase in oil and energy prices, which in turn increased the depth and extent of economic recession in the United States and some other industrial democracies. Those factors in turn have increased the likelihood that severe economic problems may arise in Eastern Europe, which could lead to serious political problems.

Over time, deepening economic problems could undermine the legitimacy of the democratic idea, despite the fact that the majority of the populations in these countries understand that this is a transitional phenomenon. Extremists of the left or the right could use such problems to jeopardize any progress in these countries toward the building of democratic and free market–oriented institutions.

Thus, while the transforming events of 1989–1990 have led to enormous progress in Eastern Europe toward freedom and a reduction of the Soviet military threat, this progress is fragile and reversible. The opportunities for secure peace and human betterment inherent in this current transition to an achievable—but not yet realized— new Europe require a prudent, coordinated, and competent foreign policy by the Western powers—including a reunited Germany.

A Design for Transition to the New Europe

Western leaders recognized in 1990 the importance of helping Eastern Europe attain full democracy with successful economic institutions— a shift that would increase the prospects for peace in Europe. President Bush had said in December 1989, "The task before us is to consolidate the fruits of this peaceful revolution and provide the architecture for continued peaceful change."[15] For that reason the sixteen member-countries of the Atlantic Alliance and others in Western Europe have taken initiatives to help the East European countries as they embark on the promising but difficult voyage of transition. The industrial democracies in the Group of Twenty-four (G-24) countries have acted to coordinate their assistance for Eastern Europe, providing emergency food supplies and other financial help. From the start of the transitional process the European Community took the lead in coordinating these financial contributions and seeking to remove barriers to trade with the East European countries. By the end of 1989, the G-24 countries had committed over $14 billion in grants, credits, guarantees, food aid, and technical assistance to Poland and Hungary alone.[16]

In late 1989 a new multilateral organization was proposed, the European Bank for Reconstruction and Development (EBRD). It quickly pledged capital of approximately $12 billion to be used for economic development and, according to U.S. Secretary of State Baker, "to assist the political and economic transformation of these countries. No other international institution has the goal of promoting democracy, pluralism, and the rule of law."[17] In November 1989 the United States established a new national program to "Support East European Democracy" (the SEED Act). This program proposed a three-year commitment of $928 million for humanitarian assistance and support for democratic institution-building, technical training, environmental improvement, and economic aid. In addition the United States established the Polish Stabilization Fund, the Polish Enterprise Fund, and the Hungarian Enterprise Fund as efforts "designed to promote entrepreneurial activity" in those transitional countries (see table 10–2).[18]

TABLE 10–2
OVERVIEW OF INSTITUTIONS AIDING THE EAST
EUROPEAN TRANSITIONS, 1989–1991

Organization	Description	Estimated Aid, 1989–1990
Support for East European Democracies (SEED)	Enacted by U.S. legislation in 1989; works to coordinate aid from both private and public sources, stresses long-term structural change over simple relief aid.	$928 million over three years from U.S.; undisclosed from other sources.
Western Bilateral Aid Commitments	Includes commitments from the 24 democracies in the OECD.	Over $4 billion in direct assistance.
European Reconstruction and Development Bank	Multilateral development bank; currently under French leadership; operations began in 1991.	$12 billion capital fund.
World Bank Institutions (IMF, IFC)	Promote development by selective loans and advice on economic restructuring.	$5 billion loan to Eastern Europe; approximately half to Poland.

SOURCES: Data on SEED from Department of State, "Support for East European Democracies" (Washington, D.C.: January 1990). Data on Western Bilateral Aid Commitments from *Washington Post*, January 27, 1990. Data on European Reconstruction and Development Bank from *Washington Post*, February 23, 1990. Data on World Bank from *Washington Post*, February 23, 1990.

The commitment displayed by the United States and Western Europe to democracy in Eastern Europe reflects the Western perception of this as a major historical opportunity for peace, for the reduction of armaments, and perhaps for a future opening to full democracy in the Soviet Union. This commitment may also reflect a broad understanding that the "new Europe" is still being built, rather than an accomplished fact. There may be an unspoken concern that the prospects for democracy in East European countries are precarious, both internally and perhaps because of the threat that the Soviet regime might move to reassert hegemony over them and promote the resurgence of their remaining national Communist parties.

When will the "new Europe" have been achieved? When most or all the countries of Eastern Europe are governed by democratic political institutions and have made substantial progress toward the modern combination of free markets and functioning social welfare institutions. Also, when the transitional process in the Soviet Union has led to the establishment of democracy there, which in turn results in sharply reduced Soviet offensive strategic and conventional forces, then it can be said that the new Europe has been achieved.

Until then, it must be understood that while the dramatic and hopeful events of the years 1989 and 1990 have opened the way to a new Europe, it is not yet a reality. This understanding implies the need for new ideas and a conceptualization of the institutional arrangements during the transition to the new Europe—a transition that may take five, ten, or more years. For this reason it is necessary to envision a sensible and balanced architecture of European-Atlantic engagement, which can make reunified Germany more likely to remain a steadfast and constructive partner of the West and can make the ultimate goal of democracy in all of Europe more likely to be achieved. The starting point for such an effort, however, must be the realistic understanding of the lessons to be drawn from the evolution of the European-Atlantic institutions in the post–World War II era.

Lessons from the Evolution of the European-Atlantic Institutions

In the years immediately following World War II, as Western hopes for a functioning collective security system under United Nations auspices were disappointed by the actions of the Soviet Union in Europe, Western nations established a variety of new institutions to meet their perceived needs in the emerging international political system. A brief review of the evolution of these diverse institutions will provide a useful perspective on Europe's needs during the next transition years.

TABLE 10-3

EVOLUTION OF EUROPEAN-ATLANTIC INSTITUTIONS, 1948–1986

March 1948	BRUSSELS PACT—established to extend collective security among treaty signatories. Became a foundation for NATO. Members: Belgium, France, Luxembourg, the Netherlands, the U.K.
July 1948	ORGANIZATION FOR EUROPEAN ECONOMIC COOPERATION (OEEC)—instituted in connection with the Marshall Plan to promote European economic cooperation. Members: Austria, Belgium, Denmark, France, Greece, Iceland, Ireland, Italy, Luxembourg, the Netherlands, Norway, Portugal, Spain, Sweden, Switzerland, Turkey, the U.K., West Germany.
April 1949	NORTH ATLANTIC TREATY ORGANIZATION (NATO)—treaty signed to provide members with mutual security assistance. Members: Belgium, Canada, Denmark, France, Iceland, Italy, Luxembourg, the Netherlands, Norway, Portugal, the U.K, the U.S.; Greece (1952), Turkey (1952), West Germany (1955), Spain (1982).
December 1949	COUNCIL FOR MUTUAL ECONOMIC ASSISTANCE (CMEA, COMECON)—created to coordinate the integration of East European states. Members: Bulgaria, Czechoslovakia, Hungary, Poland, Romania, the Soviet Union; Albania (1949–1961), the GDR (1950), Mongolia (1962), Cuba (1972), Vietnam (1978).
July 1949	COUNCIL OF EUROPE—established to encourage unity and cooperation among European democracies. Members: Belgium, Denmark, France, Ireland, Italy, Luxembourg, the Netherlands, Norway, Sweden, the U.K.; Greece (1949), Turkey (1949), Iceland (1950), West Germany (1951), Austria (1956), Cyprus (1961), Switzerland (1963), Malta (1965), Portugal (1976), Spain (1977), Liechtenstein (1978).
August 1952	EUROPEAN COAL AND STEEL COMMUNITY (ECSC)—created by the Treaty of Paris (1951), it was formed to facilitate economic interdependence and thus reduce the chance of war. Members: Belgium, France, West Germany, Italy, Luxembourg, the Netherlands.

(continued)

TABLE 10-3 (continued)

May 1955	WESTERN EUROPEAN UNION (WEU)—established to consider mutual economic and security concerns. Members: Belgium, France, West Germany, Italy, Luxembourg, the Netherlands, the U.K.; Portugal (1989), Spain (1989).
May 1955	WARSAW PACT —organized in response to NATO to provide mutual security assistance among the East European states. Members: Albania (until 1961), Bulgaria, Czechoslovakia, East Germany, Hungary, Poland, Romania, the Soviet Union.
January 1958	EUROPEAN ECONOMIC COMMUNITY (EEC)—founded by the members of the ECSC under the Treaty of Rome (1957), they intended it to guarantee certain rights among member-states and to strengthen economic cooperation.
January 1958	EUROPEAN ATOMIC ENERGY COMMUNITY (EURATOM)—formed in conjunction with the EEC to regulate peaceful atomic applications.
May 1960	EUROPEAN FREE TRADE ASSOCIATION (EFTA)—created to eliminate internal trade barriers and expand world trade. Members: Finland, Iceland, Norway, Sweden, Switzerland; Austria (1961). It included six members in 1990.
September 1961	ORGANIZATION FOR ECONOMIC COOPERATION AND DEVELOPMENT (OECD)—replaced the OEEC; expanded beyond solely European focus and added development aid to its responsibilities. Members: participants in the OEEC were joined by Australia, Canada, Finland, Japan, New Zealand, the U.S. It included twenty-four members in 1990.
July 1967	EUROPEAN COMMUNITY (EC)—formed in 1967 by the merger of the ECSC, EEC, and EURATOM, it is a supranational body charged primarily with integrating the economies of the member-states. By 1992, members plan to practice complete economic freedom in transactions among themselves. Members: beyond the participants in the ECSC, members include the U.K. (1973), Denmark (1973), Ireland (1973), Greece (1981), Portugal (1986), Spain (1986). It included twelve members in 1990.

TABLE 10-3 (continued)

July 1973	CONFERENCE ON SECURITY AND COOPERATION IN EUROPE (CSCE)—culminated with the signing of the Helsinki Final Act on August 1, 1975. The act is intended as a framework for improving cultural, economic, humanitarian, and security cooperation. The act has no legal authority over its signatories but rather seeks compliance by moral persuasion. Members: all European states except Albania, plus the U.S. and Canada. It included thirty-four members in 1990.
January 1984	CONFERENCE ON DISARMAMENT IN EUROPE (CDE)— the conference adopted, upon adjournment in September 1986, a set of confidence- and security-building measures intended to reduce the chances of war in Europe. Members: same membership as of the CSCE.

SOURCES: Department of State, "Conference on Disarmament in Europe" (Washington, D.C.: December 1986), and "Helsinki Final Act: Tenth Anniversary" (Washington, D.C.: July 1985). *The Europa World Year Book, 1989* (Kent, England: Rochester Limited, 1989). Paxton, John, ed., *The Statesman's Year-Book* (New York: St. Martin's Press, 1988). Kaplan, Morton A., *The Rationale for NATO* (AEI–Hoover Policy Study 8, August 1973).

Defense and Deterrence. Once the Western powers understood that the post–World War II era still posed dangers, their first concern was defense and deterrence. In 1948 France and Britain formed a bilateral defensive alliance that was later extended into the Brussels Pact, to provide collective security to its six signatory West European countries (see table 10–3). This alliance in turn laid the foundation for the North Atlantic Treaty Organization, established among twelve countries in 1949, when the United States made the unprecedented decision to participate in a peacetime military alliance.

After North Korea's attack on South Korea in June 1950 and the ensuing fears of a Soviet attack against Western Europe, NATO transformed itself from an essentially political commitment to an alliance with a multinational, fully integrated military command and assigned forces. Hundreds of thousands of U.S. troops were deployed to Europe, providing both immediate defensive strength and a guarantee of full U.S. commitment to Europe's defense.[19] NATO subsequently added members, bringing its total membership to sixteen— all democracies.

The original Brussels Pact of 1948 was transformed in 1955 into the Western European Union, a treaty organization established to ensure the mutual security of the European member states. By 1989 the Western European Union included nine members—who belonged also to NATO and the European Community—and was perceived as a potential source of increased military-security cooperation among members of the European Community. While the NATO Treaty explicitly confined the area of mutual guarantee to the territories of the member states, the Western European Union security agreement permitted its nine member-states to cooperate in areas of mutual interest outside their immediate territories. After the 1990 Iraqi invasion of Kuwait, for example, the Western European Union functioned as a coordinating entity among European states as they decided to contribute military or other support to the multinational political-military coalition opposing Iraq.

Political Cooperation. After establishing organizations for defense and deterrence in 1948, the European countries founded the Council of Europe in 1949. Its purpose was to bring about greater cooperation among the West European countries and to encourage political democracy and the observance of human rights. Germany's admission to the Council of Europe in 1951 constituted an important step in its reconciliation with Western Europe. Neutral Austria joined in 1956, after the withdrawal of Soviet troops in 1955, and by 1980 the Council of Europe included the twelve members of the European Community along with a number of other European democracies, including neutral states.[20]

The council includes a committee of ministers of the individual member governments, a parliamentary assembly selected by the national legislatures of the member states, a European commission of human rights, and a European court of human rights. Its headquarters near the French-German border in Strasbourg, France, were intended to encourage and symbolize a new era of peace between France and Germany and among all the countries of Europe. Beginning in 1985, the Council of Europe sought to strengthen its cooperation with the European Community and the United States and, simultaneously, to expand its contacts with Eastern Europe. After that time the council's parliamentary assembly also took a special interest in fostering worldwide democracy. It organized a major international conference on parliamentary democracy in 1987, which brought together representatives from some sixty-five countries.

Because of the council's symbolic role, its established interests in fostering democracy, its independence of any military alliance, and its neutral European democracy member-states, it is the ideal institution to be the bridge of political association with Eastern Europe in its transition to democracy. In November 1990 the council marked the fortieth anniversary of its Human Rights Charter and admitted Hungary as the first member from the post-Communist countries of Eastern Europe.[21]

Another institutional focus for political cooperation in Europe has been the Conference on Security and Cooperation in Europe. The Soviet Union first proposed such a conference in 1954, and for years the West viewed it as a Soviet initiative to divide the United States from Europe. But with the coming of U.S.-Soviet détente, Germany's *Ostpolitik* in the early 1970s, and the Soviet decision to permit the United States and Canada to participate in the CSCE, negotiations under CSCE auspices began in July 1973. They concluded with the signing of the Helsinki Final Act, on August 1, 1975.

That CSCE agreement ratified the existing borders of Europe and thereby reinforced the international commitment the Soviet Union had received from Germany as a result of the Eastern Treaties of 1970. But it also established standards and goals on issues of security, disarmament, economic cooperation, and human rights. After the opening of the Berlin Wall in 1989, U.S. Secretary of State James Baker observed that

> in 1975, the governments of Eastern Europe may not have taken seriously their commitments to respect a wide range of fundamental human rights, [but] their populations did. The standards of conduct set by the Helsinki Final Act are increasingly being met by international pressure and domestic ferment. The peoples of Poland, of Hungary, of Czechoslovakia, of Bulgaria, and of East Germany . . . have freed themselves.[22]

The commitments undertaken as part of the 1975 Helsinki Final Act could not be enforced by any CSCE signatory state against another, and for fourteen years they seemed to have little effect in loosening the grip of the East European Communist regimes. Nevertheless, the Helsinki Final Act provided a basis of legitimacy for domestic groups in East European countries seeking to hold their governments to the human rights standards they had agreed upon in 1975. One example is the Charter '77 organization in Czechoslovakia, one of whose members, Vaclav Havel, became first the interim president and later the democratically elected president of his country.

In December 1989, U.S. Secretary of State Baker noted that:

> the CSCE process has made its most distinctive mark in the field of human rights. One fundamental right, however, is

207

not yet fully institutionalized. This is the right for people to choose in regular, free, open, multiparty elections, those who will govern them. This is the ultimate human right, the right that secures all others. Without free elections, no rights can be long guaranteed. With free elections no rights can be long denied. . . . Free elections should now become the highest priority in the CSCE process.[23]

This proposal points the way to a major opportunity for using the CSCE process on behalf of political democracy and freedom in the coming years.

Economic Cooperation. Institutions for economic cooperation were the third type established. The Organization for European Economic Cooperation was launched in July 1948 to promote and facilitate European economic coordination in administering the U.S. assistance funds provided under the Marshall Plan. The success of that cooperative experience, along with the vision of such French and German political leaders as Robert Schumann, Jean Monnet, and Konrad Adenauer concerning defeated Germany's need for reconciliation and reintegration with Western Europe, provided the basis for establishing in 1952 Europe's first common market—the European Coal and Steel Community.[24]

Among its six founding members were France, West Germany, and Italy. The establishment of the European Coal and Steel Community marked the beginning of true political reconciliation between France and Germany. As the proposals were being launched in the spring of 1950, the architect of this idea, Jean Monnet, said they "provide a basis for the building for a new Europe through the concrete achievement of a supranational regime within a limited but controlling area of economic efforts."[25]

West German Chancellor Adenauer, while agreeing with the importance of economic cooperation, told the West German Parliament in June 1950, "the importance of this project is above all political and not economic."[26] In other words, membership on an equal basis with five European democracies in an organization for economic cooperation politically signified the return of Germany to democratic Europe, overcoming its status as a defeated and occupied aggressor country. In the same way, during the 1990s the increasing association of post-Communist Eastern Europe with the European Community and other West European economic institutions could help Eastern Europe move closer to the West politically, institutionally, and economically.

In 1957 the success of their first effort at economic integration led the six countries to conclude the Treaty of Rome, which in 1958 established the European Economic Community (EEC) to extend and strengthen this economic cooperation. In 1967, merger treaties brought together the three European communities—ECSC, EEC, and EURATOM—together as the European Community. Since then, the European Community has been governed by four multinational institutions, combining elements of supranational authority on most economic issues with intergovernmental agreement. Such agreement is required by the EC Council of Ministers and is guaranteed through provisions permitting individual governments to veto most major EC proposals they oppose.[27]

In 1973 the original six members of the European Community agreed to the entry of the United Kingdom, Denmark, and Ireland. The European Community grew further in the 1980s, reaching a membership of twelve by 1986. The European Community adopted the Single European Act in 1986, calling for the establishment of a full single market among the twelve member-states by the end of 1992. As of 1988, the European Community constituted a major economic and political unit with a combined population of 320 million, a combined gross national product of $4.7 trillion, and annual exports and imports of roughly $890 billion.[28]

The original organization for cooperation in distributing Marshall Plan aid evolved in 1961 into the Organization for Economic Cooperation and Development (OECD). It added development assistance for third-world countries to its mandate and later expanded beyond Europe to include the major industrial democracies. By 1990 it included twenty-four countries, and as the G-24 it continued to play an important role in development assistance while also coordinating the provision of economic aid for the transitional countries of Eastern Europe.

In October 1990 the leadership of the European Community agreed they would do the following: (1) create a European central bank in 1994, looking toward the creation of a common European currency sometime during the 1990s; (2) enhance the legislative powers of the European Parliament; (3) create a European citizenship and strive to reach more decisions by majority vote, rather than permit vetoes by individual governments. All of these measures would be geared to establishing greater momentum toward an eventual European political union.[29] Germany and France led the way in supporting these proposals, among the first major diplomatic initiatives of the reunified Germany.

By late 1990, Austria, Turkey, and Cyprus had applied for membership in the European Community, Sweden had announced plans to do so, and Norway was reportedly considering similar action.[30] As of November 1990, however, the European Community decided to "deepen" its existing institutions and the extent of cooperation among its current members before admitting any new ones. This decision was motivated primarily by the challenges that the European Community faced as it moved toward a single European market in 1992. For the East European countries seeking EC admission, however, it meant having to wait until some time into the future for full membership.

Arms Reduction and Confidence-building. The fourth phase in the evolution of these European-Atlantic institutions involved the varied international efforts for arms reduction and confidence-building cooperation. These have included U.S.-Soviet bilateral agreements in the 1960s on nuclear testing and nonproliferation, U.S.-Soviet bilateral agreements since the 1970s to limit offensive strategic weapons and defensive systems, and a range of ongoing U.S.-Soviet negotiations. In 1990 these negotiations included talks on strategic arms reductions (START), on defense and space, on nuclear testing, and on chemical weapons and missile technology proliferation.[31] The 1987 U.S.-Soviet agreement to remove all intermediate-range nuclear warheads based in Europe was being implemented even before the dramatic events of 1989–1990 created the perception in Western Europe of major opportunities for additional arms reductions.

In 1973 all the NATO and Warsaw Pact member-countries began negotiations on Mutual and Balanced Force Reductions (MBFR) in Europe. The Western objective was to deal with the large conventional forces superiority of the Warsaw Pact by "eventually establishing parity at lower levels in the form of a common collective ceiling on each side's military manpower."[32] But differences concerning the total size of existing Warsaw Pact military forces—with Western estimates being higher than the Warsaw Pact was willing to admit—caused these negotiations to go on inconclusively for years, eventually to be supplanted by two more sets of East-West negotiations.

The first, from 1984 to 1986, under the auspices of the CSCE, reached agreement on confidence- and security-building measures that were intended to lower the risks of armed conflict arising from misunderstandings of military maneuvers in Europe. The confidence-building measures agreed upon by all thirty-five CSCE states in September 1986 included:

> Forty-two–day prior notification of certain military activities above the threshold of 13,000 troops or 300 tanks; exchange

of annual forecasts of notifiable activities; prohibition on exercises involving more than 75,000 troops, unless forecast two years in advance; mandatory observation of exercises above 17,000 troops; and on-site inspection (both on the ground and from the air) as a means of verification.[33]

As of 1989, according to the U.S. State Department, implementation of this confidence-building system was "encouraging." The Warsaw Pact reported "between 21 and 25 notifiable activities per year, while NATO had reported between 14 and 20 such activities annually, although Eastern observation programs have been much more limited than NATO and neutral, nonaligned programs."[34]

Negotiations among all CSCE member-states (reduced from thirty-five to thirty-four with German reunification) continued through 1990 on further confidence-building measures. In addition, the separate 1990 agreement between NATO and the Warsaw Pact to pursue conversations on "open skies" continued to provide another means of expanding confidence-building arrangements between the two armed coalitions.[35]

In 1989 NATO and the Warsaw Pact began negotiations in Vienna on the reduction of conventional armed forces in Europe, which became known as the CFE talks. These negotiations succeeded the long stalled MBFR talks, and for the West the objective remained the same—to seek increased security and to reduce the chances of surprise attack in Europe, from the Atlantic Ocean to the western region of the Ural Mountains (that is, including the western 1,600 miles of Soviet territory), by decreasing the conventional armed forces deployed by both sides in that region.

The United States and Soviet Union reached agreement in February 1990 on new upper limits for the number of troops each could station in Europe in the context of a final CFE treaty. The remaining differences were resolved following German reunification and further U.S.-Soviet negotiations in October 1990. As a result, on November 19, 1990, the twenty-two NATO and Warsaw Pact countries concluded a Treaty on Conventional Forces in Europe and signed it at the Paris summit meeting of the thirty-four CSCE member-states.[36] The November 1990 CFE treaty, when ratified by all signatories and fully implemented by 1994, will restrict both sides to an equal number of heavy weapons in the region from the Atlantic to the western boundary of the Ural Mountains. If implemented, the CFE treaty will limit both sides according to the specifications shown in table 10–4.

The CFE treaty also includes measures to provide for the verification of compliance, and it calls for the destruction of all disallowed

211

TABLE 10–4

TREATY ON CONVENTIONAL FORCES IN EUROPE, NOVEMBER 19, 1990

Weapons	Alliance/ Country	1988 Level	Treaty Limit
Tanks	NATO	22,000	20,000
	Warsaw Pact	60,000	20,000
	U.S. forces	5,700	13,300
	Soviet forces	46,000	13,300
Armored vehicles	NATO	27,000	30,000
	Warsaw Pact	63,000	30,000
	U.S. forces	5,500	20,000
	Soviet forces	45,000	20,000
Artillery pieces	NATO	21,000	20,000
	Warsaw Pact	61,000	20,000
	U.S. forces	2,650	13,700
	Soviet forces	47,000	13,700
Helicopters	NATO	2,000	2,000
	Warsaw Pact	3,000	2,000
	U.S. forces	700	1,500
	Soviet forces	2,800	1,500
Combat aircraft	NATO	6,300	6,800
	Warsaw Pact	14,000	6,800
	U.S. forces	800	5,150
	Soviet forces	11,000	5,150

NOTES: No country can have more than about two-thirds of the alliance's total in most categories. Treaty limit figures are maximums allowed by 1994. Actual figures could be lower.
SOURCE: *U.S. delegation to negotiations on the Conventional Armed Forces in Europe Treaty*; as published in the *New York Times*, November 20, 1990.

military equipment still located in the zones designated by the treaty on the day of signature. The hopes for the CFE treaty were expressed by U.S. Secretary of State James Baker, who said in October 1990 that it would "match last fall's political revolutions in Central and Eastern Europe with a military revolution as well . . . [and accelerate] the construction of a new, more stable and legitimate European order, politically and militarily."[37]

A number of the participants in the CSCE meeting where the CFE treaty was signed viewed it as part of the opening of a new era in Europe. Some compared it to the Congress of Vienna in 1815 and the 1919 Versailles peace conference. Chancellor Kohl of Germany called the CSCE conference a part of building "a Europe of eternal peace." In the last two centuries, Kohl continued, "Europe and my country in particular became the epicenter of worldwide catastrophes."[38] President Mitterrand of France added:

> It is the first time in history that we witness a change in depth of the European landscape that is not the outcome of a war or bloody revolution. . . . We do not have sitting here either victors or vanquished, but free countries equal in dignity.[39]

Critics of the 1990 CFE treaty point to a major irony: whereas the force levels it establishes would have been viewed as a major breakthrough in 1988 before the unraveling of East European communism in 1989–1990, in the post-1990 context the treaty as signed might provide multilateral and indeed Western endorsement for a higher level of national and Soviet combat forces among the former Warsaw Pact countries than might otherwise have resulted from the decisions of the newly independent governments of Hungary, Poland, and Czechoslovakia. Further, by establishing numbers of Soviet forces permitted west of the Urals, the CFE treaty might reinforce the Soviet central government's position on maintaining its military forces inside Belorussia, the Ukraine, and other Soviet republics that declared self-rule in 1990 and attempted to limit the military forces stationed by the Soviet central government on their territories.

Skeptics also observe that the U.S. government published a report in August 1990 showing the Soviet Union had by then transported between 7,000 and 8,000 tanks and more than 6,000 artillery pieces into storage facilities east of the Ural Mountains, as a way of avoiding their destruction under the terms of the treaty.[40] And with verification procedures having been a major stumbling block during the nearly two years of negotiations, critics of the CFE treaty contend that the procedures agreed upon will not provide adequate information for determining the precise extent of Soviet compliance with the terms of the treaty.[41] Missing from the 111-page CFE treaty—which specifies a twenty-two–nation Joint Consulting Group to verify the military information provided by the signatories—was aerial inspection, considered crucial by the United States for effective verification.[42]

Concern about verification was reinforced on the day the CFE treaty was signed; the national security advisor to President Bush publicly questioned the accuracy of some Soviet-supplied military forces data.[43] In December 1990, British Minister of Defense Tom King expressed "great concern" whether the CFE treaty was proceeding with "the degree of control and accuracy that was intended."[44] He said the latest NATO calculations showed that more than 78,000 Soviet tanks, armored vehicles, artillery pieces, and rocket launchers, along with 800 combat aircraft, had been moved east of the Ural Mountains. As a result, the Soviet military forces that would remain in being after the implementation of the CFE treaty were expected to be much larger than was assumed when the treaty was signed. Therefore, King said, it was "a matter of some urgency" for NATO to draw up a new military strategy.[45]

On the date the CFE treaty was signed, November 19, 1990, all twenty-two NATO and Warsaw Pact states were required to submit an inventory of their military forces remaining in the region from the Atlantic to the western side of the Urals. The treaty provided for a ninety-day period of verification, and if there were questions concerning the inventory's accuracy or about other issues they would have to be resolved before ratification by the national parliaments.

Beginning in the early 1980s the U.S. Congress required that the president submit annual classified and public reports on Soviet compliance with arms control agreements it had reached with the United States. All these presidential reports subsequently contended that the Soviet Union had in many cases violated existing arms control agreements and continued to do so in the Gorbachev era. In February 1990, President Bush reported to the U.S. Congress that "serious concerns about [Soviet] noncompliance remain," but he also indicated that "the Soviet Union now appears to be willing to take significant action to resolve some U.S. concerns."[46]

The problem of Soviet noncompliance was studied by an independent panel of experts who reported to President Reagan in 1984 that "over a twenty-five–year span the Soviets had violated a substantial number of arms control commitments."[47] In his December 1985 report to the U.S. Congress, President Reagan said:

> There is a pattern of Soviet noncompliance. As documented in this and previous reports, the Soviet Union has violated its legal obligation under or political commitment to: the SALT I ABM treaty and Interim Agreement, the SALT II Agreement, the limited Test Ban Treaty of 1963, the Biological and Toxin Weapons Convention (1970), the General Protocol on Chemical Weapons, and the Helsinki Final Act (1975).[48]

An important exception to that pattern might be the 1987 U.S.-Soviet agreement to eliminate intermediate-range nuclear launchers—the INF treaty. But even in that case, it came to light in early 1990 that a number of intermediate-range missiles had been secretly transferred to the military forces in several East European Communist countries. Only the unraveling of the former Communist regimes brought this transfer to light in 1990, and the Soviet Union responded to the U.S. protest by declaring this had taken place without its knowledge.[49]

This history explains why the Western countries consider verification such an important issue in the CFE context. It also explains why Soviet performance in the matter of the CFE treaty might be viewed as a key indicator of the degree of change in Soviet foreign policy. After closer examination of the Soviet-submitted CFE data, the U.S. government in December 1990 noted the following reported serious problems:

> The Soviets declared at least 20,000 fewer weapons than Western officials believed they had, and also mislabeled some weapons, possibly to exempt them from destruction. They said the Soviets also appear to have transferred some undeclared arms outside the region after the treaty was signed, an action the treaty does not permit.[50]

In addition, since naval weapons are not covered in the CFE treaty, the Soviet Union reportedly "designated three regular Army divisions as units of naval infantry" to exempt these tens of thousands of combat personnel from the limitations. By early 1991 it was evident that Soviet hard-line elements, especially in the military, were opposed to full implementation of the CFE treaty.[51]

Notwithstanding the divergent Western views about Soviet compliance with the 1990 CFE treaty, it is quite possible that the treaty will create the public impression of a major and irreversible reduction of military forces in Europe, barring any shift by the Soviet Union to an overtly threatening posture. Although the CFE negotiations have been held between NATO and the Warsaw Pact, they were signed in the context of the November 1990 CSCE summit meeting. As a result, there will be a natural tendency for some in both East and West to ascribe the CFE treaty to the CSCE process of dialogue and negotiation. That tendency will in turn be used by the Soviet Union to increase gradually the role of the CSCE on security issues, with the corollary assumption that the role of NATO will decline.

Here one can expect the full resources of Soviet diplomacy to focus on newly reunified Germany, with important attention also to France and perhaps to Italy. They will be urged to "grasp the historic opportunity" of moving "beyond the blocs" and match the hopeful optimism of the new era in international relations. Alone or in concert they will be urged to reinforce the security role of the CSCE and steadily to reduce the role of NATO.

215

To repeat, this is not a hidden objective of the Soviet Union. It is one that the Soviets have proclaimed in different ways for more than three decades and that Gorbachev has reaffirmed. The Soviet Union emphasizes that the withering away and ultimate dismantling of NATO is an objective it seeks in the cause of peace, as it defines this term.

Parallel Communities for Freedom and Peace

During the past four decades the nations of the Atlantic Alliance have accomplished their major objectives; they have preserved peace with freedom in their own countries and, by the example of their political and economic success, inspired movements for freedom in many countries, including countries of the contiguous Communist world. As this historical overview outlines, four types of institutions evolved to help bring about this result: institutions for defense and deterrence; institutions for political cooperation and the affirmation of democracy and human rights; institutions for economic cooperation; and institutions and negotiating arrangements to achieve arms reduction and confidence-building cooperation among hostile countries and coalitions.

Despite the inevitable range of stresses and the differences of viewpoint among the sovereign, cooperating, democratic countries, for more than four decades the historical record of these institutions has been one of progress through consensual decision making and shared, core democratic political values. Instead of conflicting with each other in purpose, these four types of institutions have served to complement each other and to provide the political leadership of the democracies with a broader range of opportunities to maintain peace with freedom while seeking new relationships with the Warsaw Pact countries. Ultimately that resulted in a lowering of tensions, normalization, and the unraveling of many European Communist regimes.

Since the new Europe has not yet been achieved but rather is in the process of being created in the formerly Communist countries of the East, the institutional design for this era of transition to a Europe "whole and free" should be one of parallel communities for freedom and peace. As summarized in the following table, this architecture for Europe in transition would include four elements that would be explicitly understood and perceived as the institutional framework for the next years.

Cooperation for Defense and Deterrence. Each of the four elements is important, but the success of all rests on the first—the institutions

216

TABLE 10–5

DESIGN FOR PARALLEL COMMUNITIES OF FREEDOM AND PEACE

COOPERATION FOR DEFENSE AND DETERRENCE

North Atlantic Treaty Organization: to remain with its integrated military command, but forces to be reduced through reciprocal, verified agreements; NATO to increase its role in arms control and reduction, and in the independent verification of agreements

Western European Union: established in 1955 as an organization for defense cooperation; currently includes 9 countries, which are also members of EC and NATO

POLITICAL COOPERATION TO AFFIRM DEMOCRACY AND HUMAN RIGHTS

Council of Europe

CSCE, Council for Security and Cooperation in Europe

ECONOMIC COOPERATION FOR PROSPERITY AND TRANSITIONS TO MARKET ECONOMIES

European Community

Group of 24 or OECD: Organization for Economic Cooperation and Development

European Bank for Reconstruction and Development

World Bank and the International Monetary Fund

Bilateral programs among industrial democracies and East European countries

ARMS REDUCTION AND CONFIDENCE-BUILDING COOPERATION

CSCE Confidence- and Security-building Measures negotiations: includes the United States and Canada, plus all European states except Albania

CSCE conflict resolution center: established November 1990, in Vienna

Conventional Forces Europe agreement of November 1990 and further negotiations: includes all 16 NATO and 6 Warsaw Pact countries

Strategic Arms Reduction Talks: negotiations between the U.S. and Soviet Union on strategic arms, defense, space, and nuclear testing

SOURCE: Author.

for defense and deterrence. To reassure the Soviet Union about its defensive intentions, NATO would not expand its membership to include former Warsaw Pact countries in the foreseeable future.

NATO would remain what it has been, a political-military coalition among sixteen sovereign states with an integrated military command and forces considered adequate to deter any form of attack from the Soviet Union. NATO could, however, play an increased role in arms control and arms reduction issues, including assisting in the independent verification of CFE and any other arms control, arms reduction, or confidence-building agreements that might be reached under CSCE or other auspices.

Will NATO still be needed in the aftermath of the 1990 CFE treaty and the likely dissolution of the Warsaw Pact, as newly independent East European governments seek to reduce their military obligations to the Soviet Union? The U.S. government gave one answer to this question by noting in November 1990 that "even after withdrawals from Hungary, Czechoslovakia, Poland, and Germany, the Soviet Union will still retain by far the largest standing army in Europe. There is no guarantee that the size of Soviet forces will continue to diminish or that they would refrain from reentering Eastern Europe should the political climate change."[52] The counsel of prudence is that NATO should continue to exist as a deterrent military alliance until the process of democratic transition has been successfully accomplished in Eastern Europe and the Soviet Union, and until the Soviet Union has substantially reduced its strategic and conventional forces to a level consistent with the defense of its own territory. In the meantime, the sum of NATO military forces must be able to deter existing Soviet nuclear and conventional military capabilities.

The NATO alliance also serves the vital political function of keeping the United States engaged in the defense of Europe. If the widely perceived trends toward a more benign Soviet foreign policy and an age of "eternal peace" in Europe continue, significant political pressure will come from both major political parties in the United States to reduce sharply the level, cost, and risk of the U.S. political commitment in Europe. If NATO were in effect abandoned or permitted to become an entirely ornamental institution by the European members, it would accelerate U.S. withdrawal from Europe; such a diminution might signify to the United States that the burden no longer needed to be carried, and that Europe was no longer committed to mutual defense.

The Atlantic Alliance has also played a key role as the focal point for German military participation and planning since the rearmament of West Germany. This "internationalization" of the German armed forces and of those of other NATO members has made a subtle but politically important contribution to the contemporary sense of mutual trust among the West European member-states. It is precisely in the next years, as the new Germany becomes more active and independent in its foreign policy, that it will be important to all NATO member-states—and even, arguably, to the Soviet Union—for the German armed forces to remain fully involved in a multinational alliance of democracies that includes the United States.[53]

Equally important to political-military trust among the West European states is their security alliance with the United States—a nation able to balance the massive military capabilities of the Soviet Union, and of such military preponderance over any West European state combination that they are freed from balance of power calculations with respect to each other. This has contributed to the European movement toward greater political and economic unity and to the assumption that relations among the European democracies will be peaceful. Perhaps the trends toward European unity have advanced so far that these positive effects—some of them subliminal—would endure past the demise of NATO; but this is not a certainty in this time of historical transition.

At the same time, the members of the European Community are likely to strengthen their own security cooperation under the auspices of the Western European Union (WEU) and the European Community. It is even possible that the Soviet Union will seek to encourage emphasis on this "European pillar" as an alternative to NATO in the next years and that some in France and Germany may be tempted to move in that direction. While increased European military cooperation in WEU is desirable, using it as a replacement for NATO would be a mistake because WEU, even with the nuclear forces of the United Kingdom and France, cannot in any way match the strategic nuclear forces of the Soviet Union. The de facto removal of the U.S. strategic deterrent, as part of the arrangement for the defense of Europe, would not be in the interests of either Europe or the United States.

The Western European Union can play an important role in enhancing the political and security cooperation of the EC states, as proposed by France and Germany—provided this role is played within the context of NATO. But it is also unlikely to admit any former Warsaw Pact countries to membership, to avoid giving the Soviet Union cause to fear the strengthening and expansion of an armed coalition against itself as a result of the political changes in Eastern Europe.

Political Cooperation to Affirm Democracy and Human Rights. An affirmative effort should be made to establish relations of political cooperation on behalf of democracy and human rights with all the post-Communist countries and those in transition. The Council of Europe can and should admit to membership those East European countries that have made a transition to functioning political democracy—as it admitted Hungary in November 1990—and the Council of Europe should also be directly and actively involved in supporting prodemocratic institution-building in all the countries of the East.

On November 21, 1990, in concluding their summit meeting the CSCE member-states proclaimed a Charter of Paris for a New Europe, affirming

> steadfast commitment to democracy based on human rights and fundamental freedoms, prosperity through economic liberty and social justice, and equal security for all countries. . . . Full respect for these precepts is the bedrock on which we will seek to construct the new Europe. . . . We undertake to build, consolidate, and strengthen democracy as the only system of government of our nations.[54]

The CSCE states also took the first steps toward establishing permanent institutions by agreeing that a secretariat for the entire organization should be headquartered in Prague, that a new center for the resolution of interstate conflicts should be based in Vienna, and that Warsaw would be the site of a CSCE group that would monitor future elections within the member-states.

Thus in its political dimension the CSCE can be important both in continuing to monitor the human rights standards of the Helsinki Final Act and in moving forward to encourage free and democratic elections. This encouragement would be of great importance for Bulgaria, Romania, Yugoslavia, and the Soviet Union, all of which have a long way to go toward the standard of free and fair national elections endorsed by CSCE in the Charter of Paris.

Economic Cooperation for Prosperity and Transitions to Free Market–Oriented Economies. During the 1970s the East European Communist regimes and the Soviet Union received tens of billions of dollars in Western aid and financial credits. None of this enormous flow of resources brought about fundamental improvements in the political or economic practices in those countries. The transitional countries of Eastern Europe need economic help from the West, and it is important that G-24 and the European Community have taken the lead in coordinating this assistance effort. But the industrial democracies in G-24 have decided to link large-scale economic assistance to progress toward democracy, as measured by fully free and fair national elections, by the reestablishment of civil society, and by the observance of human rights. Therefore, it is likely that no assistance beyond humanitarian help for serious crisis conditions will be provided to regimes such as those in Bulgaria, Romania, and the Soviet Union as long as they seek only partial openings, while the national Communist parties seek to remain in de facto political control.

Although the European Community intends not to admit any new countries to full membership until the single European market has been achieved among the current twelve countries, nevertheless associate-member status could be extremely useful for countries that are establishing genuine democratic institutions. It would perhaps fall to the European Bank for Reconstruction and Development to provide a focal point for more than financial assistance, for the broader and deeper understanding of free market and social market institutions that are necessary for all the countries in transition.

While the World Bank and the International Monetary Fund also have important roles to play in the economic transitions, it is more likely that bilateral relationships such as those with Germany and the United States will be important in helping to provide support for free market institution-building and access to the private sector investment of capital that could make an enormous political difference in the transitional countries of Eastern Europe. The CSCE also has an economic dimension, which could possibly provide a forum for the nations of the West to share with those of the East ideas and practical proposals for the transition to market economies.

Arms Reduction and Confidence-building Cooperation. In addition to those agreements on confidence- and security-building measures (CSBM) signed at the 1990 CSCE summit, continuing negotiations on this issue appear likely to result in further agreements. There may also be negotiations on further reductions in conventional forces in Europe. The NATO and former Warsaw Pact countries and some combination of other European states—under CSCE auspices, or including all thirty-four CSCE members—might initiate efforts to negotiate a CFE II treaty, for the reduction of armed personnel as well as weapons.

The course that could lead to a stable peace would be reciprocal and verifiable agreements building on genuine good faith compliance with the agreements already made. Therefore another important reason for keeping NATO intact during the transitional years is that the sixteen NATO member-nations, with their shared political-mili-

221

tary experience and staffs, could be more effective in working to-gether to bring about further constructive agreements.

If the transitional process continues moving as it has through 1990, it is likely that Poland, Czechoslovakia, and Hungary will function as independent sovereign states rather than as Soviet mili-tary allies. Until they begin a full transition to democracy, Bulgaria and Romania will likely side with the Soviet Union on a number of issues. Arms reduction and confidence-building negotiations con-ducted thus under the auspices of CSCE could produce a lineup of approximately thirty-one democratic countries in favor of sensible further steps and three countries clustering around the views of the Soviet Union. With NATO intact that result would be likely; but if NATO were in gradual dissolution and if the Soviet Union were successfully able to move Germany or France or any other major NATO countries toward its position, it is more likely that the Soviet Union could promote future arms reduction and confidence-building measures that might undermine peace and Western interests.

Most probably, irrespective of negotiations on European issues, the United States and the Soviet Union will continue their negotia-tions on strategic arms reduction, defense systems, space technology, and other issues over the next years. Presumably progress in the European arena will be reflected in progress on bilateral U.S.-Soviet negotiations, but not necessarily.

Conclusion

This proposed four-part architecture for Europe in transition builds upon the success of the past four decades and is entirely consistent with the political values and expressed political preferences of all members of the Atlantic Alliance, including Germany. If this concep-tualization of parallel communities, striving for the same overarching purposes of peace and freedom, is clearly understood by both the Atlantic Alliance and the German leadership, and if it is promoted by the consistent and reliable support of the United States, there is a far higher probability that German reunification will have the positive consequences discussed earlier.

But confusion among the leaders of the West or of Germany could blight such a success. A mistaken assumption that a full transition to a new Europe and an era of peace have already arrived could lead to a desire for new arrangements for their own sake. Then the Soviet Union might be able to use the CSCE process and the interests of individual European leaders and states, including Ger-many, to gradually move Germany away from full membership and partnership in the Atlantic Alliance.

The prospects for a positive historical evolution have been increased by the continuation of close German-French cooperation in the European Community, by the reelection of Kohl and the CDU-CSU–FDP coalition in December 1990, by firm and unwavering U.S. support for German reunification in NATO—as was made evident by the actions during the critical months of 1989–1990 of the U.S. Ambassador Vernon Walters, Secretary of State James Baker III, and President George Bush—and by the questions about future Soviet foreign policy raised by the visable shift of the Gorbachev regime in the direction of the hard-line Communist factions. This shift was made evident by the violent repression in the Baltic republics in early 1991 and the sudden shrinkage of glasnost.

If there were also conceptual agreement among the major Western powers on an international, institutional framework of the type proposed in this study—maintaining a realistic level of Western military-political cohesion and also opening the way for significant reciprocal, verified force reductions and new political, economic, and security cooperation with the countries beyond the former iron curtain—then this framework would help the new Germany pursue a positive foreign policy and avoid neutralization, in any form.

Given the decision of the German people in the December 1990 elections to return Chancellor Kohl and his party to office, and given the decades of strong commitment by the Christian Democratic, Christian Social Union, and Free Democratic parties to Germany's integration with democratic Europe, a bright future can certainly lie ahead for the relationship between Germany and the Atlantic Alliance. And freedom, peace, democracy, and free markets would be more likely to thrive in Eastern Europe and, some day perhaps, in the Soviet Union.

Appendix 1

Treaty on the Final Settlement with Respect to Germany, September 12, 1990

The Federal Republic of Germany, the German Democratic Republic, the French Republic, the Union of Soviet Socialist Republics, the United Kingdom of Great Britain and Northern Ireland, and the United States of America,

Conscious of the fact that their peoples have been living together in peace since 1945;

Mindful of the recent historic changes in Europe which make it possible to overcome the division of the continent;

Having regarded to the rights and responsibilities of the Four Powers relating to Berlin and to Germany as a whole, and the corresponding wartime and post-war agreements and decisions of the Four Powers;

Resolved in accordance with their obligations under the Charter of the United Nations to develop friendly relations among nations based on respect for the principle of equal rights and self-determination of peoples, and to take other appropriate measures to strengthen universal peace;

Recalling the principles of the Final Act of the Conference on Security and Cooperation in Europe, signed in Helsinki;

Recognizing that those principles have laid firm foundations for the establishment of a just and lasting peaceful order in Europe;

Determined to take account of everyone's security interests;

Convinced of the need finally to overcome antagonism and to develop cooperation in Europe;

Confirming their readiness to reinforce security, in particular by adopting effective arms control, disarmament and confidence-building measures; their willingness not to regard each other as adversaries but to work for a relationship of trust and cooperation; and accordingly their readiness to consider positively setting up appropriate institutional arrangements within the framework of the Conference on Security and Cooperation in Europe;

Welcoming the fact that the German people, freely exercising their right of self-determination, have expressed their will to bring about the unity of Germany as a state so that they will be able to serve the peace of the world as an equal and sovereign partner in a united Europe;

Convinced that the unification of Germany as a state with definitive borders is a significant contribution to peace and stability in Europe;

Intending to conclude the final settlement with respect to Germany;

Recognizing that thereby, and with the unification of Germany as a democratic and peaceful state, the rights and responsibilities of the Four Powers relating to Berlin and to Germany as a whole lose their function;

Represented by their Ministers for Foreign Affairs who, in accordance with the Ottawa Declaration of February 13, 1990, met in Bonn on May 5, 1990, in Berlin on June 22, 1990, in Paris on July 17, 1990, with the participation of the Minister for Foreign Affairs of the Republic of Poland, and in Moscow on September 12, 1990;

Have agreed as follows:

Article 1

(1) The united Germany shall comprise the territory of the Federal Republic of Germany, the German Democratic Republic, and the whole of Berlin. Its external borders shall be the borders of the Federal Republic of Germany and the German Democratic Republic and shall be definitive from the date on which the present Treaty comes into force. The confirmation of the definitive nature of the borders of the united Germany is an essential element of the peaceful order in Europe.

(2) The united Germany and the Republic of Poland shall confirm the existing border between them in a treaty that is binding under international law.

(3) The united Germany has no territorial claims whatsoever against other states and shall not assert any in the future.

(4) The Governments of the Federal Republic of Germany and the German Democratic Republic shall ensure that the constitution of the united Germany does not contain any provision incompatible with these principles. This applies accordingly to the provisions laid down in the preamble, the second sentence of Article 23, and Article 146 of the Basic Law for the Federal Republic of Germany.

(5) The Governments of the French Republic, the Union of the Soviet Socialist Republics, the United Kingdom of Great Britain and Northern Ireland, and the United States of America take formal note of the corresponding commitments and declarations by the Governments of the Federal Republic of Germany and the German Democratic Republic and declare that their implementation will confirm the definitive nature of the united Germany's borders.

Article 2

The governments of the Federal Republic of Germany and the German Democratic Republic reaffirm their declarations that only peace will emanate from German soil. According to the constitution of the united Germany, acts tending to and undertaken with the intent to disturb the peaceful relations between nations, especially to prepare for aggressive war, are unconstitutional and a punishable offense. The governments of the Federal Republic of Germany and the German Democratic Republic declare that the united Germany will never employ any of its weapons except in accordance with its constitution and the Charter of the United Nations.

Article 3

(1) The Governments of the Federal Republic of Germany and the German Democratic Republic reaffirm their renunciation of the manufacture and possession of and control over nuclear, biological, and chemical weapons. They declare that the united Germany, too, will abide by these commitments. In particular, rights and obligations arising from the Treaty on the Non-Proliferation of Nuclear Weapons of July 1, 1968, will continue to apply to the united Germany.

(2) The government of the Federal Republic of Germany, acting in full agreement with the Government of the German Democratic Republic, made the following statement on August 30, 1990, in Vienna at the Negotiations on Conventional Armed Forces in Europe:

"The Government of the Federal Republic of Germany undertakes to reduce the personnel strength of the armed forces of the united Germany to 370,000 (ground, air, and naval forces) within three to four years. This reduction will commence on the entry into force of the first CFE agreement. Within the scope of this overall ceiling no more than 345,000 will belong to the ground and air forces which, pursuant to the agreed mandate, alone are the subject of the Negotiations on Conventional Armed Forces in Europe. The federal government regards its commitment to reduce ground and air forces as a significant German contribution to the reduction of conventional armed forces in Europe. It assumes that in follow-on negotiations the other participants in the negotiations, too, will render their contribution to enhancing security and stability in Europe, including measures to limit personnel strengths."

The government of the German Democratic Republic has expressly associated itself with this statement.

(3) The governments of the French Republic, the Union of Soviet Socialist Republics, the United Kingdom of Great Britain and Northern Ireland, and the United States of America take note of these statements by the governments of the Federal Republic of Germany and the German Democratic Republic.

Article 4

(1) The governments of the Federal Republic of Germany, the German Democratic Republic, and the Union of Soviet Socialist Republics state that the united Germany and the Union of Soviet Socialist Republics will settle by treaty the conditions for and the duration of the presence of Soviet armed forces on the territory of the present German Democratic Republic and of Berlin, as well as the conduct of the withdrawal of these armed forces which will be completed by the end of 1994, in connection with the implementation of the undertaking of the Federal Republic of Germany and the German Democratic Republic referred to in paragraph 2 of Article 3 of the present treaty.

(2) The governments of the French Republic, the United Kingdom of Great Britain and Northern Ireland, and the United States of America take note of this statement.

Article 5

(1) Until the completion of the withdrawal of the Soviet armed forces from the territory of the present German Democratic Republic and of Berlin in accordance with Article 4 of the present treaty, only German territorial defense units which are not integrated into the alliance structures to which German armed forces in the rest of German territory are assigned will be stationed in that territory as armed forces of the united Germany. During that period and subject to the provisions of paragraph 2 of this Article, armed forces of other states will not be stationed in that territory or carry out any other military activity there.

(2) For the duration of the presence of Soviet armed forces in the territory of the present German Democratic Republic and of Berlin, armed forces of the French Republic, the United Kingdom of Great Britain and Northern Ireland, and the United States of America will,

upon German request, remain stationed in Berlin by agreement to this effect between the government of the united Germany and the governments of the states concerned. The number of troops and the amount of equipment of all non-German armed forces stationed in Berlin will not be greater than at the time of signature of the present treaty. New categories of weapons will not be introduced there by non-German armed forces. The government of the united Germany will conclude with the governments of those states which have armed forces stationed in Berlin treaties with conditions which are fair taking account of the relations existing with the states concerned.

(3) Following the completion of the withdrawal of the Soviet armed forces from the territory of the present German Democratic Republic and of Berlin, units of German armed forces assigned to military alliance structures in the same way as those in the rest of German territory may also be stationed in that part of Germany, but without nuclear weapon carriers. This does not apply to conventional weapon systems which may have other capabilities in addition to conventional ones but which in that part of Germany are equipped for a conventional role and designated only for such. Foreign armed forces and nuclear weapons or their carriers will not be stationed in that part of Germany or deployed there.

Article 6

The right of the united Germany to belong to alliances, with all the rights and responsibilities arising therefrom, shall not be affected by the present treaty.

Article 7

(1) The French Republic, the Union of Soviet Socialist Republics, the United Kingdom of Great Britain and Northern Ireland, and the United States of America hereby terminate their rights and responsibilities relating to Berlin and to Germany as a whole. As a result, the corresponding, related quadripartite agreements, decisions, and practices are terminated and all related Four Power institutions are dissolved.

(2) The united Germany shall have accordingly full sovereignty over its internal and external affairs.

Article 8

(1) The present treaty is subject to ratification or acceptance as soon as possible. On the German side it will be ratified by the united Germany. The treaty will therefore apply to the united Germany.

(2) The instruments of ratification or acceptance shall be deposited with the government of the united Germany. That government shall inform the governments of the other contracting parties of the deposit of each instrument of ratification or acceptance.

Article 9

The present Treaty shall enter into force for the united Germany, the French Republic, the Union of Soviet Socialist Republics, the United Kingdom of Great Britain and Northern Ireland, and the United States of America on the date of deposit of the last instrument of ratification or acceptance by these states.

Article 10

The original of the present treaty, of which the English, French, German, and Russian texts are equally authentic, shall be deposited with the government of the Federal Republic of Germany, which shall transmit certified true copies to the governments of the other contracting parties.

Agreed Minute to the Treaty on the Final Settlement with Respect to Germany of September 12, 1990

Any questions with respect to the application of the word "deployed" as used in the last sentence of paragraph 3 of Article 5 will be decided by the government of the united Germany in a reasonable and responsible way taking into account the security interests of each contracting party as set forth in the preamble.

For the Federal Republic of Germany
HANS-DIETRICH GENSCHER

For the German Democratic Republic
LOTHAR DE MAIZIÈRE

For the French Republic
ROLAND DUMAS

For the Union of Soviet Socialist Republics
EDUARD SHEVARDNADZE

For the United Kingdom of Great Britain and Northern Ireland
DOUGLAS HURD

For the United States of America
JAMES W. BAKER III

Letter from Foreign Minister Hans-Dietrich Genscher (Federal Republic) and Prime Minister Lothar de Maizière (German Democratic Republic) to the foreign ministers of the United States, France, Great Britain, and the Soviet Union, concerning the Treaty on the Final Settlement with Respect to Germany.

Mr. Foreign Minister,

In connection with the signing today of the Treaty on the Final Settlement with Respect to Germany, we would like to inform you that the governments of the Federal Republic of Germany and the German Democratic Republic declared the following in the negotiations:

1. The Joint Declaration of June 15, 1990, by the governments of the Federal Republic of Germany and the German Democratic Republic on the settlement of outstanding property matters contains, inter alia, the following observations:

The expropriations effected on the basis of occupation law or sovereignty (between 1945 and 1949) are irreversible. The governments of the Soviet Union and the German Democratic Republic do not see any means of revising the measures taken then. The government of the Federal Republic of Germany takes note of this in the light of the historical development. It is of the opinion that a final decision on any public compensation must be reserved for a future all-German parliament.

According to Article 41 (1) of the treaty of August 31, 1990, between the Federal Republic of Germany and the German Democratic Republic establishing German unity (Unification Treaty), the aforementioned Joint Declaration forms an integral part of the Treaty. Pursuant to Article 41 (3) of the Unification Treaty, the Federal Republic of Germany will not enact any legislation contradicting the part of the Joint Declaration quoted above.

2. The monuments dedicated to the victims of war and tyranny which have been erected on German soil will be respected and will enjoy the protection of German law. The same applies to the war graves, which will be maintained and looked after.

3. In the united Germany, too, the free democratic basic order will be protected by the Constitution. It provides the basis for ensuring that parties which, by reason of their aims or the behavior of their adherents, seek to impair or abolish the free democratic basic order as well as associations which are directed against the constitutional order or the concept of international understanding, can be prohibited. This also applies to parties and associations with National Socialist aims.

4. On the treaties of the German Democratic Republic, the following has been agreed in Article 12 (1) and (2) of the treaty of August 31, 1990, between the Federal Republic of Germany and the German Democratic Republic establishing German unity:

"The contracting parties agree that, as part of the process of establishing German unity, the international treaties concluded by the German Democratic Republic shall be discussed with the contracting parties in terms of the protection of bona fide rights, the interests of the states concerned and the treaty obligations of the Federal Republic of Germany as well as in the light of the principles of a free democratic basic order founded on the rule of law and taking into account the responsibilities of the European Communities in order to regulate or ascertain the continuance, adjustment, or termination of such treaties.

The united Germany shall lay down its position on the continuance of international treaties of the German Democratic Republic after consultations with the respective contracting parties and with the European Communities insofar as their responsibilities are affected."

Accept, Mr. Foreign Minister, the assurances of our high consideration.

Appendix 2

Treaty between the Federal Republic of Germany and the Union of Soviet Socialist Republics on Good-Neighborliness, Partnership, and Cooperation, November 9, 1990

The Federal Republic of Germany and the Union of Soviet Socialist Republics,

Conscious of their responsibility for the preservation of peace in Europe and in the world,

Desiring to set the final seal on the past and, through understanding and reconciliation, render a major contribution toward ending the division of Europe,

Convinced of the need to build a new, united Europe on the basis of common values and to create a just and lasting peaceful order in Europe including stable security structures,

Convinced that great importance attaches to human rights and fundamental freedoms as part of the heritage of the whole of Europe and that respect for them is a major prerequisite for progress in developing that peaceful order,

Reaffirming their commitment to the aims and principles enshrined in the United Nations Charter and to the provisions of the Final Act of Helsinki of August 1, 1975, and of subsequent documents adopted by the Conference on Security and Cooperation in Europe,

Resolved to continue the good traditions of their centuries-long history, to make good-neighbourliness, partnership, and cooperation the basis of their relations, and to meet the historic challenges that present themselves on the threshold of the third millennium,

Having regard to the foundations established in recent years through the development of cooperation between the Union of Soviet Socialist Republics and the Federal Republic of Germany as well as the German Democratic Republic,

Moved by the desire to further develop and intensify the fruitful and mutually beneficial cooperation between the two States in all fields and to give their mutual relationship a new quality in the interests of their peoples and of peace in Europe,

Taking account of the signing of the Treaty of September 12, 1990, on the Final Settlement with Respect to Germany regulating the external aspects of German unity,

Have agreed as follows.

Article 1

The Federal Republic of Germany and the Union of Soviet Socialist Republics will, in developing their relations, be guided by the following principles:

They will respect each other's sovereign equality, territorial integrity, and political independence.

They will make the dignity and rights of the individual, concern for the survival of mankind, and preservation of the natural environment the focal point of their policy.

They reaffirm the right of all nations and States to determine their own fate freely and without interference from outside and to proceed with their political, economic, social, and cultural development as they see fit.

They uphold the principle that any war, whether nuclear or conventional, must be effectively prevented and peace preserved and developed.

They guarantee the precedence of the universal rules of international law in their domestic and international relations and confirm their resolve to honor their contractual obligations.

They pledge themselves to make use of the creative potential of the individual and modern society with a view to safeguarding peace and enhancing the prosperity of all nations.

Article 2

The Federal Republic of Germany and the Union of Soviet Socialist Republics undertake to respect without qualification the territorial integrity of all States in Europe within their present frontiers.

They declare that they have no territorial claims whatsoever against any State and will not raise any in the future.

They regard and will continue to regard as inviolable the frontiers of all States in Europe as they exist on the day of signature of the present Treaty.

234

Article 3

The Federal Republic of Germany and the Union of Soviet Socialist Republics reaffirm that they will refrain from any threat or use of force which is directed against the territorial integrity or political independence of the other side or is in any other way incompatible with the aims and principles of the United Nations Charter or with the CSCE Final Act.

They will settle their disputes exclusively by peaceful means and never resort to any of their weapons except for the purpose of individual or collective self-defense. They will never and under no circumstances be the first to employ armed forces against one another or against third States. They call upon all other States to join in this nonaggression commitment.

Should either side become the object of an attack the other side will not afford any military support or other assistance to the aggressor and resort to all measures to settle the conflict in conformity with the principles and procedures of the United Nations and other institutions of collective security.

Article 4

The Federal Republic of Germany and the Union of Soviet Socialist Republics will seek to ensure that armed forces and armaments are substantially reduced by means of binding, effectively verifiable agreements in order to achieve, in conjunction with unilateral measures, a stable balance at a lower level, especially in Europe, which will suffice for defense but not for attack.

The same applies to the multilateral and bilateral enhancement of confidence-building and stabilizing measures.

Article 5

Both sides will support to the best of their ability the process of security and cooperation in Europe on the basis of the Final Act of Helsinki adopted on August 1, 1975, and, with the cooperation of all participating States, develop and intensify that cooperation further still, notably by creating permanent institutions and bodies. The aim of these efforts is the consolidation of peace, stability, and security and the coalescence of Europe to form a single area of law, democracy, and cooperation in the fields of economy, culture, and information.

Article 6

The Federal Republic of Germany and the Union of Soviet Socialist Republics have agreed to hold regular consultations with a view to further developing and intensifying their bilateral relations and coordinating their positions on international issues.

Consultations at the highest political level shall be held as necessary but at least once a year.

The Foreign Ministers will meet at least twice a year.

The Defense Ministers will meet at regular intervals.

Other ministers will meet as necessary to discuss matters of mutual interest.

The existing mixed commissions will consider ways and means of intensifying their work. New mixed commissions will be appointed as necessary by mutual agreement.

Article 7

Should a situation arise which in the opinion of either side constitutes a threat to or violation of peace or may lead to dangerous international complications, both sides will immediately make contact with a view to coordinating their positions and agreeing on measures to improve or resolve the situation.

Article 8

The Federal Republic of Germany and the Union of Soviet Socialist Republics have agreed to substantially expand and intensify their bilateral cooperation, especially in the economic, industrial, and scientific-technological fields and in the field of environmental protection, with a view to developing their mutual relations on a stable and long-term basis and deepening the trust between the two States and peoples. They will to this end conclude a comprehensive agreement on the development of cooperation in the economic, industrial, and scientific-technological fields and, where necessary, separate arrangements on specific matters.

Both sides attach great importance to cooperation in the training of specialists and executive personnel from industry for the development of bilateral relations and are prepared to considerably expand and intensify that cooperation.

Article 9

The Federal Republic of Germany and the Union of Soviet Socialist Republics will further develop and intensify their economic cooperation for their mutual benefit. They will create, as far as their domestic legislation and their obligations under international treaties allow, the most favorable general conditions for entrepreneurial and other economic activity by citizens, enterprises, and governmental as well as nongovernmental institutions of the other side.

This applies in particular to the treatment of capital investment and investors.

Both sides will encourage the initiatives necessary for economic cooperation by those directly concerned, especially with the aim of fully exploiting the possibilities afforded by the existing treaties and programs.

Article 10

Both sides will, on the basis of the Agreement of July 22, 1986, concerning Economic and Technological Cooperation, further develop exchanges in this field and implement joint projects. They propose to draw on the achievements of modern science and technology for the sake of the people, their health, and their prosperity. They will promote and support parallel initiatives by researchers and research establishments in this sphere.

Article 11

Convinced that the preservation of the natural sources of life is indispensable for prosperous economic and social development, both sides reaffirm their determination to continue and intensify their cooperation in the field of environmental protection on the basis of the agreement of October 25, 1988.

They propose to solve major problems of environmental protection together, to study harmful effects on the environment, and to develop measures for their prevention. They will participate in the development of coordinated strategies and concepts for a transborder environmental policy within the international, and especially the European, framework.

Article 12

Both sides will seek to extend transport communications (air, rail, sea, inland waterway, and road links) between the Federal Republic of Germany and the Union of Soviet Socialist Republics through the use of state-of-the-art technology.

Article 13

Both sides will strive to simplify to a considerable extent, on the basis of reciprocity, the procedure for the issue of visas to citizens of both countries wishing to travel, primarily for business, economic, and cultural reasons and for purposes of scientific and technological cooperation.

Article 14

Both sides support comprehensive contacts among people from both countries and the development of cooperation among parties, trade unions, foundations, schools, universities, sports organizations, churches and social institutions, women's associations, environmental protection, and other social organizations and associations.

Special attention will be given to the deepening of contacts between the parliaments of the two States.

They welcome cooperation based on partnership between municipalities and regions and between Federal States and Republics of the Union.

An important role falls to the German-Soviet Discussion Forum and cooperation among the media.

Both sides will facilitate the participation of all young people and their organizations in exchanges and other contacts and joint projects.

Article 15

The Federal Republic of Germany and the Union of Soviet Socialist Republics, conscious of the mutual enrichment of the cultures of their peoples over the centuries and of their unmistakable contribution to Europe's common cultural heritage, as well as of the importance of cultural exchange for international understanding, will considerably extend their cultural cooperation.

Both sides will give substance to and fully exploit the agreement on the establishment and work of cultural centers.

Both sides reaffirm their willingness to give all interested persons comprehensive access to the languages and cultures of the other side and will encourage public and private initiatives.

Both sides strongly advocate the creation of wider possibilities for learning the language of the other country in schools, universities, and other educational institutions and will for this purpose assist the other side in the training of teachers and make available teaching aids, including the use of television, radio, audio-visual, and computer technology. They will support initiatives for the establishment of bilingual schools.

Soviet citizens of German nationality as well as citizens from the Union of Soviet Socialist Republics who have their permanent abode in the Federal Republic of Germany and wish to preserve their language, culture, or traditions will be enabled to develop their national, linguistic, and cultural identity. Accordingly, both sides will make possible and facilitate promotional measures for the benefit of such persons or their organizations within the framework of their respective laws.

Article 16

The Federal Republic of Germany and the Union of Soviet Socialist Republics will advocate the preservation of cultural treasures of the other side in their territory.

They agree that lost or unlawfully transferred art treasures which are located in their territory will be returned to their owners or their successors.

Article 17

Both sides stress the special importance of humanitarian cooperation in their bilateral relations. They will intensify this cooperation with the assistance of the charitable organizations of both sides.

Article 18

The Government of the Federal Republic of Germany declares that the monuments to Soviet victims of the war and totalitarian rule erected on German soil will be respected and be under the protection of German law.

The same applies to Soviet war graves; they will be preserved and tended.

The Government of the Union of Soviet Socialist Republics will guarantee access to the graves of Germans on Soviet territory, their preservation and upkeep.

The responsible organizations of both sides will intensify their cooperation on these matters.

Article 19

The Federal Republic of Germany and the Union of Soviet Socialist Republics will intensify their mutual assistance in civil and family matters on the basis of the Hague Convention relating to Civil Procedure to which they are signatories. Both sides will further develop their mutual assistance in criminal matters, taking into account their legal systems and proceeding in harmony with international law.

The responsible authorities in the Federal Republic of Germany and the Union of Soviet Socialist Republics will cooperate in combating organized crime, terrorism, drug trafficking, illicit interference with civil aviation and maritime shipping, the manufacture or dissemination of counterfeit money, and smuggling, including the illicit transborder movement of works of art. The procedure and conditions for mutual cooperation will be the subject of a separate arrangement.

Article 20

The two Governments will intensify their cooperation within the scope of international organizations, taking into account their mutual interests and each side's cooperation with other countries. They will assist one another in developing cooperation with international, especially European, organizations and institutions of which either side is a member, should the other side express an interest in such cooperation.

Article 21

The present Treaty will not affect the rights and obligations arising from existing bilateral and multilateral agreements which the two sides have concluded with other States. The present Treaty is directed against no one; both sides regard their cooperation as an integral part and dynamic element of the further development of the CSCE process.

Article 22

The present Treaty is subject to ratification; the instruments of ratification will be exchanged as soon as possible in. . . .

The present Treaty will enter into force on the date of exchange of the instruments of ratification.

The present Treaty will remain in force for twenty years. Thereafter it will be tacitly extended for successive periods of five years unless either Contracting Party denounces the Treaty in writing subject to one year's notice prior to its expiry.

Notes

CHAPTER 1: INTRODUCTION

1. *Washington Times*, February 2, 1990.

2. Chancellor Helmut Kohl, *A Ten-Point Program for Overcoming the Division of Germany and Europe*, speech to the German Parliament (Bundestag) November 28, 1989 (text distributed by the Federal Republic of Germany); and Thomas L. Friedman, "U.S. Backing West Germany's Unity Idea," *New York Times*, February 7, 1990.

3. Friedman, *New York Times*, February 7, 1990.

4. Paul Lewis, "Accord in Ottawa," *New York Times*, February 14, 1990.

5. Stalin's proposal as summarized by Michael Balfour, in *West Germany: A Contemporary History* (New York: St. Martins Press, 1982), p. 182.

6. Ibid., p. 185.

7. The countries are Albania, Bulgaria, Czechoslovakia, East Germany, Hungary, Poland, Romania, Yugoslavia, North Korea, and China; simultaneous failed efforts include Greece, Turkey, the Philippines, and the not-yet-successful Soviet-aided war for Indochina begun in 1945 by the Indochinese Communist party.

8. See for example Max Singer, "The Decline and Fall of the Soviet Empire," *National Review*, July 9, 1990.

9. U.S. Department of Defense, *Soviet Military Power* (Washington, D.C.: 1989).

10. My recent book, *The Twilight Struggle: The Soviet Union v. the United States Today*, Washington, D.C.: American Enterprise Institute Press, 1990, reaches this conclusion after an analysis of Soviet and U.S. foreign policies in the five wars (Afghanistan, Cambodia, Mozambique, Angola, and Nicaragua) on three continents from 1979 to 1989. The eleven new pro-Soviet regimes established during the 1970s are as follows, with the first five underlined to signify that in those countries armed anti-Communist resistance movements have fought the consolidation of Communist rule for many years: <u>Afghanistan</u>, <u>Cambodia</u>, <u>Angola</u>, <u>Mozambique</u>, <u>Nicaragua</u>, Ethiopia, South Yemen, Vietnam, Laos, Guinea-Bisseau, and Grenada (until 1983).

11. Former Director of the CIA William F. Casey made the estimate in 1986; see William F. Casey, *Scouting the Future* (Washington, D.C.: Heritage Foundation, 1989). Senator Hatch provided a public estimate in early 1990: Orrin Hatch, *Washington Times*, February 5, 1990.

12. A.M. Rosenthal, "Germany—Hidden Words," *New York Times*, February 4, 1990.

CHAPTER 2: GERMANY IN THE CONTEXT OF INTERNATIONAL POLITICS, 1945–1955

1. The text of the Ottawa statement by the foreign ministers of West Germany, East Germany, Britain, France, the United States, and the Soviet Union, is in the *New York Times*, Feb. 13, 1990.

2. Michael Balfour, *West Germany: A Contemporary History* (New York: St. Martins Press, 1982), p. 116.

3. Wolfgang Leonhard, *Child of the Revolution* (Chicago: Henry Regnery, 1959), p. 303.

4. Balfour, *A Contemporary History*, p. 114.

5. Ibid., pp. 113–14.

6. Ibid.

7. Blaine Harden, "Polish Ethnic Tension Rails Campaign," *Washington Post*, February 17, 1990.

8. Balfour, *A Contemporary History*, p. 121.

9. Quoted from Eleanor Lansing Dulles, *One Germany or Two?* (Stanford: Hoover Institution Press, 1970), pp. 288–89.

10. Balfour, *A Contemporary History*, p. 135.

11. Paul H. Nitze, *From Hiroshima to Glasnost* (New York: Grove Weedenfeld, 1989), pp. 46–70, offers new insights into the genesis of the Marshall Plan.

12. Robert G. Neumann, *European and Comparative Government* (New York: McGraw-Hill, 1960), p. 478.

13. Gerhard Loewenberg, "The Development of the Germany Party System," in Karl H. Cerny, ed., *Germany at the Polls* (Washington, D.C.: AEI Press, 1978), p. 7.

14. Ibid., p. 8.

15. Neumann, *Comparative Government*, p. 473. The March 1990 Berlin election results were published in the *New York Times*, March 1990.

16. Balfour, *A Contemporary History*, p. 141.

17. Ibid., p. 158.

18. Ibid., pp. 144–45.

19. Quoted in U.S. Department of State, "NATO Alliance at Forty" (Washington, D.C., May 1989), p. 1.

20. Balfour, *A Contemporary History*, p. 171.

21. Ibid., p. 174.

22. Ibid., p. 177.

23. Ibid., p. 178.

24. Dulles, *One Germany or Two?*, pp. 272–73.

25. Natalie Grant, *Deception, A Tool of Soviet Foreign Policy* (Washington, D.C.: The Nathan Hale Institute, 1987), pp. 37–8.

26. William G. Hyland, "The Soviet Union and Germany," in Wolfram F. Hanrieder, *West German Foreign Policy: 1949–1979* (Boulder, Colo.: Westview Press, 1980), p. 116.

CHAPTER 3: FROM CONFRONTATION TO NORMALIZATION, 1955–1975

1. Gen. Jan Sejna, "Arms Control and Soviet Strategy," in Joseph Douglass, ed., *Why the Soviets Violate Arms Control Treaties* (New York: Pergamon, 1988), p. 131.

2. Michael Balfour, *West Germany: A Contemporary History* (New York: St. Martins Press, 1982), p. 199.

3. John A. Reed, Jr., *Germany and NATO* (Washington, D.C.: National Defense University Press, 1987), pp. 84–93.

4. Ibid.

5. Ibid.

6. These and subsequent quotations from Soviet sources on Berlin are from Hans Speier, *Divided Berlin* (New York: Prager, 1961), p. 40.

7. Ibid.

8. Balfour, *A Contemporary History*, p. 203.

9. Speier, *Divided Berlin*, p. 64.

10. Ibid.

11. Ibid., p. 152.

12. Harry Rositzke, *The KGB: The Eyes of Russia* (New York: Doubleday, 1981), p. 139.

13. Ibid., p. 139.

14. Hans-Peter Schwarz, "Adenauer's *Ostpolitic*," in Wolfram F. Hanrieder, ed., *West German Foreign Policy: 1949–79* (Boulder, Colo.: Westview Press, 1980), p. 132.

15. These remarks were made at a meeting with a group of German-American leaders attended by the author in Bonn, West Germany, October 1989.

16. Balfour, *A Contemporary History*, p. 217.

17. Ibid., p. 209.

18. Karl Kaiser, "The New *Ostpolitic*," in Hanrieder, ed., *West German Foreign Policy*, p. 149.

19. Balfour, *A Contemporary History*, p. 235.

20. Ibid., p. 235. In 1971 about 25,000 people of German origin left Poland and in 1972 about 13,000 left. The West German government believed about 250,000 wanted to leave. Ibid., p. 247. This issue would also return in 1990.

21. Gordon R. Weihmiller, Dusko Doder, *U.S. Soviet Summits* (Lanham, Md.: University Press of America, 1986), pp. 141–51.

22. Balfour, *A Contemporary History*, p. 247.

CHAPTER 4: DOMESTIC POLITICS AND FOREIGN POLICY, 1975–1989

1. This conceptualization of three stages comes from Steven F. Szabo, "Political Shifts in West Germany," *Current History*, November 1988, pp. 361–62.

2. Michael Balfour, *West Germany: A Contemporary History* (New York: St. Martins Press, 1982), p. 253.

3. Gerhard Wettig, "The Political Dimension of Soviet Strategy," in Ray

S. Cline, James Arnold Miller, and Roger E. Kanet, eds., *Western Europe and Soviet Global Strategy* (Boulder, Colo.: Westview Press, 1987), p. 44.

4. Ibid., p. 45.

5. Henry Kissinger, *Years of Upheaval* (London: Weidenfeld & Nicholson, 1982), pp. 236–39.

6. Szabo, "Political Shifts," p. 362.

7. James Hoagland, "Helmut Schmidt, Germany, and the World," in "Book World," *Washington Post*, February 18, 1990.

8. Szabo, "Political Shifts," p. 362.

9. Walter F. Hahn, "NATO and Germany," *Global Affairs*, Winter 1990, p. 7.

10. Ibid.

11. Ibid., pp. 8, 9.

12. At the start of the reunification process in 1989, Soviet spokesmen offered this as an explicit Soviet condition. See *Washington Post*, November 11, 1989. After six-power talks on German reunification, this position was again reaffirmed by Gorbachev himself. See *New York Times*, May 26, 1990.

13. *Deutschland Nachrichten*, June 14, 1989.

14. Constantine Menges, "Central America and Its Enemies," *Commentary*, August 1981.

15. Balfour, *A Contemporary History*, p. 272.

16. *Frankfurter Allgemeine Zeitung*, October 27, 1989.

17. Ibid.

18. Wolfram Hanrieder, *Germany, America, Europe: Forty Years of German Foreign Policy* (New Haven, Connecticut: Yale University Press, 1989), p. 500.

19. Jeffrey Gedmin, "The Amazing Effrontery of Willy Brandt," *Wall Street Journal*, March 15, 1990.

20. Jeffrey Gedmin, "East Germany's Disappearing Future," *Problems of Communism*, March–April 1990, p. 87.

21. This "double zero" agreement involved the elimination not only of missiles in the range of 600–3,400 miles but also those in the range of 300–600 miles.

22. SPD Party Congress, *Resolution on Peace and Disarmament Policy*, adopted at Münster, August 30–September 2, 1988 (English text in author's possession), pp. 1–7.

23. Ibid.

24. SPD, *European Security 2000—A Comprehensive Concept for European Security from a Social-Democratic Point of View* (Bonn: July 1989).

25. SPD Party Congress, *Resolution*.

26. This is the "Adenauer concept" as quoted by Hahn, "NATO and Germany," p. 5.

27. Excerpts from the "Resolution of the Thirty-sixth National Convention of the Christian Democratic Union [CDU]," *CDU Foreign Policy Platform*, June 13–15, 1988, pp. 2–5; there is no date for the English language printing of the platform.

28. Although much of the promised destruction of INF missile launchers

occurred from 1987 to 1990, the United States experienced Soviet obstruction in setting up its detection equipment, and in March 1990, 135 INF missiles were revealed to be in East Germany, Hungary, and Czechoslovakia. The Soviets contended they had not known that their military had turned these over to the national armies. See *Washington Times*, March 14, 1990.

29. German Chancellor Helmut Kohl gave this figure of 10 million visitors from East Germany in his speech to the Bundestag on German reunification, "A Ten-Point Program for Overcoming the Division of Germany and Europe" (official text of English translation by the West German embassy), November 28, 1989, p. 5.

30. "NATO: The View from Europe," *Public Opinion*, May–June 1989, vol. 12, no. 1 (Washington, D.C.: American Enterprise Institute), p. 21.

31. Poll data come from 1984 and 1988, in "Germany Adrift," *Wall Street Journal*, January 31, 1989.

32. *Public Opinion*, March–April 1988, p. 30.

33. *Public Opinion*, May–June 1989, p. 25.

34. Ibid., p. 26.

35. Ibid., p. 25.

36. SPD, "Majority Parliamentary Question" (English text, printed document), March 9, 1989, p. 3.

37. Personal conversation with U.S. Ambassador Vernon Walters, October 1989, Bonn, Germany.

Chapter 5: The Democratic Opening of Eastern Europe, 1989–1990

1. The literature on communism in Eastern Europe is extensive. Among the best treatments of the initial stage of taking power is that by Hugh Thomas, *Armed Truce* (New York: Athenaeum, 1987); see also Jacques Rupnik, *The Other Europe: The Rise and Fall of Communism in East Central Europe* (New York: Pantheon Books, 1989); Zbigniew Brzezinski, *Soviet Bloc: Unity and Conflict* (Cambridge, Mass.: Harvard University Press, 1967, revised edition 1981); Zbigniew Brzezinski, *The Grand Failure: The Birth and Death of Communism in the Twentieth Century* (New York: McMillan/Collier, 1989); Adam Ulam, *Expansion and Coexistence: Soviet Foreign Policy, 1917 to 1973* (New York: Holt, Rinehart & Winston, 1974).

2. Timothy Garton-Ash, *The Polish Revolution: Solidarity 1980–1982* (London: Jonathan Cape, 1983).

3. Jackson Diehl, "The Communists Lose Control of the Process," *Washington Post*, January 14, 1990.

4. Ibid.

5. Ibid.

6. Flora Lewis, "Mr. Jaruzelski Smiles," *New York Times*, September 12, 1989.

7. Ference Feher, *Hungary 1956 Revisited* (Boston: Allen and Unwin, 1983).

8. Blaine Harden, "Refugees Force a Fateful Choice," *Washington Post*, January 14, 1990.

9. Center for Security Policy, "Toward a Free and Independent Hungary," no. 90-42, Washington, D.C., May 3, 1990.

10. Alex R. Alexiev, "The Soviet Campaign Against the INF: Strategy, Tactics, and Means," *Orbis* (Summer 1985), pp. 319–50.

11. Jackson Diehl, "Leipzig's Leaders Prevent a Blood Bath," *Washington Post*, January 14, 1990.

12. Ibid.

13. Ibid.

14. Ibid.

15. Ibid.

16. *Time*, January 1, 1990, p. 59.

17. Mary Battiata, "Police Riot Sticks Spawn a Revolution," *Washington Post*, January 14, 1990.

18. Ibid.

19. Ibid.

20. *The Economist*, June 23, 1990, p. 46.

21. John Bell, *The Bulgarian Communist Party: From Blazoevto to Zhivkov* (Stanford: Hoover Institution Press, 1985).

22. Blaine Harden, "An Unlikely Rebel Leads a Palace Coup," *Washington Post*, January 14, 1990.

23. Ibid.

24. Quoted in Kjell Engelbrekt, "Trade Unions and Their Potential to Mobilize," *Report on Eastern Europe*, May 4, 1990.

25. Quoted in *New York Times*, Feb. 4, 1990.

26. Radio Free Europe/Radio Liberty, *Daily Report*, June 7, 1990.

27. Quoted by Georgie Anne Geyer, "Futile Farce in Bulgaria," *Washington Times*, June 18, 1990.

28. Quoted in Chuck Sudetic, "Sharply Split, Bulgaria Votes Again Tomorrow," *New York Times*, June 16, 1990.

29. Ibid.

30. "Bulgarian Elections Get Violent," *Washington Times*, June 18, 1990.

31. Ibid.

32. Ibid.

33. Ion Pacepa, *Red Horizons: Chronicles of a Communist Spy Chief* (Washington, D.C.: Regnery Gateway, 1987); David Funderburk, *Pinstripes and Reds: An American Ambassador Caught between the State Department and the Romanian Communists, 1981–1985* (Washington, D.C.: Selous Foundation Press, 1987). Pacepa was a senior-level defector from the Romanian intelligence service, and Funderburk was the former U.S. ambassador to Romania.

34. Mary Battiata, Blaine Harden, "A Balkan Dictator Seals His Own Doom," *Washington Post*, January 14, 1990.

35. Ibid.

36. Evidence for this includes a broadcast in France on January 1, 1990, in which this claim is made by some Romanians associated with the new regime. Furthermore, Ceausescu's former ambassador to the United States, now a high-ranking National Salvation Front official, said that a group of

Romanian Communist party members and top military officers had prepared plans for the takeover "months in advance" and was prepared "to seize any opportunity" to implement them. See Radio Free Europe/Radio Liberty, *Report on Eastern Europe*, June 1, 1990, p. 55. A Hungarian general also confided to a Western journalist that the Hungarian military in cooperation with the Soviet Union had provided help to the Romanian military during the critical events. See also, Lally Weymouth, "Reds Beneath the Velvet," *Washington Post*, March 18, 1990.

37. Juliana Pilon, "A Revolution Hijacked," *Uncaptive Minds*, January–February 1990, pp. 36–38.

38. *New York Times*, May 8, 1990.

39. Crisula Stefancescu, "Free Romanian Television 'Losing Its Credibility,' " *Report on Eastern Europe*, March 23, 1990, pp. 24–29.

40. Mihai Sturdza, "How Dead is Ceausescu's Secret Police Force?" *Report on Eastern Europe*, April 13, 1990, pp. 28–36.

41. Pilon, "Hijacked," pp. 36–38.

42. Keith Schuette, president of the Republican international group, in the *Washington Post*, May 26, 1990.

43. Center for Security Policy, "Not Free, Not Fair: An Assessment of the 20 May, 1990 Elections in Romania," no. 90-59, Washington, D.C., June 14, 1990, pp. 1–4.

44. Celestine Bohlen, "Romanians Ponder Burst of Violence," *New York Times*, June 16, 1990.

45. Ibid.

46. Charles Krauthammer, *National Review*, June 25, 1990.

47. *Die Welt*, April 12, 1990, no. 12.

48. *Washington Post*, January 20, 1990.

49. *New York Times*, May 31, 1990.

50. Quoted in Weymouth, "Reds Beneath the Velvet."

51. David Remnick, "Warsaw Pact Alliance to Dissolve April 1," *Washington Post*, February 12, 1991.

Chapter 6: The Road to German Reunification

1. *The Economist* (London), June 17, 1989, p. 53.

2. John Goshko, "Gorbachev Visit May Boost East Berlin," *Washington Post*, September 16, 1989.

3. Ibid.

4. Serge Schmemann, "Authorities Storm Protests in Cities of East Germany," *New York Times*, October 9, 1989.

5. As quoted in Robert J. McCartney, "Tens of Thousands Protest in East Germany," *Washington Post*, October 10, 1989.

6. Goshko, "Gorbachev Visit."

7. *Time*, November 20, 1989, p. 30.

8. Blaine Harden, "Warsaw Pact Warms against Border Shifts," *Washington Post*, October 28, 1989.

9. Ibid.

10. Ibid.

11. Robert J. McCartney, "East Germany Announces Amnesty for Escapees," *Washington Post*, October 28, 1989.

12. "East Germans Pour across the Border," *New York Times*, November 6, 1989.

13. "East German Refugees Filled with Hope, Fear," *Washington Post*, November 13, 1989.

14. Comments at a luncheon meeting with Chancellor Kohl in Bonn, West Germany, October 27, 1989, an on-the-record discussion attended by the author.

15. Chancellor Helmut Kohl, *A Ten-Point Program for Overcoming the Division of Germany and Europe*, speech to the German parliament (Bundestag), November 28, 1989 (text in English as distributed by the Federal Republic of Germany).

16. Deutsche Press Agentur, Hamburg, November 11, 1989; in Foreign Broadcast Information Service, *Western Europe*, November 13, 1989, p. 9.

17. Ibid.

18. *Deutschland-Nachrichten* (New York), November 30, 1989.

19. *Deutschland-Nachrichten* (New York), December 20, 1989.

20. Heritage Foundation, *U.S.S.R. Monitor*, December 1989, p. 1.

21. Michael Dobbs, "Changes Proved to Be Bonus for Gorbachev," *Washington Post*, November 10, 1989.

22. Ibid.

23. David Remnick, "Soviets Accept Wall's Fall, Not Reunification," *Washington Post*, November 11, 1989.

24. In *Kyodo* (Tokyo), as cited in Foreign Broadcast Information Service, *Soviet Union*, November 15, 1989, p. 24.

25. David Remnick, "Soviets Clear East Berlin Policy Shift," *Washington Post*, November 10, 1989.

26. "Gorbachev Rejects Changes in Europe's Post-War Borders," *Washington Post*, December 2, 1989.

27. John M. Goshko and Debra Devroy, "Moscow Warned on Use of Force," *Washington Post*, November 11, 1989.

28. Ibid.

29. "Bush Won't Rule Out New Troop Cuts Abroad," *Washington Post*, November 24, 1989.

30. Peter Conradi, "Push for German Reunification Too Risky for Now, Mitterrand Warns," *Washington Times*, December 7, 1989.

31. *Washington Post*, March 21, 1990.

32. Etienne Huygens, "Despite Denials, Secret Police Appear Strong," *Washington Inquirer*, January 12, 1990.

33. "East German Groups Demand Proof on Disbanding of the Secret Police," *Washington Times*, January 9, 1990.

34. Interview in *Bunte* (Germany), January 16, 1990.

35. "Attempt to Set Up New Secret Police Eroded Confidence, Kohl Says," *Washington Post*, January 18, 1990.

36. Serge Schmemann, "East German Party Purges Ex-Leaders," *New York Times*, January 22, 1990.

37. "East German Party Expels Forty Leaders," *Washington Post*, January 22, 1990.

38. Marc Fisher, "East German Communists Drop Opposition to Reunification," *Washington Post*, January 31, 1990.

39. Lally Weymouth, "Putting the Brakes on Reunification?" *Washington Post*, February 4, 1990.

40. Ibid.

41. Michael Dobbs, "Gorbachev Shifts on Unification," *Washington Post*, January 31, 1990.

42. Ibid.

43. Thomas L. Friedman, "Gorbachev Accepts Deep Cuts in Europe if Forces Are Equal," *New York Times*, February 10, 1990. This would mean reducing U.S. forces in Central Europe from 255,000 to 195,000 and Soviet forces in the same zone from 565,000 to 195,000.

44. Ibid.

45. Craig R. Whitney, "Kohl Says Moscow Agrees Unity Issue is Up to Germans," *New York Times*, February 11, 1990.

46. Ibid.; meaning, presumably, the Stalin "peace note" of 1952; see chapter 2.

47. Don Oberdorfer, "West Gives Soviets German Unity Plan," *Washington Post*, February 13, 1990.

48. Paul Lewis, "West and Soviets Agree with Two Germanys on Rapid Schedule for Unification Talks: Gorbachev Accepts Bush Troop Ceiling," *New York Times*, February 14, 1990.

49. Francis X. Clines, "Gorbachev Voices New Reservations on German Unity," *New York Times*, February 21, 1990.

50. Excerpts from "Gorbachev's Remarks on German Unification in Europe," *New York Times*, February 21, 1990.

51. Marc Fisher, "Germanys Take Steps to Unify Currencies," *Washington Post*, February 14, 1990.

52. Serge Schmemann, "Kohl Stomps As if Germanys Were One," *New York Times*, February 21, 1990.

53. Serge Schmemann, "Bonn's Politicians Invade East Germany," *New York Times*, February 9, 1990.

54. Wolfgang G. Gibowski, *East Germans Voting for Freedom in United Germany* (Mannheim, Germany: Forschungsgruppe Wahlen, 1989), p. 5.

55. Quoted in Henry Kamm, "German Losers Reject Victor's Invitation," *New York Times*, March 20, 1990.

56. Serge Schmemann, "Mandate for Unity As Soon As Possible," *New York Times*, March 19, 1990.

57. Glenn Frankel, "East Germany Party Head Leaves Post," *Washington Post*, March 27, 1990. In November 1990, similar allegations were made against Lothar de Maizière.

58. Serge Schmemann, "East Germans Form 'Grand Coalition,' " *New*

York Times, April 10, 1990. Marc Fisher, "East German Parties Agree on Coalition," *Washington Post*, April 10, 1990.

59. Ferdinand Protzman, "The East Germans Issue an Apology for Nazis' Crimes," *New York Times*, April 13, 1990.

60. Ibid.

61. Ibid.

62. Ferdinand Protzman, "Bonn Offers East a Generous Rate in Unifying Money," *New York Times*, April 24, 1990.

63. Henry Kamm, "East German Leader Rejects Subsidiary Role in Unity Talks and Reassures Moscow," *New York Times*, April 20, 1990.

64. *Washington Post*, May 14, 1990.

65. *Washington Post*, May 17, 1990.

66. *New York Times*, May 19, 1990.

67. Quoted in Marc Fisher, "Market Economy, Unification Sought," *Washington Post*, March 19, 1990.

68. *New York Times*, May 22, 1990.

69. *New York Times*, April 7, 1990.

70. *New York Times*, April 12, 1990.

71. David Remnick, "East Berlin, Soviet Split on NATO," *Washington Post*, April 30, 1990.

72. Edward Cody, "France, West Germany Urge European Unity," *Washington Post*, April 20, 1990.

73. David Hoffman, "Bush, Mitterrand Agree to Hold a NATO Summit," *Washington Post*, April 20, 1990.

74. Edward Cody, "Europeans to Seek New Union," *Washington Post*, April 29, 1990.

75. *New York Times*, May 4, 1990.

76. Jim Hoagland, "Kremlin Seen Rethinking Alliances," *Washington Post*, April 29, 1990.

77. *Washington Post*, May 6, 1990.

78. Marc Fisher, "Kohl Rejects Soviet 'Negotiation Poker,' " *Washington Post*, May 9, 1990.

79. Radio Free Europe/Radio Liberty, *Daily Report*, May 14, 1990, p. 5.

80. Celestine Bohlen, "Warsaw Alliance Split on Germany," *New York Times*, March 18, 1990.

81. *New York Times*, May 24, 1990.

82. *Washington Times*, May 24, 1990.

83. Bill Gertz, "Kohl Agrees to Provide Aid to the Soviets," *Washington Times*, May 21, 1990.

84. Marc Fisher, "Soviet Encourages Bonn on Arms Talks, German Unification," *Washington Post*, May 24, 1990.

85. Michael Dobbs, "Gorbachev Issues Warning over Plan to Include Unified Germany in NATO," *Washington Post*, May 26, 1990.

86. *Washington Times*, May 29, 1990.

87. *Washington Post*, May 30, 1990.

88. R. W. Apple, Jr., "Besieged at Home, Gorbachev Arrives in U.S. for Summit," *New York Times*, May 31.

89. Ibid.

90. *Washington Post*, June 1, 1990.

91. Excerpts from the Joint Press Conference, *New York Times*, June 4, 1990.

92. As quoted in the *New York Times*, June 5, 1990.

93. *New York Times*, June 6, 1990.

94. Thomas L. Friedman, "U.S. Will Press the Soviets to Accept Plan on Germany," *New York Times*, June 5, 1990.

95. *New York Times*, June 7, 1990.

96. Francis X. Clines, "Warsaw Pact Pronounces the End of Ideological Conflict with the West," *New York Times*, June 8, 1990.

97. "NATO Overture to a Rival," *New York Times*, June 9, 1990.

98. Andrew Borowiec, "East German Leader Meets Bush Today," *Washington Times*, June 11, 1990.

99. Ibid.

100. Edward Cody, "Kohl, Mitterrand Urge West to Aid Gorbachev," *Washington Post*, June 23, 1990.

101. Craig R. Whitney, "European Leaders Back Kohl's Plea for Soviet Aid," *New York Times*, June 27, 1990.

102. Estimate made to the author by a senior U.S. official concerned with Germany in October 1989.

103. Ferdinand Protzman, "East Germans Add to Unity Pressure," *New York Times*, June 18, 1990.

104. Serge Schmemann, "Kohl Says Ballot by Germanys Gains Momentum for '90," *New York Times*, June 19, 1990.

105. Marc Fisher, "Bonn Outlines Blueprint for Political Unification," *Washington Post*, June 27, 1990.

106. Bill Keller, "Gorbachev Yields on Alliance Roles in a New Germany," *New York Times*, June 13, 1990.

107. Ferdinand Protzman, "Bonn Welcomes New Soviet Shift," *New York Times*, June 14, 1990.

108. "Kremlin Ties German Unity to Joining Collective Alliance," *Washington Times*, June 15, 1990.

109. David Hoffman, "Soviets Propose Retaining Four Powers Role in Germany," *Washington Post*, June 23, 1990.

110. Ibid.

111. Ibid.

CHAPTER 7: REUNIFICATION AND CONTINUING COMMITMENT TO THE ATLANTIC ALLIANCE

1. "Bush: The Enemy Is Unpredictability, Instability," *Washington Post*, February 26, 1990.

2. Ferdinand Protzman, "Germans in Talks on Political Unity," *New York Times*, July 7, 1990.

3. Craig R. Whitney, "NATO Leaders Proclaim End of Cold War," *New York Times*, July 7, 1990.

4. R. Geoffrey Smith, "Kohl's Surprising Pledge Called Gesture to Moscow," *Washington Post,* July 7, 1990.

5. "Text of the Declaration after the NATO Talks," *New York Times,* July 7, 1990.

6. Ibid.

7. Ibid.

8. Ibid.

9. Jim Hoagland, "Bush's NATO Success Advances U.S. Goals," *Washington Post,* July 7, 1990.

10. "Declaration after the NATO Talks."

11. Bill Keller, "Shevardnadze Says Moves Pave Way to a 'Safe Future' for Europe," *New York Times,* July 7, 1990.

12. "Comments by Soviets on NATO," *New York Times,* July 7, 1990.

13. Craig R. Whitney, "Kohl Will Meet Gorbachev Today on Unity," *New York Times,* July 14, 1990.

14. Serge Schmemann, "Gorbachev Clears Way for German Unity, Dropping Objection to NATO Membership," *New York Times,* July 17, 1990.

15. Ibid.

16. Ibid.

17. Thomas L. Friedman, "Two Germanys Vow to Accept Border with the Poles," *New York Times,* July 18, 1990.

18. Schmemann, "Gorbachev Clears Way."

19. Josef Joffe, "One and a Half Cheers for German Reunification," *Commentary,* June 1990.

20. U.S. Department of Defense, Defense Intelligence Agency Report, February 1990, in *Washington Times,* April 23, 1990.

21. Josef Joffe, "The Future of Germany," paper given at the American Enterprise Institute, March 1990, p. 27.

22. Joffe, "One and a Half Cheers," pp. 31–32.

23. Wolfram F. Hanrieder, *Germany, America, Europe: Forty Years of German Foreign Policy* (New Haven: Yale University Press, 1989).

Chapter 8: Reunification and de Facto Neutralization

1. John Kegan, *The Second World War* (New York: Viking, 1990).

2. Ibid.

3. Ibid.

4. Wolfgang Seiffert, "Soviet Political Strategy toward the Federal Republic of Germany," in Raymond S. Cline, James Arnold Miller, Roger E. Kanet, eds., *Western Europe and Soviet Global Strategy* (Boulder, Colo.: Westview Press, 1987), p. 135.

5. William G. Hyland, "The Soviet Union and Germany," in Wolfran F. Hanrieder, *West German Foreign Policy: 1949–1979* (Boulder, Colo.: Westview Press, 1980), pp. 111–12.

6. Michael Balfour, *West Germany: A Contemporary History* (New York: St. Martin's Press, 1983), p. 201.

7. Department of State, *The CSCE Process*, September 1985, p. 1.

8. Hyland, "Soviet Union and Germany," p. 119.

9. Hans Graf Huyn, *Die Doppelfalle: Das Risiko Gorbatschow* (München: Universitas Verlag, 1989).

10. Joseph Douglass, *Why the Soviets Violate Arms Control Agreements* (New York: Pergamon, 1988), p. 50.

11. Anatoliy Golitsyn, *New Lies for Old: The Communist Strategy of Deception and Disinformation* (New York: Dodd, 1984).

12. *Facts on File: Weekly World News Digest*, New York, vol, 9, p. F2.

13. Gerhardt Wettig, *The Role of Military Power in Soviet Policy* (Cologne, Germany: Bundesinstitut für Ostwissenschaftlische und Internationale Studien, 1989), p. 21.

14. Ibid.

15. Ibid.

16. Ibid.

17. Evan G. Galbraith, "Softening of the Germans," *National Review*, May 22, 1987, pp. 34–5.

18. Ibid, p. 35.

19. For a discussion of these complex negotiations and the results of the agreements concluded in 1988, see my recent book, *The Twilight Struggle: The Soviet Union v. the United States Today* (Washington, D.C.: AEI Press, 1990).

20. John Lenscowski, "Military Glasnost and Strategic Deception," *International Freedom Review*, Winter 1990, vol. 3, no. 2, pp. 10–11.

21. Theo Summer, "Through German Eyes," *The National Interest*, Spring 1988, p. 4.

22. Walter Momper, "Berlin, Germany, Europe," speech given in Washington, D.C., February 26, 1990, p. 5.

23. *Deutschland-Nachrichten*, December 7, 1989.

24. Steven F. Szabo, "The German Social Democrats and Defense after the 1987 Elections," *SAIS Review*, Summer–Fall 1987, vol. 7, no. 2, p. 58.

25. Lally Weymouth, "Germany's Urge to Merge," *Washington Post*, March 4, 1990.

26. Glenn Frankel, "NATO Tries to Change with Time," *Washington Post*, July 5, 1990.

27. Evan Galbraith, "Softening of the Germans," p. 35.

28. For perspective on the Soviet-French relationship from the inception of the Mitterrand presidency, see Michael J. Sodaro, "Moscow and Mitterrand," *Problems of Communism*, August 1982, pp. 20–36.

29. *Washington Post*, February 9, 1990.

30. Simon Serfaty, ed., *The Foreign Policy of the French Left* (Boulder, Colo.: Westview Press, 1979).

31. Hyland, "Soviet Union and Germany," p. 115.

32. Michael R. Gordon, "Nunn Proposes Sharp U.S. Military Cuts in Europe," *New York Times*, April 20, 1990.

33. Ibid.

34. Pat Schroeder, "Bring Our Troops Back Home—And Save a Few Billion," *Washington Post*, June 24, 1990.

35. Patrick Buchanan, "Tripwire or Stabilizing Nexus?" *Washington Times*, May 9, 1990.

36. Rosemary Fiscarelli, "Europe is Grabbing the Spoils of Peace," *New York Times*, March 9, 1990.

37. For example, 150,000 people demonstrated against the war in Bonn in late January 1991; see Stephen Kinzer, "Antiwar Protest Is Staged in Bonn," *New York Times*, January 27, 1991, p. 17.

38. Marc Fisher, "Germany Pledges $5.5 Billion More toward Gulf War," *Washington Post*, January 30, 1991.

39. Clyde Haberman, "As Allies Use Its Bases, Ankara Faces an Implicit Threat from Iraq," *New York Times*, January 27, 1991.

40. NBC Network News, broadcast of February 8, 1991.

41. Republican staff, U. S. Senate, Committee on Foreign Relations, "Saddam's Foreign Legion-Corporations Marching to Saddam's Call," January 31, 1991, typescript.

42. Central Intelligence Agency, "Eastern Europe: Long Road Ahead to Economic Well-Being," presented to the U.S. Congress, Joint Economic Committee, May 16, 1990, p. 33.

43. Douglas L. Clark, "Soviets Halt Troop Pullout from East Germany," *Report on Eastern Europe*, vol. 1, no. 22, June 1, 1990, pp. 28–31.

44. CIA, "Long Road Ahead," p. 32.

45. Center for Security Policy, "Energy Leverage: Moscow's Ace in the Hole," Washington, D.C., paper no. 90-20, March 1, 1990, Press Release accompanying publication of this analysis.

46. Ibid. See table 3, p. 9.

47. Ibid., p. 2.

48. Ibid., p. 2.

49. Michael Dobbs, "Changes Prove to Be Bonus for Gorbachev," *Washington Post*, November 10, 1989, p. 1.

50. CIA, "Long Road Ahead," p. 32.

51. Jeane Kirkpatrick, "Germany's Diplomatic Thrust," *Washington Post*, July 9, 1990.

52. Joseph Joffe, "Germany and NATO," AEI conference paper, March 1990, Washington, D.C., p. 34.

53. Theo Sommer, "Through German Eyes," *The National Interest*, Spring 1988, p. 8.

54. Jim Hoagland, "France—Still on Guard," *Washington Post*, July 12, 1990.

55. Henry Kissinger, "Delay is the Most Dangerous Course," *Washington Post*, February 9, 1990.

56. Stanley Hoffmann, "Today's NATO—and Tomorrow's," *New York Times*, May 27, 1990.

57. Henry Kissinger, "Germany, Neutrality, and the 'Security System' Trap," *Washington Post*, April 15, 1990.

58. Letter from President Gorbachev to President Bush as cited in David Hoffman, "Gorbachev's Appeals for Aid Show Increased Urgency," *Washington Post*, July 14, 1990.

59. Marc Fisher, "Kohl Views Soviet Trip as Way to Unity," *Washington Post*, July 14, 1990.

60. Evan Galbraith, "Heading toward a Neutral Germany?" *Washington Times*, July 3, 1989.

61. President Gorbachev in an interview by *Time*, June 4, 1990, p. 33.

62. Henry A. Kissinger, "Germany, Neutrality, and the 'Security System' Trap," *Washington Post*, April 15, 1990.

63. Lev Navrovzov, "The West Still Stuck at Munich, September 30, 1938," *New York City Tribune*, January 22, 1990.

64. Ambassador Evan Galbraith, "The Soviet Domination of Europe," address given to the Conservative Political Action Conference, February 23, 1989, Washington, D.C., p. 4.

65. Gorbachev, interview in *Time*, p. 31.

66. Brian Beedham, "The Future of the Warsaw Pact," in *Reshaping Western Security*, Richard Perle, ed. (Washington, D.C.: AEI Press, 1991).

CHAPTER 9: THE EAST EUROPEAN AND GERMAN TRANSFORMATIONS—
CONCEPTUAL PERSPECTIVES

1. James N. Rosenau, *Turbulence in World Politics: A Theory of Change and Continuity* (Princeton, N.J.: Princeton University Press, 1990), p. 8.

2. Zbigniew K. Brzezinski, *The Grand Failure: The Birth and Death of Communism in the Twentieth Century* (New York: McMillan, 1990), p. 129.

3. In their seminal work, Gabriel Almond and G. Bingham Powell, Jr., *Comparative Politics: A Developmental Approach* (Boston: Little, Brown and Co., 1966), the authors discuss the generic characteristics and types of political systems, making a clear distinction among authoritarian, totalitarian, and democratic types of systems. They make it clear that no "model of political growth" is inevitable. See pp. 299–332.

4. Henry R. Nau, *The Myth of America's Decline: Leading the World Economy in the 1990s* (Oxford: Oxford University Press, 1990), p. 4.

5. Rosenau, *Turbulence*, p. 11.

6. I experienced the impact of this television coverage in German, French, Swiss, and British reporting while in Europe in August, September, and October 1989.

7. William M. Brinton, "The Role of Media in a Telerevolution," in William M. Brinton and Allen Rinzler, eds., *Without Force or Lies: Voices from the Revolution of Central Europe in 1989–1990* (San Francisco: Mercury, 1990), pp. 459, 467.

8. Rosenau, *Turbulence*, pp. 10–13.

9. Crane Brinton, *Anatomy of Revolution* (New York: Random House, 1965).

10. Sidney Tarrow, " 'Aiming at a Moving Target': Social Science and the Recent Rebellions in Eastern Europe," *PS: Political Science and Politics*, March 1991, pp. 12–18, provides a comprehensive overview of the social science literature on social mobilization and offers his interpretation of its relevance to the events of 1989 in Eastern Europe.

11. Gale Stokes, in his presentation, "Modes of Opposition to the Stalinist Model in Eastern Europe, 1945–1989," George Washington University, March 26, 1991.

12. Adam Michnik, "The Moral and Spiritual Origins of Solidarity," in Brinton and Rinzler, eds., *Without Force or Lies*, p. 242.

13. Ibid., pp. 242–43.

14. Stokes, "Modes of Opposition."

15. Vaclav Havel, "The Power of the Powerless," in Brinton and Rinzler, eds., *Without Force or Lies*, pp. 52, 63.

16. Brzezinski, *The Grand Failure*, pp. 114–28 describes the "self-emancipation" of Poland; see also Constantine C. Menges, *The Political Evolution of Poland, 1980–1990: Implications for Eastern Europe* (Washington, D.C.: Program on Transitions to Democracy, December 1990).

17. For an overview of the human results of these Communist regimes, see Constantine C. Menges, *The Twilight Struggle: The Soviet Union v. The United States Today* (Washington, D.C.: AEI Press, 1990).

18. Among those works documenting Soviet complicity in the attempted assassination is Paul Henze, *The Attempt to Shoot the Pope* (New York: Charles Scribner and Sons), 1983; Claire Sterling, *The Time of the Assassins* (New York: Holt, Rinehart and Winston, 1983).

19. Brzezinski, *The Grand Failure*, p. 130.

20. Ibid., p. 131.

21. Vaclav Havel, Address to the joint session of the U.S. Congress, February 1990, in Brinton and Rinzler, eds., *Without Force or Lies*, p. 492.

22. Henry Nau, *The Myth of America's Decline*, p. 5.

23. This description came from a member of Poland's Solidarity organization, Leszek Kolakowski; cited in Joshua Muravchik, *Exporting Democracy: Fulfilling America's Destiny* (Washington, D.C.: AEI Press, 1991).

24. Brzezinski, *The Grand Failure*, p. 138.

25. Ibid., p. 141; the discussion of economic integration comes also from chapter 12 of this excellent analysis.

26. As phrased by Z (anonymous), "To the Stalin Mausoleum," *Daedalus*, January 1990; cited in Brinton and Rinzler, eds., *Without Force or Lies* p. 412.

27. Ibid., p. 416.

28. Ibid.

29. Michnik, "Origins of Solidarity," p. 244. For one analysis of the process of transition in Spain, see Constantine C. Menges, *Spain: The Struggle for Democracy Today* (Beverly Hills, Calif.: Sage, 1978).

30. Brzezinski, *The Grand Failure*, p. 240–41 offers as a very low estimate the figure of 54 million persons killed for political reasons in all of the Communist countries since 1917, of which those in Eastern Europe are a smaller part.

31. For an overview of the wars fought by five pro-Soviet regimes aided by 300,000 combat troops from the Soviet Union, Cuba, and Vietnam, see Menges, *The Twilight Struggle*.

32. Karen J. Holsti, *International Politics: A Framework for Analysis* (Englewood Cliffs, N.J.: Prentice-Hall, 1983), chapter 6.

33. Helmut Kohl, "A Ten-Point Program for Overcoming the Division of Germany and Europe," English text of speech to the West German Bundestag, November 28, 1989, pp. 9–10; reproduction by the Embassy of the Federal Republic of Germany, Washington, D.C.

34. Bruce Russett and Harvey Starr, *World Politics: The Menu for Choice* (New York: W. H. Freeman, 1989), p. 153.

35. Richard E. Neustadt and Ernest R. May, *Thinking in Time* (New York: The Free Press, 1986), p. 251ff.

36. Chancellor Helmut Kohl, "Statement on the Fiftieth Anniversary of the Outbreak of World War II, September 1, 1939," to the German Bundestag, September 1, 1989, English text reproduced by the Embassy of the Federal Republic of Germany.

37. Kohl, "A Ten-Point Program," p. 11.

38. James N. Rosenau, "Moral Fervor, Systematic Analysis, and Scientific Consciousness in Foreign Policy Research," in Austin Ranney, ed., *Political Science and Public Policy* (Chicago: Markham, 1968), p. 205.

39. Ibid., p. 211.

40. Ibid., p. 215.

41. Havel, Address to the U.S. Congress, p. 488.

42. *Washington Post*, December 12, 1990.

43. Brzezinski, *The Grand Failure*, p. 269.

44. Quoted in Charles Gati, "Central Europe Is Scared," *New York Times*, February 14, 1991.

CHAPTER 10: TOWARD THE NEW EUROPE

1. President Bush, *Proposal for a Free and Peaceful Europe*, U.S. Department of State current policy no. 1179, p. 2; speech delivered in the Federal Republic of Germany on May 31, 1989.

2. Marc Fisher and David Remnick, "Kohl, Gorbachev Sign Historic Treaty of Nonaggression," *Washington Post*, November 10, 1990.

3. See Jeane J. Kirkpatrick, *The Withering Away of the Totalitarian State . . . and Other Surprises* (Washington, D.C.: The AEI Press, 1990).

4. Serge Schmemann, "Germans Fear Becoming Eastern Europe's 'Keeper,' " *New York Times*, December 9, 1990, and Clyde Haberman, "Europe Supports $2.4 Billion Plan to Assist Kremlin," *New York Times*, December 15, 1990, reported the EC and U.S. commitments. Roger Robinson of the Center for Security Policy, appearing on Cable News Network, November 30, 1990, provided an estimate of total aid commitments received by the Soviet Union, June–December, 1990.

5. William Drozdiak, "EC Agrees to Establish the European Central Bank," *Washington Post*, October 29, 1970.

6. Alan Riding, "Regional Reforms Planned for Europe," *New York Times*, December 8, 1990. The quotation from the concluding declaration of the December 14–15, 1990, European Community summit and a summary of its decisions is provided in William Drozdiak, "Europeans Closer to Single Currency," *Washington Post*, December 16, 1990.

7. William Drozdiak, "Mitterrand, Kohl Stepping Up Pace without Britain," *Washington Post*, November 3, 1990.

8. Ibid.

9. Horst Teltschik, "Neither 'Political Dwarf' nor 'Superpower': Reflections on Germany's New Role in Europe," *German Comments* (Bonn, Germany, 1990), pp. 19–21.

10. Commission on Security and Cooperation in Europe, *Elections in Central and Eastern Europe*, Washington, D.C., July 1980, p. 19.

11. Marc Fisher, "Grateful Germans Vote to Keep Kohl," *Washington Post*, December 3, 1990.

12. Charles Gati, "Central Europe is Scared," *New York Times*, February 14, 1991.

13. Ibid.

14. William Safire, "Cold War II Has Begun," *New York Times*, February 14, 1991.

15. As quoted in Secretary of State James Baker III, *A New Europe, A New Atlanticism: Architecture for a New Era*, U.S. Department of State, Bureau of Public Affairs current policy no. 1233; speech delivered on December 12, 1989.

16. Secretary of State James Baker III, *Imperatives of Economic Reform: Change in Soviet and East European Economies*, U.S. Department of State current policy no. 1270, p. 9; statement to the House Ways and Means Committee, April 18, 1990.

17. Ibid.

18. Ibid., p. 8.

19. Lawrence S. Kaplan, *NATO and the United States* (Boston: Twayne, 1988), pp. 33–52.

20. Among other possible sources, see U.S. Department of State, *The Council of Europe*, June 1987.

21. "Council of Europe Seeks Others' Assistance," *New York Times*, November 6, 1990, p. A13.

22. Secretary of State Baker, *A New Europe, A New Atlanticism: Architecture for a New Era*, U.S. Department of State, Bureau of Public Affairs, current policy no. 1233, pp. 1 and 5; speech delivered on December 12, 1989.

23. Ibid., p. 5.

24. Neil Nugent, *The Government and Politics of the European Community* (Durham, North Carolina: Duke University Press, 1989), chapters 1, 2.

25. Ibid., p. 30.

26. Ibid., p. 32.

27. Ibid. For an informed discussion of the evolution of the European Community and its institutions, see chapters 3–8.

28. U.S. Department of State, *The European Community*, April 1990, p. 1.

29. Drozdiak, "European Central Bank."

30. Alan Riding, "A Stronger New Profile for the European Twelve," *New York Times*, November 4, 1990.

31. U.S. Department of State, *U.S. Soviet Relations: Arms Control Negotiations*, March 1990, p. 1.

32. U.S. Department of State, *Arms Control: Mutual and Balanced Force Reductions*, May 1986, p. 1.

33. U.S. Department of State, *Confidence- and Security-building Measures Negotiations*, March 1989, p. 1.

34. Ibid.

35. The United States proposed an "open skies" regime on May 12, 1989, which was approved by NATO on December 15, 1989, and agreed upon in principle with the Warsaw Pact in February 1990. See U.S. Arms Control and Disarmament Agency, *Open Skies: Basic Elements*, official text (Washington, DC: Office of Public Affairs, 1990).

36. For background on these negotiations see U.S. Arms Control and Disarmament Agency, *CFE Negotiation on Conventional Armed Forces in Europe*, November 5, 1990.

37. Secretary of State James Baker III, statement of October 4, 1990, as quoted in the *Washington Post*, October 5, 1990.

38. Alan Riding, "The New Europe," *New York Times*, November 20, 1990.

39. Ibid.

40. U.S. Department of Defense, *Soviet Military Power*, August 1990.

41. For a summary of the major criticisms of the CFE treaty see Center for Security Policy, *Agenda for the CSCE Meetings in Paris: Three Steps Backward for European Security?*, November 14, 1990, Paper no. 90, p. 107.

42. Alan Riding, "Arms Pact to Codify Europe's New Power Balance," *New York Times*, November 18, 1990.

43. Ibid. U.S. National Security Advisor Brent Scowcroft raised these questions.

44. David White, "Concern about Vanishing Arms," *London Financial Times*, December 7, 1990.

45. Ibid. See also RFE/RL, *Soviet/East European Report*, April 1, 1991, pp. 1–2.

46. President George Bush, "Soviet Non-compliance with Arms Control Agreements," Report to the U.S. Congress, the White House, Office of the Press Secretary, February 23, 1990, p. 1.

47. President Ronald Reagan, "Soviet Noncompliance with Arms Control Agreements," Report to the U.S. Congress, the White House, Office of the Press Secretary, December, 23, 1985, p. 1.

48. Ibid.

49. "Missile-Inspection Technicality Provokes Top Level Protest to Soviets," *Washington Post*, March 19, 1990; R. Jeffrey Smith, "Missile Shifts Not Reported to Negotiators," *Washington Post*, April 6, 1990; Sven F. Kraemer, "Moscow's Disinformation Adds Insult to Injury Caused by Its Arms Control Cheating," Center for Security Policy, press release, Washington, D.C., March 19, 1990.

50. R. Jeffrey Smith, "U.S., Soviets Disagree on Arms Cuts," *Washington Post*, December 17, 1990.

51. Ibid. See also RFE/RL, *Soviet/East-European Report*, April 1, 1991, pp. 1–2.

52. U.S. Arms Control and Disarmament Agency, *CFE Negotiation on Conventional Armed Forces in Europe*, p. 1.

53. See the argument made in Michael Sodaro, *Moscow, Germany and the West, from Khrushchev to Gorbachev* (Ithaca, N.Y.: Cornell University Press, 1991).

54. R. W. Apple, Jr., "34 Lands Proclaim a United Europe in Paris Charter," *New York Times*, November 22, 1990.

Bibliography

BOOKS

Almond, Gabriel, and G. Bingham Powell, Jr. *Comparative Politics: A Developmental Approach*. Boston: Little, Brown and Co., 1966.

Ardagh, John. *Germany and the Germans: An Anatomy of Society Today*. New York: Harper & Row, 1987.

Bahr, Egon, and Dieter S. Lutz, eds. *Gemeinsame Sicherheit: Bd. 2*. Frankfurt, Germany: Nomos, 1987.

Balfour, Michael. *West Germany: A Contemporary History*. New York: St. Martin's Press, 1983.

Brinton, Crane. *Anatomy of Revolution*. New York: Random House, 1965.

Brinton, William, M., and Allen Rinzler, eds. *Without Force or Lies: Voices for the Revolution of Central Europe in 1989–1990*. San Francisco: Mercury, 1990.

Brzezinski, Zbigniew. *The Grand Failure: The Birth and Death of Communism in the Twentieth Century*. New York: Macmillan, 1990.

———. *The Soviet Block: Unity and Conflict*. Cambridge, Mass.: 1981.

Buchan, Alastair. *NATO in the 1960s*. New York: Fredrick A. Praeger, 1960.

Burant, Stephen R. *East Germany: A Country Study*. Washington, D.C.: Library of Congress, 1987.

Burns, Arthur F. *The United States and Germany: A Vital Partnership*. New York: Council on Foreign Relations, 1986.

Calleo, David P. *Beyond American Hegemony*. New York: Basic Books, Inc., 1987.

Carpenter, Ted Galen, ed. *NATO at Forty: Confronting a Changing World*. Lexington, Ky.: Lexington Books, 1990.

Casey, William F. *Scouting the Future*. Washington, D.C.: Heritage Foundation, 1989 (compiled by Herbert E. Meyer).

Cerny, Karl H. *Germany at the Polls: The Bundestag Election of 1976*. Washington, D.C.: American Enterprise Institute, 1978.

Cline, Ray S., James Arnold Miller, and Roger E. Kanet. *Western Europe in Soviet Global Strategy*. Boulder, Colo.: Westview Press, 1987.

Cooney, James A., and others, eds. *Deutsch-amerikanische Beziehungen*. Germany: Campus, 1989.

Crozier, Brian. *The Gorbachev Phenomenon: "Peace" and the Secret War.* London: Claridge Press, 1990.

———. *Strategy of Survival.* London: Institute for the Study of Conflict, 1978.

Dankert, Jochen. *Die Aussenpolitik Frankreichs: V. Republik.* East Germany: Staatsverlag, 1989.

Davis, Jacquelyn K., and others. *The INF Controversy: Lessons for NATO Modernization and Transatlantic Relations.* New York: Pergamon, 1989.

Deutschen Bischofskonferenz. *Gerechtigkeit schafft Frieden.* Bonn: Herausgeber, 1983.

———. *Out of Justice, Peace.* Dublin: Irish Messenger Publications, 1983.

Deutscher Gewerkschaftsbund. *Parlament der Arbeit, Ordentlicher Bundeskongress Hamburg 25.-31. 5. 1986.* Frankfurt: Deutscher Gewerkschaftsbund, 1986.

Douglass, Joseph D., Jr. *Why the Soviets Violate Arms Control Treaties.* New York: Pergamon, 1988.

Dulles, Eleanor Lansing. *One Germany or Two: The Struggle at the Heart of Europe.* Stanford: Hoover Institution Press, 1970.

Dunn, Keith A. *In Defense of NATO: The Alliance's Enduring Value.* Boulder, Colo.: Westview Press, 1990.

Ebenstein, William. *Today's ISMS: Communism, Fascism, Capitalism, Socialism.* Englewood Cliffs, N.J.: Prentice-Hall, 1964.

Evangelischen Kirche in Deutschland. *Frieden, Versohnung und Menschenrechte* (vol. 1 & 2). Germany: Gutersloher Verlagshaus, 1978.

Friedrich Naumann Foundation. *German Identity—Forty Years After Zero.* Germany: COMDOK-Verlagsabteilung, 1987.

George, Alexander L., and others, eds. *U.S.-Soviet Security Cooperation: Achievements, Failures, Lessons.* Oxford: Oxford University Press, 1988.

Gibowski, Wolfgang G. *East German Voting Patterns for Freedom in the United Germany.* Mannheim, Germany: Forschungsgruppe Wahlen, 1990.

Grant, Natalie. *Deception: A Tool of Soviet Foreign Policy.* Washington, D.C.: The Nathan Hale Institute, 1987.

Hanrieder, Wolfram F. *Germany, America, Europe: Forty Years of German Foreign Policy.* New Haven, Conn.: Yale University Press, 1989.

———. ed. *West German Foreign Policy: 1949–1979.* Boulder, Colo.: Westview Press, 1980.

Holsti, Karen J. *International Politics: A Framework for Analysis.* Englewood Cliffs, N.J.: Prentice-Hall, 1983.

Huntington, Samuel P., and Joseph S. Nye, Jr. *Global Dilemmas.* Lanham, Maryland: Center for International Affairs, Harvard University, and University Press of America, 1985.

Huyn, Hans Graf. *Die Doppelfalle: Das Risiko Gorbatschow.* München: Universitas Verlag, 1989.

International Institute for Strategic Studies. *The Military Balance: 1987–1988*. Great Britain: Easter Press Ltd., 1988.

————. *The Military Balance: 1988–1989*. Great Britain: Brassey's, 1989.

Kanarowski, Stanley M. *The German Army and NATO Strategy*. Washington, D.C.: National Defense University, 1982.

Kegan, John. *The Second World War*. New York: Viking, 1990.

Kissinger, Henry. *Years of Upheaval*. London: Widenfeld & Nicholson, 1982.

Konrad-Adenauer-Stiftung. *Die Westpolitik der DDR*. Melle: Verlag Ernst Knoth, 1989.

Lapp, Peter Joachim. *Die Blockparteien im Politischen System der DDR*. Melle: Verlag Ernst Knoth, 1988.

Lebovic, James H. *Deadly Dilemmas: Deterrence in U.S. Nuclear Strategy*. New York: Columbia University Press, 1990.

Leonhard, Wolfgang. *Child of the Revolution*. Chicago: Henry Regnery, 1959.

Linden, Carl A. *The Soviet Party-State: The Politics of Ideocratic Despotism*. New York: Praeger, 1983.

Mager, N. H., and Jacques Katel. *Conquest Without War*. New York: Simon & Schuster, 1961.

Menges, Constantine C. *Spain: The Struggle for Democracy Today*. Beverly Hills, Calif.: Sage, 1978.

————. *The Twilight Struggle: The Soviet Union v. the United States Today*. Washington, D.C.: AEI Press, 1990.

Moodie, Michael. *The Dreadful Fury: Advanced Military Technology and the Atlantic Alliance*. Foreword by Senator Sam Nunn. New York: Praeger, 1989.

Mujal-Leon, Eusebio M. *European Socialism and the Conflict in Central America*. New York: Praeger, 1989.

Müller, Helmut M., Karl Friedrich Krieger, and Hanna Vollrath. *Schlaglichter der Deutschen Geschichte*. Mannheim, Germany: Bibliographisches Institut, 1986.

Murovchik, Joshua. *Exporting Democrary: Fulfilling America's Destiny*. Washington D.C.: AEI Press, 1991.

Nau, Henry R. *The Myth of America's Decline: Leading the World Economy in the 1990s*. Oxford: Oxford University Press, 1990.

Nerlich, Uwe, and James A. Thomson, eds. *The Soviet Problem in American-German Relations*. New York: Crane, 1985.

Neumann, Robert G. *European and Comparative Government*. New York: McGraw-Hill, 1960.

Nitze, Paul H. *From Hiroshima to Glasnost: At the Center of Decision—A Memoir*. New York: Grove Weidenfeld, 1989.

Phillips, Ann L. *Soviet Policy toward East Germany Reconsidered: The Postwar Decade*. Westport, Conn.: Greenwood Press, 1986.

Ranney, Austin, ed. *Political Science and Public Policy*. Chicago: Markham, 1968.

Reed, John A., Jr. *Germany and NATO*. Washington, D.C.: National Defense University, 1987.

Rogner-Francke, Andrea. *Die SED und die deutsche Geschichte*. Melle: Verlag Ernst Knoth, 1987.

Rosenau, James. *Turbulence in World Politics: A Theory of Change and Continuity*. Princeton, N.J.: Princeton University Press, 1990.

Rosenau, James, Vincent Davis, and Maurice A. East. *The Analysis of International Politics*. Glencoe, Ill.: Free Press, 1972.

Rositzke, Harry. *The KGB: The Eyes of Russia*. New York: Doubleday, 1981.

Rupnik, Jacques. *The Other Europe: The Rise and Fall of Communism in East-Central Europe*. New York: Pantheon Books, 1989.

Russet, Bruce M., and Harvey Starr. *World Politics: The Menu for Choice*. New York: W. H. Freeman, 1989.

Sloan, Stanley, Jr., ed. *NATO in the 1990s*. Foreword by William W. Roth, Jr. New York: Pergamon, 1989.

Smyser, W. R. *Restive Partners: Washington and Bonn Diverge*. Foreword by Paul H. Nitze. Boulder, Colo.: Westview Press, 1990.

Sodaro, Michael J. *Moscow, Germany and the West, from Khruschev to Gorbachev*. Ithaca, N.Y.: Cornell University Press, 1991.

Sodaro, Michael J., and Sharon L. Wolchik. *Foreign and Domestic Policy in Eastern Europe in the 1980s: Trends and Prospects*. New York: St. Martin's Press, 1983.

Sommer, Theo, ed. *Perspektiven: Europa im 21 Jahrhundert*. Germany: Argon, 1989.

Speier, Hans. *Divided Berlin*. New York: Praeger, 1961.

Staar, Richard F., ed. *United States–East European Relations in the 1990s*. Philadelphia: Taylor and Francis, 1989.

Stent, Angela E. *From Embargo to Ostpolitik: The Political Economy of West German–Soviet Relations, 1955–1980*. Cambridge, England: Cambridge University Press, 1981.

Stent, Angela E., ed. *Economic Relations with the Soviet Union: American and West German Perspectives*. Boulder, Colo.: Westview Press, 1985.

Thomas, Hugh. *Armed Truce: The Beginnings of the Cold War 1945–1946*. New York: Atheneum, 1987.

Ulam, Adam. *Expansion and Coexistence: Soviet Foreign Policy, 1917 to 1973*. New York: Holt, Rinehart & Winston, 1968.

Veen, M. J., and B. Vogel. *Extremism on the Rise? The New Challenges Facing the Major Parties in the Federal Republic of Germany*. Bonn: Konrad Adenauer Foundation, 1989.

Warner, Edward L., III, and David A. Ochmanek. *Next Moves: An Arms Control Agenda for the 1990s*. New York: Council on Foreign Relations, 1989.

Weihmiller, Gordon R., and Dusko Doder. *U.S.-Soviet Summits: An Account of East-West Diplomacy at the Top, 1955–1985*. New York: University Press of America, 1986.

ARTICLES AND DOCUMENTS

Adomeit, Hannes. "The German Factor in Soviet Westpolitik." *Annals of the American Academy of Political and Social Science* (Summer 1985): 15–28.

Alexiev, Alex R. "The Soviet Campaign against the INF: Strategy, Tactics, and Means." *Orbis* (Summer 1985): 319–50.

Beedham, Brian. "The Future of the Warsaw Pact." Paper given at conference, The United States and Europe in the 1990s. American Enterprise Institute, Washington, D.C., March 5–8, 1990.

Buchanan, Patrick. "Tripwire or Stabilizing Nexus?" *Washington Times*. May 9, 1990.

Bush, George. "Statement on Signing the Support for East European Democracy (SEED) Act of 1989, November 28, 1989." *Weekly Compilation of Presidential Documents*. December 4, 1989.

Center for Security Policy. "Energy Leverage: Moscow's Ace in the Hole." Washington, D.C. March 1, 1990.

Central Intelligence Agency. "Eastern Europe: Long Road Ahead to Economic Well-Being." Paper presented to the U.S. Congress, Joint Economic Committee, May 16, 1990.

Christliche demokratische Union. "CDU Foreign Policy Platform." Resolution of the Thirty-sixth National Convention of the Christian Democratic Union, June 13–15, 1988.

Croan, Melvin. "The Politics of Division and Détente in East Germany." *Current History* (November 1985): 369–72.

Crozier, Brian. "The Enduring Soviet Global Threat." *Global Affairs* (Summer/Fall 1990).

Friedmann, Bernhard. "The Reunification of Germany as a Security Concept." *Atlantic Community Quarterly* (Summer 1987): 118–22.

Galbraith, Evan G. "Heading toward a Neutral Germany?" *Washington Times*. July 3, 1989.

———. "Softening of the Germans." *National Review* (May 22, 1987): 34–35.

Griffith, William E. "Superpower Problems in Europe: A Comparative Assessment." *Orbis* (Winter 1986): 735–52.

Hahn, Walter F. "NATO and Germany." *Global Affairs* (Winter 1990): 1–18.

Joffe, Josef. "The End of the Postwar Order and the Future of European Security." Paper given at the American Enterprise Institute, Washington, D.C., March 7, 1990.

Kissinger, Henry. "Germany, Neutrality and the 'Security System' Trap." *Washington Post*. April 15, 1990.

Kohl, Helmut. "A Ten-Point Program for Overcoming the Division of Germany and Europe." Speech presented to the Bundestag, November 28, 1989 (text distributed by the Federal Republic of Germany).

———. "Statement on the Fiftieth Anniversary of the Outbreak of

World War II." Speech presented to the Bundestag, September 1, 1989.

Lenzcowski, John. "Military Glasnost and Strategic Deception." *International Freedom Review* (Winter 1990).

Menges, Constantine C. "NATO and Geopolitics." *Global Affairs* (Summer/Fall 1990).

NATO Information Services. *NATO and the Warsaw Pact: Force Comparisons* (Brussels, 1984).

Peters, Susanne. "The Germans and the INF Treaty: Ostrich Policy towards an Unresolvable Strategic Dilemma." *Arms Control* (May 1989): 21–42.

Pond, Elizabeth. "Andropov, Kohl, and the East-West Issues." *Problems in Communism* (July/August 1983): 35–45.

Schroeder, Pat. "Bring Our Troops Back Home—and Save a Few Billion." *Washington Post.* June 24, 1990.

Sodaro, Michael J. "Moscow and Mitterrand." *Problems of Communism* (July/August 1982): 20–36.

Sommer, Theo. "Through German Eyes." *National Interest* (Spring 1988).

Sozial Demokratische Partei Deutschlands. *European Security 2000—A Comprehensive Concept for European Security for a Social-Democratic Point of View* (Bonn: July 1989).

Stent, Angela E. "The USSR and Germany." *Problems of Communism* (September/October 1981): 1–24.

Stokes, Gale. "Modes of Opposition to the Stalinist Model in Eastern Europe." Presentation at George Washington University, March 26, 1991.

Szabo, Stephen F. "The German Social Democrats and Defense after the 1987 Elections." *SAIS Review* (Summer-Fall 1987).

———. "Political Shifts in West Germany." *Current History* (November 1988): 361–62.

Tarrow, Sidney. " 'Aiming at a Moving Target': Social Science and the Recent Rebellions in Eastern Europe." *PS: Political Science and Politics* (March 1991).

Teltschik, Horst. "Neither 'Political Dwarf' nor 'Superpower': Reflections on Germany's New Role in Europe." *German Comments* (Bonn: 1990): 19–21.

Ullman, Richard H. "The Covert French Connection." *Foreign Policy* (Summer 1989): 3–33.

United States Department of State. *Atlas of NATO* (Washington, D.C.: Department of State, 1985).

Voight, Karsten, "Die Vereinigung Europas-Westeuropäische Integration und grosseuropäische Kooperation." *Europa Archiv,* 1988.

"The Warsaw Appeal: A Programme of Military Détente from the Atlantic to the Urals; What Proposals Did the Political Consultive Committee of the Warsaw Treaty Countries Put Forward at the

Conference?" *New Times: A Soviet Weekly of World Affairs* (July 1988): 5–8.

Wetting, Gerhardt. *Die NATO im amtlichen sowjetischen Denken und Handeln.* Bundesinstitut fur Ostwissenschaftlische und Internationale Studien (Cologne, Germany: 1989).

———. *The Role of Military Power in Soviet Policy.* Bundesinstitut fur Ostwissenschaftlische und Internationale Studien (Cologne, Germany: 1989).

Weymouth, Lally, "Germany's Urge to Merge." *Washington Post.* March 4, 1990.

Zielonka, Jan. "Toward a More Effective Policy for Human Rights in Eastern Europe." *Washington Quarterly* (Autumn 1988): 199–220.

About the Author

Constantine C. Menges, who is currently Distinguished Visiting Professor of International Relations at George Washington University, was a resident scholar at the American Enterprise Institute while writing this book. From 1981 to 1986 he served as special assistant to the president for national security affairs and as national intelligence officer at the CIA. He has also been deputy assistant secretary of education, a staff member of the Hudson Institute and the Rand Corporation, and a professor at the University of Wisconsin. His articles have appeared in *Commentary*, the *New Republic*, the *Wall Street Journal*, the *New York Times*, and elsewhere. His book *Inside the National Security Council* (Simon & Schuster, 1988, paperback 1989) analyzes the presidency and the making of foreign policy based on his own foreign-policy experience during the Reagan years, and his *Twilight Struggle* (AEI Press, 1990) deals with U.S.-Soviet relations in regard to five continuing international conflicts. He is also the author of *Spain: The Struggle for Democracy Today* (Sage, 1978).

A refugee from the Nazi regime as a child, Mr. Menges has returned as a visitor to Germany each year for the past quarter century. With Professor Otto Kirchheimer in 1965 he was the co-author of "Treason and Freedom of the Press in a Democratic State," an analysis of the *Spiegel* affair, West Germany's major national security scandal. During the building of the Berlin Wall he assisted East Germans in fleeing to the West, and in 1989 he was one of a group of German and American experts who met with Chancellor Kohl only days before the Wall came down.

Index

troops in East Germany, 2, 25,
105–6, 112, 119, 126, 139–40
two-plus-four talk proposals by,
112–13
use of Brezhnev doctrine by, 170
violates Atlantic Charter, 14–15
violation of agreements by, 14
on West German NATO membership, 3, 26–27
on West German rearmament, 26–
27
Spain, 34
SPD. *See* Social Democratic party
(*Sozial demokratische Partei
Deutschlands:* SPD)
SPD-FPD coalition, 39, 40–41, 43
Stalin, Joseph, 13
actions to annex territory (1945),
14, 134
dictatorial regime of, 6, 8–9, 178
political technique of, 19
proposal for German reunification
(1952), 2–3, 25–26
START. *See* Strategic arms reduction
(START)
Stokes, Gale, 171
Stoltenberg, Gerhard, 106–7, 147
Strategic arms reduction (START),
210
Stresemann, Gustav, 18
Syria, 8

Tarrow, Sidney, 169–70
Teltschik, Horst, 194
Terrorism, Soviet, 6, 28–29, 42
Thatcher, Margaret, 86
on proposed EC union, 104
reluctance to accept German reu-
nification, 140
Tocqueville, Alexis de, 169, 178
Treaty, German-Soviet (1990), 124–
25
Treaty of Bonn (1952), 26
Treaty of Cooperation and Friend-
ship, French-Soviet (1990), 193
Treaty of Economic Unification, West
and East Germany (1990), 101–
2, 225–32
Treaty of Friendship, French-Ger-
man (1963), 34
Treaty of Friendship and Coopera-

tion, Germany (reunified)-So-
viet (1990), 3–4, 190, 233–40
Treaty of Nonaggression, West Ger-
many–Soviet Union (1970), 36
Treaty of Paris (1951), 24
Treaty of Rome (1958), 89, 209
Treaty of Western Union (1948), 22
Treaty on Conventional Forces in
Europe (CFE Treaty), 1990, 46,
193, 211–12
criticism of, 213
Soviet noncompliance with, 214–
15
troop limits in context of, 211
Treaty on Intermediate Nuclear
Forces, United States-Soviet
(1987). *See* INF Treaty (1987)
Truman, Harry
position on East European reconstruction of, 16–17
position on existence of NATO, 22
Turkey, 17, 42, 141
Two-plus-four talks
defined, 96
effectiveness of, 184
as formal reunification bargaining
process, 180
progress, of, 102–3
Soviet position during June 1990,
111–13
Soviet proposals for reunification
during, 104–5, 124

UDF. *See* United Democratic Front
(UDF), Bulgaria
Ulbricht, Walter, 13, 31, 45
United Democratic Front (UDF), Bulgaria, 75
United Kingdom, 141
United States
assurances related to German reunification, 108–9
conciliation toward Soviet Union
(1990), 105
economic assistance to Europe
(1945–1947), 17
efforts at détente of, 36–38
goal for reunified Germany, 117
policy on Germany (1946), 16–17
position on German reunification,
2

A NOTE ON THE BOOK

This book was edited by Cheryl Weissman
of the staff of the AEI Press.
The index was prepared by Shirley Kessel.
The text was set in Palatino, a typeface designed by
the twentieth-century Swiss designer Hermann Zapf.
Coghill Composition Company, of Richmond, Virginia,
set the type, and Edwards Brothers Incorporated,
of Ann Arbor, Michigan, printed and bound the book,
using permanent acid-free paper.

The AEI PRESS is the publisher for the American Enterprise Institute for Public Policy Research, 1150 17th Street, N.W., Washington, D.C. 20036: *Christopher C. DeMuth,* publisher; *Edward Styles,* director; *Dana Lane,* assistant director; *Ann Petty,* editor; *Cheryl Weissman,* editor; *Susan Moran,* editorial assistant (rights and permissions). Books published by the AEI PRESS are distributed by arrangement with the University Press of America, 4720 Boston Way, Lanham, Md. 20706.